Adversarialism and Consensus?

The Professions' Construction of Solicitor and Family Mediator Identity and Role

―――

Lisa C. Webley

Dissertation Series

qp

Quid Pro Books

The *Dissertation Series* of Quid Pro Books makes globally available, in a high-quality format, original research from select theses and dissertations in law and society, legal history, sociology, philosophy, and political science. Compelling research is now accessible and affordable, presented in readable and citable form. All monographs in the Series feature detailed contents, true footnotes, legible charts and graphs, extensive bibliographies, and available digital platforms. Paperback imprints are also available for bulk order and classroom adoptions; please email *info@quidprolaw.com*. The current title is available in a digital edition from online retailers worldwide.

Adversarialism and Consensus?

The Professions' Construction of Solicitor and Family Mediator Identity and Role

Published by Quid Pro Books in 2010. Printed in the United States of America.

ISBN-10: 1610270169
ISBN-13: 9781610270168

Quid Pro, LLC
5860 Citrus Blvd., Suite D-101
New Orleans, Louisiana USA 70123
www.quidprobooks.com

qP

Publisher's Cataloging-in-Publication

Webley, Lisa C.

    Adversarialism and Consensus? The Professions' Construction of Solicitor and Family Mediator Identity and Role / by Lisa C. Webley.

        p. cm.

        Includes bibliographical references.

        Includes preface.

ISBN-13: 9781610270168

"A sociological and legal study in the UK of different professional actors in the process of divorce mediation and litigation, and the varying attitudes and practices they maintain about agreement versus adversarial approaches, in part from the ideological messages they receive from their educational and regulatory organizations."

1. United Kingdom—Law—Family law. 2. United Kingdom—Alternative dispute resolution. 3. Law—Divorce mediation practice. I. Title

Adversarialism and Consensus?

The Professions' Construction of Solicitor and Family Mediator Identity and Role

———

Lisa C. Webley

Dissertation Series

Quid Pro Books
New Orleans, Louisiana

To Jan, Paul and Jemma Webley
and to my nieces Caitlin and Natasha

Table of Contents

Abstract

This study considers the messages that the Law Society of England and Wales and the UK College of Family Mediators transmit to their members about the professional approach they should adopt in divorce matters. The study employs a grounded theory method to analyse the training, accreditation, best practice statements and codes of conduct generated by the two professional bodies.

The study examines the extent to which the training, accreditation and codes of conduct of family solicitors and family mediators privilege adversarial or consensus based approaches to divorce for their clients, in the light of statements made around the time of the passage of the Family Law Bill, which suggested a dichotomy in professional approach by these two professional groups. It considers further the nature of professional identity for each of the professional groupings, as constructed through the messages delivered by the professional bodies.

Preface and Acknowledgments

The starting point for this research was to consider whether the traditional view of adversarial directed legal practice and consensus based facilitative family mediation was a true reflection of the approaches adopted by family solicitors and family mediators in England and Wales. It sought to consider this at a macro level by examining the messages that the Law Society of England and Wales and the UK College of Family Mediators (now UK College of Mediators) transmitted to their members about the professional approach they should adopt in divorce matters.

The study employed a grounded theory method to analyse the training, accreditation, best practice statements and codes of conduct generated by the two professional bodies. It examined the extent to which the training, accreditation and codes of conduct of family solicitors and family mediators privileged adversarial or consensus based approaches to divorce for their clients, in the light of statements made around the time of the passage of the Family Law Bill in the mid 1990s, which suggested a dichotomy in professional approach by these two professional groups. It considered further the nature of professional identity for each of the professional groupings, as constructed through the messages delivered by the professional bodies.

This study was conducted over a period of ten years between 1996 and 2006 and formed the basis for my doctorate submitted at the end of 2007 to the Institute of Advanced Legal Studies, University of London under the title *Adversarialism & Consensus? The Messages Professional Bodies Transmit About Professional Approach & Professional Identity to Solicitors & Family Mediators Undertaking Divorce Matters*. The findings were up-to-date as of 31st December 2006, although many of the themes that emerged from the study remain current even if some of the detail has subsequently changed. I have taken some of these themes further, particularly the theoretical aspects, in subsequent publications, including: Webley, L.C., "Solicitors as Imagined Masculine, Family Mediators as Fictive Feminine and the Hybridisation of Divorce Solicitors," in Mortensen, R., Bartlett, F. & Tranter, K. (eds.) *Alternative Perspectives on Lawyers and Legal Ethics: Reimagining the Profession* (Sydney: Routledge-Cavendish), forthcoming August 2010; and Webley, L.C., "Gate-Keeper, Supervisor or Mentor? The Role of Professional Bodies in the Regulation and Professional Development of Solicitors and Family Mediators Undertaking Divorce Matters in England and Wales," *Journal of Social Welfare and Family Law*, forthcoming 2010.

This book is formed from the text of my doctoral thesis, with a few amendments to the tables as required by digital publishing formats, and thus follows the anatomy and style of a thesis rather than a more traditional monograph. I should be grateful to receive feedback from readers with contrary opinions as well as those who have made similar findings, and to hear of any omissions that may improve my subsequent work. I would be pleased to be given the opportunity to correct any errors in this work that are brought to my attention. Feedback is one of the engines of reflective professional practice, as the professional bodies demonstrate in their training and accreditation requirements.

My doctorate would not have reached a successful completion without the help of many people. I am extremely grateful to my supervisor Professor Avrom Sherr for his patience with what was a very lengthy PhD study, and to Doctor Bruce Butcher for his belief (on some days) that I could bring the study to a successful completion and for reminding me that the only good PhD is one that is completed. My PhD examiners Mavis Maclean from the University of Oxford and Professor Linda Mulcahy from the London School of Economics both provided much encouragement to me to publish my research, as did Liz Duff, my Head of Department and friend. Professor John Flood from the University of Westminster was particularly positive about the opportunity for me to publish my thesis in the dissertation series and facilitated this project. I am grateful to Professor Alan Childress from Tulane University for his enthusiasm for dissertation and digital publication and for his foundation of Quid Pro Books.

And finally, as always, my love and thanks go to my parents Jan and Paul Webley, my sister Jemma and my stalwart friends Ruth Baxter, Christina Norman and Sarah Turnbull for their friendship and support throughout this period and beyond. I have missed many events that I should have attended, with the excuse that I had to finish my thesis, and I thank them for allowing me to be elsewhere for so long.

— Lisa C. Webley

University of Westminster, London
June 2010

www.westminster.ac.uk/schools/law/staff/department-of-academic-legal-studies/webley,-lisa

Table of Tables

For purposes of legibility on multiple platforms, these tables have been produced and displayed in a vertical format. For the tables as laid out in a large, horizontal manner, if you prefer that presentation, please contact the author (see About the Author, to follow).

List of Abbreviations

CPE Common Professional Exam (referred to by the term *Graduate Diploma in Law* throughout the thesis)

GDL Graduate Diploma in Law

FMC Family Mediation Consultancy

Law Society Law Society of England and Wales

LLB Bachelor of Laws, undergraduate law degree

LCS Legal Complaints Service

LPC Legal Practice Course

OSS Office for the Supervision of Solicitors, now known as the Legal Complaints Service

PPC Professional Practice Consultancy

PPCt Professional Practice Consultant

PSC Professional Skills Course

SFLA Formerly the Solicitors Family Law Association, now known as Resolution

UKCFM UK College of Family Mediators

About the Author

Dr. Lisa Webley is a Reader at the University of Westminster School of Law and a Research Fellow at the Institute of Advanced Legal Studies. She has previously held positions at Birkbeck College London and the University of Exeter. Lisa is a Fellow of the Higher Education Academy and the Royal Society of Arts. She holds degrees from the University of Birmingham (LLB (Hons.) (Law with French)), the University of Westminster (MA in Legal Practice) and the Institute of Advanced Legal Studies University of London (PhD). She has a Postgraduate Diploma in Legal Practice (College of Law Chester) and a Diploma in French Law (Université de Limoges).

Much of Lisa's research is empirical and focuses on the legal profession and allied professions, equality and diversity within the legal professions, and access to justice. She has undertaken funded empirical research and consultancy for public bodies and organisations including: the European Commission; the Department for Constitutional Affairs (now MoJ); the Department for Trade and Industry (now BERR); the Law Society of England and Wales; the Legal Services Board; the Legal Services Commission; the Solicitors Pro Bono Group (now LawWorks); the UK Centre for Legal Education; and the Victoria Law Foundation & National Pro Bono Centre Australia.

Recent publications from some of those projects include: "The Next Generation of Legal Aid Solicitors – The LSC's Training Grants Scheme," in Buck, A., Pleasence, P. & Balmer N. (eds.) *Reaching Further: Innovation, Access and Quality in Legal Services* (London: The Stationery Office, 2009) (with Sylvie Bacquet, Andrew Boon, & Avis Whyte); "Women Solicitors as a Barometer for Problems within the Legal Profession – Time to Put Values before Profits?" (2007) 34(3) *Journal of Law & Society* 374-402 (with Liz Duff); *Report on the Evaluation of the Birmingham Court-based Civil Mediation Scheme* (London: The Department for Constitutional Affairs, 2006) (with Pamela Abrams and Sylvie Bacquet); "Divorce Solicitors and Ethical Approaches – The Best Interests of the Client and/or the Best Interests of the Family?" (2004) 7(2) *Legal Ethics* 231-250.

Lisa has held visiting positions at the University of Technology, Sydney Australia (2002) and the Victoria Law Foundation, Melbourne Australia (2004); a visiting professorship on the Stetson University College of Law semester in London programme (2008, 2009, 2010) and the Dickinson Penn State School of Law semester abroad programme (2004 and 2005); and a visiting professorship at Cleveland Marshall College of Law, Cleveland State University USA (2007). Her principal areas of teaching and supervision are constitutional and administrative law, judicial review, ADR, family law and research methods. She is author of two text-books: *Legal Writing* (2nd edition Routledge-Cavendish), and with Harriet Samuels, *The Complete Public Law: Text Cases and Materials* (Oxford University Press, 2009). She has written, on empirical legal research methods, Webley, L.C., "Part III Doing Empirical Legal Studies Research Chapter 38 – Qualitative Approaches to ELS," in Cane, P. & Kritzer, H. (eds.) *Oxford Handbook of Empirical Legal Research* (Oxford University Press), forthcoming 2010.

Further details of Lisa's teaching and publications are available at her webpage at the University of Westminster:

www.westminster.ac.uk/schools/law/staff/department-of-academic-legal-studies/webley,-lisa.

Lisa C. Webley

Adversarialism and Consensus?

The Professions' Construction of Solicitor and Family Mediator Identity and Role

Chapter 1: Introduction

This study considers the professional approach (some may prefer the word *paradigm* to approach) that family solicitors and family mediators are encouraged to employ in divorce situations, with reference to the cues and messages sent to them by their professional bodies. It examines whether the training, accreditation and codes of conduct of family solicitors and family mediators privilege adversarial or consensus based approaches to divorce.

The study also considers what this means as regards professional identity. This examination is made in the light of statements made around the time of the passage of the Family Law Bill, suggesting a dichotomy in professional approach by these two professional groups – adversarialism on the part of solicitors, compared with family mediators striving for consensus between the divorcing couple.

1.1 Background

Prior to the Family Law Act 1996 there was little public knowledge about family mediation.[1] Debate was restricted to practitioners in the field and a small group of academics who worked within it. Couples who wanted to begin divorce proceedings either chose to organise the divorce themselves through the special procedure,[2] went to see solicitors then conducted the divorce themselves or with the assistance of a solicitor- one for each of them as they are not permitted to instruct one solicitor to represent their joint interests. The divorce procedure for an undefended divorce is relatively straight forward assuming the couple can come to agreement about issues ancillary to the divorce. The divorce procedure is a set of administrative steps, which involves both parties in completing a number of forms and serving them on the other party and the court, in accordance with a timetable, along with payment of the court fee.[3] Thus the couple may complete the divorce process themselves without the

---

[1] Haynes illustrated this point around the time of the passage of the Family Law Bill 1995 by reference to where family mediation services were indexed in the Yellow Pages (or equivalent) in each city he visited on his speaking tours. He reports that family mediation services were often wrongly indexed and advertised in the meditation section, leading him to conclude that few people understood what mediation was nor had spotted and reported the error. See the introduction of Haynes, J. *The Fundamentals of Family Mediation* (New York: Albany State University and New York Press, 1994) for details.

[2] The Solicitors Family Law Association Divorce Procedure Fact Sheet at www.sfla.org.uk/ factsheetdisplay.php?id=18. The SFLA has subsequently been renamed Resolution.

[3] Divorce proceedings are started when the court receives the divorce petition, a statement of arrangements for children (if applicable), a statement on the advice given on reconciliation, the marriage certificate and the fee (assuming that the Petitioner is not fee exempt) from the Petitioner. The court will then send the petition and the statement of arrangements for children along with an acknowledgement of service form to the Respondent. The Respondent has eight days from receipt to complete and return the acknowledgement of service. This asks

assistance of a solicitor, even though the 'proceedings' are legal ones. Couples who are having difficulty in reaching an agreement in relation to either the divorce itself, or matters ancillary to the divorce, would often instruct solicitors to act on their behalf.

The courts are still involved in divorce issues, notwithstanding the move towards alternative dispute settlement and notwithstanding the relative ease with which a couple may obtain a divorce. Aside for the declaration of the end of the marriage – the *decrees nisi* and *absolute*, Genn found that fifty-six per cent of respondents with divorce or separation problems had a court decision or order, by far the highest percentage of all forms of civil justice legal issues considered in her study.[4] This may be attributable to the need to involve the courts in order for the marriage to be legally terminated, but it may also be because people expect to involve the courts in divorce matters.[5] This can be contrasted with the decline in ancillary financial relief orders whereby the parties to the action ask the court to decide the financial provision in the case rather than deciding the financial issues themselves.[6] It could be suggested that one of the more legally complex areas of divorce is financial and property provision, the area that one would consider ripe for court order rather than negotiated settlement. Judicial statistics indicate that during 2005, there were 151,654 divorce petitions lodged, which resulted in 142,393 *decrees absolute*.[7] There were over 50,000 ancillary relief consent orders, the largest number of court orders other than *decrees nisi* and *absolute*. These orders are made at the request of the divorcing couple. In relation to court orders made by the judiciary, there were 15,468 maintenance orders in respect of children, although most child maintenance issues

---

the Respondent to confirm whether he or she agrees with the basis of the court's jurisdiction, intends to defend the divorce petition, objects to paying any costs that are claimed within the petition and agrees with the arrangements that have been proposed for the children. If the Respondent wishes to defend the divorce, called an Answer, then a defence must be filed within twenty-nine days from the receipt of the divorce papers from the court. If the divorce is undefended then the court sends a copy of the Respondent's acknowledgement to the Petitioner (or his/her solicitor) who then draws up an affidavit confirming the Petition is true. This is sent to the court in order for a date to be set for the decree nisi. A judge will look through the papers to decide whether the ground for divorce has been met. If so, the judge certifies that a decree nisi should be given, and the parties are informed of the date on which the decree will be made. The couple do not need to attend court on that day. The judge on that date will look through the papers and will check the statement for arrangements for children. If there is no dispute about the arrangements for the children and the judge is satisfied with them, then normally the decree nisi will be pronounced. If the judge is concerned he may ask the parties to attend an appointment to clarify these issues first. The Petitioner may apply for the decree nisi to be made absolute six weeks and one day after the decree nisi was pronounced.

[4] Genn, H. *Paths to Justice: What Do People Think About Going To Law?* (Oxford: Hart Publishing, 1999) at 115.

[5] As suggested by Douglas, G. *Resolving Family Disputes*, The Nuffield Seminars in Civil Justice, Seminar 4, 4th March 2002 at 5.

[6] As discussed by Douglas, G. *id.* Discussed further in Barton, C. and Bissett-Johnson, A 'The Declining Number of Ancillary Financial Relief Orders' (2000) *Family Law* 94.

[7] See *Judicial Statistics 2005* (London: Department for Constitutional Affairs, 2006) at 60-62.

since April 1993 have been dealt with by the Child Support Agency. Just under 5,000 periodical payments, approximately 10,000 lump sum orders, 11,000 property adjustment orders along with around 3,000 pension sharing or attachment orders were made in that year.[8] As the figures indicate, courts are not called upon to make orders on ancillary issues in the majority of divorce cases, although when consent orders are added to other forms of order the role of the court appears more extensive. The courts remain important in terms of consent orders, to make agreements between the legally binding. The use of the courts and the role of the law as validating and enforcement mechanisms remain central to divorce.

The court is now rarely involved in a substantive way as regards the divorce itself, rather than issues ancillary to the divorce. Defended divorce petitions are extremely rare and during the passage of the Family Law Bill in 1995 there was consideration of whether it was necessary to retain this category at all. Lord Phillimore's comments are instructive in relation to the tenor of the debate,

> ...The vast majority of divorces are on the basis of behaviour and adultery.[9] Only a handful of defended divorces take place and very few of those are successfully defended. It is a sterile exercise. As was said by my noble friend Lady Faithfull, it is a traumatic experience for the children. The present existence of fault in the law does not make it more difficult in practice to obtain a divorce. It exists on paper but in practice it serves little effect to restrain a divorce......Therefore, the fault serves only to increase bitterness and acrimony... Another consequence of a defended divorce under the present law is the increased expense to the considerable detriment of the family and children.[10]

There is little support among the legal profession and the State for divorce cases to be put to evidential testing through full court hearings, although defended divorces have been retained for the time being. The traditional notion of an adversarial trial in open court with witnesses is a rarity in the divorce context, even though the rhetoric around the Family Law Bill would have suggested otherwise.

Although the number of court orders in divorce cases may be reducing, solicitors are still heavily associated with divorce, as Genn's study noted, with ninety-two per cent of respondents who were divorcing or separating stating that they had taken legal advice, of which eighty-two per cent saw a solicitor. Sixty-one per cent saw a solicitor for their first port of call for advice.[11] Having said that, as O'Donovan states,

> Divorce is another area of family law in which traditional legal methods of uncovering truth and responsibility are inapplicable. The allocation of blame and the breakdown of marriage may not be possible or fruitful,

---

[8] The exact figures are 4,721 orders for periodical payments; 9,470 lump sum orders; 10,940 property adjustment orders; 2,943 pension sharing or attachment orders; other ancillary relief consent orders 50,140. *Judicial Statistics 2005* (London: Department for Constitutional Affairs, 2006) Table 5.5 and Table 5.7 at 73-74.

[9] Lord Phillimore quotes to figure of 75% earlier on in his speech.

[10] Lord Phillimore, Hansard (HL), 11 January 1996 Column 338 and 339.

[11] Genn, H. *op. cit.* note 12 at 115.

particularly where children are involved. For law, which has one goal of stigmatising cruel behaviour such as violence, but has another goal of giving a decent burial to dead marriages, finding an appropriate method is difficult.[12]

The Family Law Act 1996 increased the profile of family mediation for divorcing couples, and this brought to the attention of the public another type of professional who may be involved with a couple who were seeking a divorce. Of course, couples had been making use of mediation services prior to this – they were well established in some parts of the country in the 1980s. Mediators had also been associated with a different way of resolving disputes. Traditionally solicitors have been perceived to be partisan advisers and advocates, and mediators as dispute settlement facilitators. The difference in professional approach has been tied in with the court versus non-court based modes of dispute settlement, even though some family mediators have been annexed to courts and worked as part of court run family mediation schemes, such as the Bristol County Court scheme that is discussed in chapter three.

Attention has switched from the notion of family justice through divorce, to procedural fairness in the divorce process, which will more often than not lead to an agreement that can be accepted by both parties.[13] This is demonstrated by the development of thinking about divorce, from that set out in the 1966 Law Commission discussion paper *Field of Choice*[14] on divorce, to the more recent report in 1988 *Facing the Future*.[15] The privatisation of divorce from court adjudicated outcomes to negotiated settlements has promoted a reconsideration of the most appropriate mode of dispute settlement for divorce matters. Family mediators highlighted that their mode of dispute settlement was well adapted to meeting the needs of people who were attempting to negotiate an agreement. Other commentators, included among them some solicitors, have sought to distinguish between mode of dispute settlement and the role of the law in reaching the outcome. They felt and feel that there is a place for the law in dispute settlement and that agreements made outside a legal framework can breed long-term inequality, particularly for women.[16] This is the point at which much of the confusion in the debate stems – the conflation of professional approach, mode of dispute settlement and the role of law in reaching a settlement.

---

[12] O'Donovan, K. *Family Law Matters* (London: Pluto Press, 1993) at 27.

[13] As demonstrated by the figures two pages previously, indicating 151,654 divorce petitions as compared to the far lower figures for ancillary relief orders. Even though not all petitions will result in a divorce (some will be withdrawn) the figures still indicate that many former couples reach agreements without the need for court orders.

[14] Law Commission, 1966 No. 6. See O'Donovan K. *op. cit.* note 12 for a discussion of divorce law and its assumptions at 110-114.

[15] Law Commission, 1998, No. 170. See O'Donovan K. *op. cit.* note 12 for a discussion of divorce law and its assumptions at 110-114 in which she discusses the development of law from guardian of justice to guardian of procedural fairness.

[16] For a discussion see Webley, L.C. *A Review of the Literature on Family Mediation in England and Wales, France, Ireland, Scotland and the United States* (London: Lord Chancellor's Advisory Committee on Legal Education and Conduct, 1998) at 86-90.

Other professionals have been invited into the publicly funded arena to assist divorcing couples with their divorce issues with the help of legal aid funding; indeed this was one of the policies behind the Family Law Act 1996 on the basis that divorce lawyers and the courts were adversarial in nature and unsuited to family disputes.[17] Whether the charge of adversarialism is a true reflection of the professional bodies' attitudes to professional approach will be considered later, however, it is certainly true that there is an impression of adversarialism. Even forty per cent of the Family Mediation Association members (who traditionally operate a co-mediation strategy of one lawyer mediator with one non-lawyer mediator) when asked whether the move towards mediation in the Family Law Act 1996 would make a difference to the way in which solicitors conducted the divorce process, stated that solicitors would become 'less adversarial'.[18] Solicitors are now also training as family mediators and taking on this role, adopting what is considered by some to be a distinct professional identity. However, the spectre of law is still evident and available where private justice cannot be reached between the parties. And it could be argued that the law is present even in negotiated agreements.[19] The confusion around professional approach, mode of dispute settlement and the role of the law is also now being heightened by professionals dual qualifying as both solicitors and family mediators.

Some lawyers have opposed the introduction of legally aided family mediation[20] as may be expected when a virtual monopoly comes under threat, while others appeared to welcome it with reservations.[21] It appears too that others have fallen victim to some of the rhetoric about the introduction of mediation as a compulsory part of the divorce process, removing any possibility of a solicitor-negotiated or court-ordered outcome. Others have confused mediation with marriage conciliation: 'Compulsory mediation is playing it far too strongly', says William Massey, a partner in the City firm of Manches. 'There are a lot of cases where there is simply no point in couples going to mediation, where there is no hope of saving the marriage.'[22] The confusion

---

[17] As discussed by Douglas, G. *op. cit.* note 5 at 6. It was also established that some divorce lawyers feel ill equipped to assist parents to help their children through the divorce and life after the divorce, Douglas, G. & Murch, M. 'Taking Account of Children's Needs in Divorce: A Study of Family Solicitors' Responses to New Policy and Practice Initiatives' (2002) Vol. 14 No. 1 *Child and Family Law Quarterly* 57, which may also suggest that there is a role for other professionals in this area.

[18] McCarthy P. & Walker J. 'Mediation and Divorce – The FMA View' February (1996) *Family Law* 109 at 112.

[19] Mnookin, R.H. & Kornhauser, L. 'Bargaining in the Shadow of the Law: The Case of Divorce' (1979) Vol. 88 No. 5 *Yale Law Journal* 950.

[20] See Tsang, L. 'Separating the issues – mediation is no longer seen as sounding the death knell for family lawyers as it appeared to do when the Family Law Bill was published in 1995' 21st July 1999 *Law Society Gazette* General News Section; *cf.* Ward, S. 'Some of the issues topping the conference agenda, as solicitors congregate to discuss "Fitting the Profession for the Future" ' 8th October 1997 *Law Society Gazette* General News Section.

[21] 'Fault Lines Rock Act' 98/05 1 February 2001 *Law Society Gazette* 26.

[22] *Ibid.* at 27.

about its function and benefits were evident around the time of the passage of the Bill and the introduction of the Family Law Act 1996.

Mediation was introduced along with the prospect of no fault divorce, and while it is easy to see how the two could go hand in hand, as some couples do seek to end their relationship without fault based recriminations in a mediation session, the two do not necessarily have to be elided. Indeed, although the legal profession has often been seen as the driver for fault based divorce, wishing to perpetuate the status quo in-keeping with their alleged adversarial divorce tactics, there are those in the profession who lamented the passing of the no-fault legislation,

> The legal profession – and divorcing couples, – hope to see no-fault divorce plans return, albeit in a more palatable form. Mr Harper says: "No fault divorce was an option for couples to divorce with dignity. Unfortunately, it had become so muddled and unworkable that the baby had to be thrown out with the bathwater."[23]

This part of the Family Law Act 1996 has yet to be introduced and is unlikely to be brought into force in the near future. Indeed, the Solicitors Family Law Association, now renamed as *Resolution*, has long championed a non-antagonistic approach to divorce, whether divorce issues are settled with the assistance of family mediators, family law solicitors, both professional groupings and/or through the courts.[24] Solicitor aided divorces need not necessarily lead to antagonism between the parties and thus Resolution considers that it is not whether divorce is fault based, nor whether solicitors are involved in the process that increases bitterness and animosity between the parties. This is a function of the couple and how their representatives choose to approach the divorce. The professional approach may, thus, be the key.

The increased attention and emphasis on family mediation is not purely a UK phenomenon and has not only been associated with a push towards no-fault divorce regimes. Family mediation has increased in scope in the Common Law world and also Civil Law jurisdictions.[25] Family mediation has received European wide endorsement as evidenced by the Council of Europe's recommendation. As Bartsch writes,

> The use of family mediation and other dispute-resolution processes, as alternatives to judicial or administrative decision-making, is capable of improving communication between members of the family, reducing conflict between parties in dispute, producing friendly settlements, providing

---

[23] *Id.*

[24] The Solicitors Family Law Association Code of Practice (now Resolution) section 2 states 'You should encourage your client to see the advantages to the family of a constructive and non-confrontational approach as a way of resolving differences. You should advise, negotiate and conduct matters so as to help the family members settle their differences as quickly as possible and reach agreement, while allowing them time to reflect, consider and come to terms with their new situation.' See www.sfla.org.uk/code_practice.php.

[25] Boulle & Nesic chart the rise of family mediation. See Boulle, L. & Nesic, M. *Mediation Principles Process Practice* (London: Butterworths, 2001).

continuity of personal contacts between parents and children, and reducing the social and economic costs of separation and divorce.[26]

The Committee of Ministers adopted Recommendation R(98) 1 on 21st January 1998 to encourage the use of family mediation by member states and to provide guidance on how family mediation should be used and carried out. The Family Law Act 1996 clearly sought to encourage family mediation in divorce in a similar way. The landscape of divorce assisted by professional intervention has changed considerably over the past decade. However, some of the assumptions about adversarial legal practice and consensus-based models of family mediation have remained relatively free from update or investigation.[27] Indeed, some are based squarely on notions of adversarial practice taken from a US tradition of zealous advocacy, rather than a British standard of 'the best interests of the client'. Further, the debate surrounding who is the client has also be reignited by the Law Society's protocol on family law, which could be considered to extend the solicitor's duty to act in the best interests of the client to include the best interest of other family members.[28] This research aims critically to analyse these assumptions.

1.2 The Research

The starting point for this research is to examine whether the traditional view of adversarial directed legal practice and consensus based facilitative family mediation is a true reflection of the approaches adopted by family solicitors and family mediators. Adversarialism has been seen as an evil in our divorce system, although this charge is by no means universal. Brown and Day-Sclater note that undermining adversarialism may be harmful rather than positive, and the move towards mediation (seen as the counter to adversarialism),

> ... can thus be seen as an attempt to deny the uncomfortable fact of family breakdown ... denying the psychological realities of loss and neglecting the psychological significance of the need to rebuild the self. ... The focus of dispute resolution and mediation should, therefore, be on containing

---

[26] Bartsch, H.-J. *Council of Europe-Leal Co-operation* (The Council of Europe, 1999) at p. 539.

[27] See Philip Lewis' study for the Lord Chancellor's Department that examined the assumptions made about lawyers in the policy literature. Lewis, P. *Assumptions about Lawyers in Policy Statements: A Survey of Relevant Research* No. 1/2000 (London: The Lord Chancellor's Department, 2000). Lewis' summary is particularly instructive as follows: 'Assumptions in proposals for divorce law reform about the degree to which lawyers increase the strains of divorce proceedings seem to understate their contribution to mitigating the effects of tensions that exist anyway. However, research supports the assumption that negotiation on financial matters through lawyers will do little to increase independent communication between the parties. But an assumption that negotiating through lawyers is associated with getting the "best deal" at the other party's expense is not generally supported by research. Research suggests that assumptions about the advice and assistance given by lawyers omit aspects of what clients ask them for in mediation and help which they provide in negotiating with outside parties. Past research did not support assumptions about the dangers which lawyers pose to mediation, though this is currently the subject of new research.'

[28] See Webley, L. 'Divorce Solicitors and Ethical Approaches – The Best Interests of the Client and/or the Best Interests of the Family?' (2005) Vol. 7 No. 2 *Legal Ethics* 231.

conflict, which means creating structure which can metabolise and transform it, rather than thinking quantitatively in terms of a reduction or denial of it.[29]

This criticism may not only be levelled at family mediation, but also towards mediatory attitudes displayed by divorce solicitors and, as Douglas suggests, the notion of clean break settlements which attempt to finalise the issues once and for all.[30]

It has been argued that the global tasks carried out by family mediators and family solicitors are different, in that solicitors see one client and generally mediators see two. In addition it could also be suggested that solicitors have a wider range of tasks to perform in theory: they advise, negotiate, draft and possibility litigate for their clients. Mediators provide information, facilitate the mediation process and the mediation itself and may draft (some do draft memoranda of understanding).[31] These tasks require a wide range of skills, some in common for both professional groupings and some distinctive. It is suggested that the professional groupings' approach to dispute settlement is distinct from their tasks and skills, aside from the sweeping generalisation that mediators adopt a 'consensus or conciliatory' approach to dispute settlement and that solicitors adopt an adversarial approach. Crudely put, traditional dispute settlement theory would suggest that solicitors approach divorce matters in adversarial and directive terms and mediators in facilitative and settlement-orientated terms. If these categorisations hold true, then solicitors and mediators indeed do have fundamentally different professional approaches. This study seeks to examine this accepted wisdom in respect of divorce in England and Wales, especially with the advent of the Family Proceeding Rules and directions which put great store on settlement between the parties rather than an adjudication by the judge. The study will focus on professional approach as defined by the professional bodies.

Previous research has been conducted on divorce, family solicitors and family mediators and their roles in the process of divorce. Research has encompassed the skills required by family solicitors and by family mediators to carry out their work effectively [32] Previous studies have tended to focus either on the role that family solicitors or family mediators perform in process terms, or on the outcome of their intervention. Others have looked at family mediation or family solicitors but have not compared the two directly.[33] Some have carried out extensive empirical studies

---

[29] Brown, J. & Day Sclater, S. 'Divorce: A Psychodynamic Perspective' in Day-Sclater, S. & Piper, C. (eds.) *Undercurrents of Divorce* (Aldershot: Dartmouth Press, 1999) at 158.

[30] Douglas, G. *op. cit.* note 5 at 7.

[31] These tasks and assumptions about what family law solicitors and family mediators are trained to do will be examined in more detail in subsequent chapters.

[32] See for family solicitors skills: Sherr, A., Lewis-Ruttley, H. & Webley, L. *A Training Skills Analysis For Family Lawyers* (London: Institute of Advanced Legal Studies, 1995). See Haynes, J. *op. cit.* note 1 and Roberts, S. 'Three Models of Family Mediation' in (eds.) Dingwall, R. & Eekelaar, J. *Divorce Mediation and the Legal Process* (Oxford: Clarendon Press, 1988) 144-149 in relation to family mediators.

[33] See Davis, G. *et al. Monitoring Publicly Funded Family Mediation: Final Report to the Legal Services*

on what family mediators or family solicitors do.[34] This study draws upon the findings of these studies in chapter three.   None have looked at the training, accreditation and codes of conduct of divorce solicitors and family mediators to examine what these say about adversarial or consensus based approaches to dispute settlement on divorce, and this will be the kernel of this thesis and its original input.

It is accepted that there will be as many professional approaches as there will be professionals working as solicitors and family mediators in England and Wales. With this in mind, this study steers away from a micro level analysis of professional approach and does not seek to extrapolate the macro from the micro. In other words, the research does not focus in-depth on a small group of professionals, from which to draw wider conclusions for the professions at a national level. Instead, the macro level, the national professional level, is the focus.   The research examines what cues the professional bodies are giving to their members, and what these indicate about the professionally acceptable best practice approaches to the work of solicitors and of mediators to divorce disputes.   It is admitted that this does not capture the subtleties of individual practice, however, it also controls for the quirks of individual professionals and the snapshot of practice that a PhD thesis can investigate.

The research has considered:

- what dispute settlement theories say about solicitor assisted divorce decision-making and mediator assisted divorce decision-making;

- what other studies reveal about the way in which family solicitors and family mediators approach divorce and what their role on divorce is (macro) and what skills solicitors and mediators use in the divorce decision-making process (micro);

- what family law solicitors' and family mediators' training reveal about how solicitors and mediators are encouraged to view their approach and their role;

- what their accreditation requirements reveal about how they are encouraged to view their approach and their role;

- what their ethical codes reveal on the same point by contrast with the ethics of litigation, negotiation and mediation.

The professions subconsciously or consciously inculcate certain values in to their members in relation to acceptable approaches to the professional project. This is achieved in a number of different ways. Professional bodies have an impact on the training regimes that their prospective members undertake; they either run or

---

Commission Legal Services Commission, 2000 for a detailed consideration of family mediators in the context of legal aid work.

[34] See Eekelaar, J., Maclean, M. & Beinart, S. *Family Lawyers: The Divorce Work of Solicitors* (Oxford: Hart Publishing, 2000) for a detailed consideration of the role and approach of family law solicitors as well as Ingelby, R., 'Chapter 3-The Solicitor as Intermediary', Dingwall, R. & Eekelaar, J. (eds.) *Divorce Mediation and the Legal Process* (New York, Oxford: Oxford University Press, 1988). See too Davis, G. *Partisans and Mediators: The Resolution of Divorce Disputes* (Oxford: Clarendon Press, 1988) for a comparison of solicitors and mediators in the context of divorce, researched at a micro level.

accredit training programmes that are a prerequisite to professional membership and practice. In the case of solicitors, they control the shape and to some extent also the content of the Graduate Diploma in Law (GDL) formerly known as the Common Professional Exam (CPE) and the Legal Practice Course (LPC). For family mediators the UK College of Family Mediators and the Law Society control the content of foundation training. While the GDL and the LPC is not the only route into the solicitors' profession, many solicitors will undertake a law degree followed by the LPC,[35] this is the one which most closely matches the mediation training route and is therefore being used as a comparator. In addition to pre-practice training there are post-practice training requirements, the training contract for solicitors and supervised practice requirements for family mediators. Professional bodies also give cues to their members through their codes of conduct and disciplinary mechanisms, indicating acceptable and non-acceptable behaviour and privileging certain approaches over others. These too will be examined in detail.

A macro analysis would not in itself complete the picture of the way in which solicitors and mediators approach divorce disputes. This research examines whether the professional ethic of solicitors is that they ought to act for their client first and foremost to the exclusion of the interests of others, which could be argued to be adversarialism in operation, or whether solicitors have moved away from this to a consensus based approach to what is best for the family. Family mediators suggest that they adopt the later, and consider the professional approach to be more accurately described as a professional ethic.[36] The literature on this area has been considered and compared with the studies of Eekelaar, Maclean and Beinart[37] on solicitors and the study by Davis *et al.*[38] on family mediators, in addition to the general literature on solicitor skills, to provide assistance on this point. In addition, training courses, accreditation requirements, best practice statements and the codes of practice have also been examined. Taken together with the literature, it is asserted that an examination of the training, accreditation and best practice requirements in addition to the codes of conduct, as extant at the 31st December 2006, should yield data on the professional approach of the two professional groupings, in the context of divorce.

1.3 Scope & Definitions

Why limit the scope of the research to divorce and why not include other forms of relationship breakdown instead? Similar issues arise for co-habiting non-married couples as they do for married couples: child contact and residence, child support,

---

[35] The Law Society's Annual Statistical Report 2006 notes that during 2005-6, 3,791 new admissions to the Roll were law graduates, 1,158 were non-law graduates who had taken the CPE/GDL prior to the LPC and the remainder came via other routes such as overseas lawyers, barristers etc. Law Society of England and Wales *Trends in the Solicitors' Profession Annual Statistical Report 2006* (London: Law Society, 2007) table 9.5 at 50.

[36] See Webley, L. (2005) *op. cit.* note 28.

[37] Eekelaar, J., Maclean, M. & Beinart, S. *op. cit.* note 34.

[38] Davis *et al op. cit.* note 33.

property and finance. As O'Donovan sets out in her chapter on *Family Forms*,[39] there are varying and various forms of families, few fulfil the idealised nuclear, married family conception of 'family' and therefore divorce is only part of a larger issue of family breakdown and of professional intervention in instances of family breakdown. However, family policies and family law privilege marriage over other forms of family union, and ascribe formalities and legal consequences to this type of relationship that are not apparent in others. It is argued by Eekelaar that there are three kinds of assumptions behind family law: predictive assumptions based on what the law considers is likely to happen, normative assumptions about what people or the majority of people believe ought to happen and value assumptions through which policy makers and the law indicate what ought to happen.[40] Law regulates marriage in a way it does not for other family groupings,[41] relying heavily on normative and value assumptions both at the inception of marriage and on divorce. Whether one adopts a positivist, functionalist, familialist, feminist, critical theory, postmodern or autopoietic theoretical approach to the role and consequences of law on the family, there is no doubt that the law has a major part to play for divorcing couples as do legal professionals and other third party professionals in the process of divorce.[42] These constrain and support divorcing couples in a way that non-married couples are not so immediately affected.

Part of the difficulty with researching in this area is the challenge of finding a consensus on terminology. It would perhaps be useful to set out the definitions to be adopted in this thesis and the reasons for this. The research considers the adversarial mode of dispute settlement, followed by the mediation mode of dispute settlement. This in itself is problematic, as it suggests that there are two distinct styles of dispute settlement. I have chosen not to use the phrase 'dispute resolution' other than for the umbrella term 'alternative dispute resolution' or where others have used it, in view of the difficulties of stating with any certainty that disputes have been resolved. Resolution suggests that a final conclusion has been reached and in family matters, particularly decision-making around children, it may need to be revisited as children grow up and the personal circumstances of family members change. 'Settlement' appears to suggest that a decision has been reached on the issue under discussion at the time, but that the 'dispute', if indeed it were a dispute, was not necessarily resolved for good.

In addition, I have had some difficulty in deciding whether the word 'dispute' is apposite in relation to decision-making around divorce. It is well documented that divorce 'disputes' are not single issue matters but rather clusters of issues relating to children, finance and property, either simultaneously, consecutively or a mixture of the two at different times in the decision-making process. Genn noted that

---

[39] O'Donovan, K. *op. cit.* note 12 at 30-33.

[40] Eekelaar, J. 'Chapter 2 – Uncovering Social Obligations: Family Law and the Responsible Citizen' in Maclean, M. (ed.) *Making Law for Families* (Oxford: Hart Publishing, 2000) at 9.

[41] Although with the introduction of civil partnerships, this is set to change for same sex relationships that have been put on a legal footing through the Civil Partnership Act 2004.

[42] As discussed by O'Donovan, K. (1993) *op. cit.* note 12 in 'Chapter 2 – The Producers of Family Law' at 18-29.

respondents in divorce proceedings during the previous five years reported family problems in fifty-nine per cent of instances, children problems in a further nineteen per cent, and money problems in nineteen per cent, in addition to the divorce itself.[43] This distinguishes family disputes from many other legally defined ones, in which generally single issues are brought before the courts, rather than multiple ones which may all have a bearing on each other and which may shift as time elapses. Douglas reports that family disputes, and particularly divorces, have added complexity as they often involve third parties as well as the couple themselves, principally children many of whom are still minors.[44] The legal system does try to take account of the children even though they could be regarded as third parties to the legal proceedings. Douglas points to the development of the law in this area as well as guidance issued to practitioners about the necessity to consider the interests of the children when dealing with divorces.[45] Other family members are not considered at present, although Douglas suggests that as the population ages, the interests of the parents of the couple and caring and financial responsibilities may also need to be considered by the courts as well as practitioners. Dispute, in the singular, does not appear to capture the complexity of the problems or issues that need to be addressed.

Other commentators, for example Boulle and Nesic, have discussed the definitional difficulties when describing family disputes, particularly in the context of mediation and have come to the conclusion that mediation is about decision-making rather than dispute settlement.[46] Some couples are indeed in 'dispute' about child contact and residence, property or finance, and the term therefore accurately reflects their situation. On the one hand, some couples are simply embarking on a decision-making process with the help of a third party who may assist their actual decision-making or may instead or additionally facilitate it. On the other hand, 'decision-making' as a term appears to imply an ease by which a decision can be made, and that belies some of the difficult negotiations that the couple and/or third party professionals, and possibly other third parties, have to go through in order to reach a settlement. Therefore, for the time being I have chosen to compromise with the phrase 'dispute settlement' which I hope conveys my meaning. This compromise was mooted by Tillet as discussed by Boulle and Nesic.[47]

1.4 Structure

In this chapter the thesis provides a background to the study and highlights some of the difficulties associated with the conflation of professional approach, professional role, mode of dispute settlement and the identity of the professional in instances in

---

[43] Genn, H. *op. cit.* note 4 at 200.

[44] Douglas notes that in 1999 the parents of a total of 148,000 children under 16 years divorced as cited in Office for National Statistics, *Social Trends* No. 31, (London: The Stationery Office, 2001) at 53, as discussed by Douglas, G. *op. cit.* note 5.

[45] Douglas, G. *op. cit.* note 5 at 3.

[46] Boulle, L. & Nesic, M. *op. cit.* note 25 at 7.

[47] Tillet, G. *Resolving Conflict – A Practical Approach,* 2nd Ed. (Sydney: Sydney University Press, 1999) at 4-6 as cited in Boulle, L. & Nesic, M. *ibid.*

which a professional is dual qualified. Chapter two outlines in detail the method adopted to answer the research question. The use of a grounded theory approach incorporates a literature review and documentary analysis of three groupings of professional documents that set out the professions' training requirements, accreditation requirements and code of conduct requirements for potential and full members of the profession. The training course requirements include details of the content of professional body approved courses and any curriculum and skills standards that must be met by individuals and institutions. The accreditation and further training standards are set to stipulate the minimum requirements to be met for full admittance to the divorce solicitors and family mediation professions. Finally, the research has considered the codes of practice and additional specialist codes for divorce solicitors and family mediators. This chapter also explains the role of the literature review in the study, including why it is positioned after the methods chapter.

Chapter three is a review of the literature on previous research on this area, in particular a review of the literature on approaches to divorce dispute settlement in respect of family mediators and divorce solicitors. Previous studies on training, on accreditation and on professional codes are examined in relation to the question to consider whether family solicitors and family mediators favour adversarialism or consensus-based approaches?

Chapter four includes the findings on the research about the training of family solicitors and family mediators. This chapter focuses on pre-entry level training. The professional bodies closely control the professional training for entry into the profession: the Law Society of England and Wales for solicitors and the UK College of Family Mediators for family mediators. The findings set out what the pre-entry training for divorce solicitors and family mediators indicates about the professions' approach to divorce dispute settlement. The chapter provides a brief description of previous research finding on pre-entry training and an outline of the research methodology employed, in order to analyse the pre-entry training of family mediators. The chapter then focuses on the professional bodies' requirements for the structure and content of academic and/or pre-practice training for would-be solicitors and would-be family mediators who have undertaken a first degree and are now undertaking pre-entry professional training. Finally, the chapter draws conclusions as regards the messages sent about the professions' approaches to divorce dispute settlement.

Chapter five sets out the findings of the research into what the full admittance accreditation requirements reveal about the professions' approaches to divorce. Both professions have post-entry accreditation requirements that must be met before members may be considered as fully qualified. This chapter focuses on the nature of those accreditation requirements and the content of any post-entry mandatory training, to consider what the requirements indicate about the professions' approach to divorce dispute settlement. The chapter begins with a brief description of previous research findings on the area. The method is then outlined in brief to put the accreditation findings in context. The chapter then moves on to consider the accreditation and content requirements (and any required further training such as the Professional Skills Course) as set by the Law Society of England and Wales for admittance as a qualified solicitor, and then for accreditation as a Law Society accredited *family* solicitor. The focus then shifts to consider the accreditation and content requirements (and if necessary further training through advanced family mediation training courses) as set by the UK College of Family Mediators for entry in to family mediation profession as a full member of the College, and then for accreditation as a *specialist* of the UK College. Finally the chapter draws conclusions about the accreditation and content requirements for divorce solicitors and family mediators as regards the professions' approach to divorce dispute settlement.

Chapter six focuses on the codes of practice for divorce solicitors and family mediators to consider what these indicate about the professions' approach to divorce dispute settlement. The chapter begins with a brief description of the previous research findings on codes of practice and conduct. The method is outlined for this part of the research. The chapter then focuses on the code of conduct for solicitors of the Law Society of England and Wales, with more detailed consideration of the additional voluntary code of practice for family solicitors carrying out family mediation. The code of practice for family mediators of the UK College of Family Mediators for family mediators is then considered. Best practice statements have also been analysed. The chapter concludes by drawing conclusions about what the codes for divorce solicitors and family mediators indicate about the professions' approach to divorce dispute settlement.

Chapter seven is the concluding chapter in this thesis. It draws together the evidence from previous research and from the research carried out during this study to consider what training, accreditation and codes of practice indicate as regards the professions' approach to divorce dispute settlement, whether they appear to privilege adversarialism or consensus based approaches. It then addresses the issue of professional identity in the light of processional approach. It sets out the core theory that has been developed through the research.

Chapter 2: Method

This chapter outlines the method employed in the research to consider what the professional bodies' training, accreditation and codes of practice requirements indicate about the way in which family solicitors' and family mediators' are encouraged to approach divorce matters. It explains the research strategy and theoretical framework, including how the empirical sources were analysed, and the nature and role of the literature review. It also considers why documents relating to training for entry into the profession, accreditation and post entry requirements, and codes of conduct and best practice statements are appropriate sources of empirical data for this study.

2.1 Research Strategy & Theoretical Framework

This study has been based on a grounded theory research method, that is to say that it has sought to develop or generate theory from the data sources using a constant comparative method. The grounded theory research method has been applied to the academic literature on the work of divorce solicitors and family mediators as well as the professional bodies' documents, although the literature has not been used as data in a strict sense, but to assist in the formulation of conceptual categories and theoretical categories. The literature review has formed part of the research phase of the study, rather than a precursor to it, and is consequently discussed after the methods chapter rather than before it. This is an accepted approach to the literature in grounded theory generation.

> [C]omparing one piece of data to another does not entirely remove the potential of intrusion of bias into interpretations. Thus, we also might turn to the literature or experience to find examples of similar phenomena. This does not mean that we use the literature or experiences as data per se. Rather, what we do is use the examples to stimulate our thinking about properties or dimensions that we can then use to examine the data in front of us.[48]

A study of this type is emergent and the literature is treated as part of the theory generation process rather than separate to it.

The study began with an understanding of the mainstream accepted position that solicitors act in an adversarial manner in divorce cases as compared with family mediators who adopted a mediatory, some would say consensus based, approach to divorce.[49]   Grounded theory purists suggest that researchers should not use a grounded theory method, if they wish to modify an existing theory rather than seek to generate a new one.[50] Having said that, there is some debate about whether one

---

[48] Strauss, A. & Corbin, J. *Basics of Qualitative Research: Techniques and Procedures for Developing Grounded Theory* 2nd Ed. (Thousand Oaks, London, New Delhi: Sage Publications, 1998) at 44-45.

[49] This is discussed in more detail in chapters 1 and 3.

[50] For a discussion of grounded theory and the theoretical divisions within the Grounded

can ever begin a study without some knowledge of previous work on the area and without a view on the theories already extant.[51] Purists employ a grounded theory method to bring a 'scientific' approach to social science study and more closely observe the rules of natural science as regards initial neutrality in respect of theories to be generated. Others are less convinced of the positivistic tendencies of grounded theory method and tend towards a more pragmatic approach to research.[52] It is asserted here, that although the study has been conducted against a backdrop of a continued debate about whether divorce solicitors and family mediators approach their work in an adversarial or consensus based manner, the method is none-the-less an appropriate one. The study has sought to consider what cues the professional bodies send to their members about appropriate professional approach and what this indicates about professional identity. Therefore, a grounded theory method is consistent with the aims of the study.

Grounded theory relies on theory emerging throughout the research, rather than hypothesis testing and verification. Instead,

> The general good of grounded theory research is to construct theories in order to understand phenomena. A good grounded theory is one that is: (1) inductively derived from data, (2) subjected to theoretical elaboration, and (3) judged adequate to its domain with respect to a number of evaluative criteria.[53]

Grounded theory thus relies on inductive reasoning.[54] The study did not seek to verify or to reject the hypothesis that solicitors approach their work in adversarial terms and that family mediators approach their work based on a consensus based model, which would have been in-keeping with an experimental model of socio-legal research.[55] An experimental design made up of a literature review, the development of a hypothesis, a data collection phase followed by analysis and the acceptance or rejection of the hypothesis, appeared to be insufficiently flexible to accommodate the analysis of documents produced by the professional bodies, which were the main source of data on the cues given by the professions. Qualitative analysis of documents required a more flexible research strategy that could be refined as more was learnt

---

Theory community, see Bryant, A. 'Grounding Systems Research: Re-establishing Grounded Theory' *Proceedings of the 35th Hawaii International Conference on System Sciences*, 2000.

[51] *Id.*

[52] *Id.*

[53] Haig, B.D. 'Grounded Theory as Scientific Method' (1995) *Philosophy of Education* at www.edu.uiuc.edu/EPS/PES-yearbook95_docs/haig.html. See further Kinach, B.M. 'Grounded Theory as Scientific Method: Haig-Inspired Reflections on Educational Research Methodology' (1995) *Philosophy of Education* at www.edu.uiuc.edu/EPS/PES-Yearbook/95_docs/kinach.html.

[54] Punch, K.F. *Introduction to Social Research* (London: Sage Publications Ltd, 1998) at 163.

[55] Grounded theory is considered to have '...led researchers from the tyranny of verifying theory and instead instructed them to focus on generating theory.' Wagenaar, H. 'The (Re-)discovery of Grounded Theory in Postpositivist Policy Research.' Paper prepared for the ESF *Workshop Qualitative Method for the Social Sciences*, Vienna, 28th-29th November 2003 at 1.

from each subsequent document during the research process. The professional bodies' documents were reviewed principally in 2003, 2004 and 2005, with some final analysis undertaken for updating purposes in 2006. To this end, grounded theory seemed to meet the need for a theoretically founded yet flexible strategy that would allow for systematic yet sensitive analysis of documentary sources. Grounded theory has an appeal to qualitative researchers because it follows the natural pattern of human enquiry. It allows the researcher to seek an understanding of an area, by developing and refining a theory as more is learnt about the area. It is pragmatic and yet theoretical.[56] In other words, grounded theory provides a framework for the whole research process and not simply a means of extracting data from documents.

But why choose grounded theory as a mode of qualitative analysis rather than the more frequently used content analysis? As Miles explains,

> The most serious and central difficulty in the use of qualitative data is that methods of analysis are not well formulated. For quantitative data, there are clear conventions the researcher can use. But the analyst faced with a bank of qualitative data has very few guidelines for protection against self-delusion, let alone the presentation of unreliable or invalid conclusions to scientific or policy-making audiences. How can we be sure than an 'earthy', 'undeniable', 'serendipitous' finding is not, in fact, wrong?[57]

Content analysis provides a framework for analysing qualitative data, but does not provide an overarching theory for the whole of the research process, unlike grounded theory. Grounded theory seeks to go further than describing the data: 'Good codes tell you something about the data in a way that ties different instances of the empirical material together. A well-chosen, evocative coding label creates a conceptual category that simultaneously describes and explains the data."[58] However, grounded theory is not without its critics and the extent to which grounded theory is distinct from descriptive 'qualitative data analysis' is a moot one. Glaser and Charmaz are still hotly debating the distinction.[59] A postmodernist or a constructivist would reject any possibility of findings being reproducible and objective in any way, all findings being the product of a local, contingent understanding by the researcher analysing the data at that time in that context, there being many realities all dependent on one's own life course.[60] However, it is

---

[56] See Glaser, B. & Strauss, A. *The Discovery of Grounded Theory: Strategies for Qualitative Research* (Chicago: Aldine, 1967).

[57] Miles M.B. 'Qualitative Data as an Attractive Nuisance: The Problem of Analysis' (1979) 24 *Administrative Science Quarterly* 590 at 591. For an analysis of Miles see Punch, K.F. *op. cit.* note 54 at 200.

[58] Wagenaar, H. *op. cit.* note 55 at 2.

[59] See Glaser, B.G. 'Constructivist Grounded Theory?' (2002) Vol. 3 No. 3 *Qualitative Sozialforschung/Forum: Qualitative Social Research* [On-line Journal] Available at www.qualitative-research.net/fqs/fqs-eng.htm *cf.* Charmaz, K. 'Grounded Theory: Objectives and Constructivist Methods' in Denzin, N.K. & Lincoln, Y.S. (eds.) *Handbook of Qualitative Research* 2nd Ed. (Thousand Oaks, California: Sage Publishing, 2000) at 509-535.

[60] For an illustration of this see Pandit, N.R. 'The Creation of Theory: A Recent Application of the Grounded Theory Method' (1996) Vol. 2 No. 4. *The Qualitative Report* at

suggested that interesting insights may still be gained through a grounded theory analysis, and that this method does seek to provide a theory of value even if not one that claims to be absolute truth.

Grounded theory offers a systematic mode of analysis, some would say a mode that comes from a quantitative tradition at its heart, and yet provides the flexibility to allow thinking to emerge and develop during the documentary research process.[61] It would, perhaps be useful, to explain the actual research process by way of illustration. Grounded theory is established after three stages of analysis. Stage one is to analyse documents, interview transcripts or observation notes to discover conceptual categories from the data. This is done by reading a document and memoing (a systematic form of note-taking) phenomena that are important in each sentence or paragraph, to come up with categories or concepts. This is repeated for each document. The notes form the first stage data for the study. The second stage of analysis is to develop relationships between these (conceptual) categories, which are known as theoretical categories, which is done by reading through the stage one notes. The final stage is to develop a core concept or theory from the theoretical categories.[62] Each stage leads to a higher abstraction from the original data.

To achieve these three stages, three coding frameworks must be followed: an open coding frame for the initial stage, and axial or theoretical coding frame for the intermediate stage and finally a selective coding frame for the final stage of analysis.[63] As Strauss and Corbin explain,

> The first step toward understanding is to be able to differentiate *among description, conceptual ordering, and theorizing*. A second step is realizing that these forms of data analysis actually build on one another, with the theory incorporating aspects of both. In brief, describing is depicting, telling a story, sometimes a very graphic and detailed one, without stepping back to interpret events or explain why certain events occurred and not others. *Conceptual ordering* is classifying events and objects along various explicitly stated dimensions, without necessarily relating the classifications to each other to form an overarching explanatory scheme. *Theorizing* is the act of constructing (we emphasize this verb as well) from data an explanatory scheme that systematically integrates various concepts through statements of relationship. A theory does more than provide understanding or paint a

---

www.nova.edu/sss/QR/QR2-4/pandit.html.

[61] It has been suggested that to be truly systematic, Grounded Theory should be generated with the aid of computer assisted techniques. Others suggest that programmes can only really be used to organize data rather than to generate codes leading to theory. For a discussion see Kelle, U. 'Theory Building in Qualitative Research and Computer Programs for Management of Textual Data.' (1997) Vol. 2 No. 2 *Sociological Research Online* at www.socresonline.org.uk/socresonline/2/2/1.html.

[62] Punch, K.F. *op. cit.* note 54 at 210.

[63] *Id.*

vivid picture. It enables users to explain and predict events, thereby providing guides to action.[64]

Having said that, grounded theory does not require these three stages to be conducted in sequence, as the data collection and analysis stages of the research are merged and become cyclical; data is collected and analysed, the theory is refined and more data is collected and analysed. The cyclical design in itself means that data could be being collected for the second data cycle at the same time as the data from cycle one is being analysed. This constant comparative method continues until the theory reaches saturation – until nothing new is added and the theory has crystallised.

The open, axial or theoretical and selective coding frames also require some explanation. Open coding is a way of analysing the documents or transcripts (often considered to be 'data' in themselves), to break it open to reveal the concepts within the document, or the policy. Open coding requires the researcher to search for indicators within the document to infer concepts from the data, at a level of abstraction one above the data itself.[65] This is undertaken through a micro-analysis of the data, line by line. The labels may be seen as descriptions of the data but this is not the main purpose of the coding exercise, as the first code is not simply a description. The concepts must be derived from and generated by the data itself rather than being predetermined, as would be more usual in quantitative analysis. Instead, open coding starts the process of theorising by labelling concepts that may later be linked in stage two to become the core theory in stage three of the analysis. Axial, sometimes known as theoretical coding, takes the analysis on to the relationship-building phase.[66]

At this point the researcher seeks to consider the concepts derived from the open coding phase, to review the links between these concepts by linking the concepts together. How the links are made will depend on the coding paradigm that the researcher accepts, if one follows Strauss' and Corbin's view that the researcher needs to undertake this phase in the light of a particular paradigm. On the other hand, Glaser criticises this standpoint and considers that true grounded theory requires the researcher to take his or her lead from the data rather than trying to impose a particular theoretical approach on the conceptual coding.[67] In this study, I

---

[64] Strauss, A. & Corbin, J. *op. cit.* note 48 at 25.

[65] The first work on this theory, which is still the classic reference, was Glaser, B. and Strauss, A. *op. cit.* note 56. Glaser and Strauss went on to develop different views on the nature of grounded theory and were unable to bring those theories together. The split continues to preoccupy writers on grounded theory.

[66] Punch notes that Strauss and Corbin refer to this stage as axial rather than theoretical coding whereas Glaser tends to refer to it as theoretical coding. *Ibid.* at 215.

[67] See Glaser, B.G. *Basics of Grounded Theory Analysis: Emergence vs. Forcing* (Mill Valley, California: Sociology Press, 1992). Bryant attributes the difference in approach to Strauss' links with the Chicago school that placed a strong emphasis on qualitative research and Glaser's adherence to the Columbia school which was more quantitatively focused. Bryant, A. *op. cit.* note 50 at 3. This debate is charted by Punch at various locations in his book but particularly at 216 as a result of Glaser's book entitled *Emergence or Forcing* which is on this very point.

have adopted Glaser's approach and taken the linkages between the concepts from the data themselves, rather than applying a particular paradigm to the analysis.

The third phase in data analysis and theory generation is selective coding. In this the researcher selects the core code or category. At this point the open coding phase must end (if it has not done so already) and the researcher must focus on this core for the remainder of the analysis. Punch explains this stage thus,

> In selective coding, therefore, the objective is to integrate and pull together the developing analysis. The theory to be developed must have a central focus, around which it is integrated. This will be the core category of the theory. It must be a central theme in the data ... In order to integrate the other categories in the data, the core category will have to be at a higher level of abstraction. Potential core categories are noted right from the start of the analysis, though final decisions about the core category should not be made too early in the analysis.[68]

This phase moves the researcher from describing the relationships between the concepts to unifying them into the higher-level core concept, which in itself becomes the theory derived from and grounded in the data. The researcher must repeat this process with new data until she reaches theoretical saturation,[69] in other words that the new data no longer produce a different perspective on the theory.

There are, it is conceded, many criticisms that may be levelled at grounded theory. Commentators such as Denzin note that grounded theory only goes part way to meeting the needs of postmodernist theories of research, as grounded theory is a product of an empirical research genre, which is subject to attack in similar ways to positivism.[70] It is suggested that this, however, assumes that the researcher considers that the core concept she has abstracted into theory, is an objective truth that has finally been discovered in a similar way to the way in which scientific principles may be established. It is suggested here, that grounded theory offers a systematic approach to qualitative analysis, a strategy for research, which does not necessarily lead to grand theories or meta-narratives. Instead, it seeks to draw out concepts from the data, to organise them and to theorise them, as is true of most forms of qualitative analysis, but seeks to do so in a structured and considered fashion.

How can grounded theory operate within the context of library based documentary research? Grounded theory has tended to be used for more traditional forms of sociological research such as interview and observational techniques. Documentary research has often been conducted using research methods that position and analyse documents in their social context. Are these two research methods mutually exclusive? It is suggested that it depends on how the document is defined in the context of grounded theory, in other words, whether the data for the purposes of grounded theory, stops at the end of the physical document, or whether grounded theory considers that the social context and purpose of the document also constitute

---

[68] Punch K.F. *op. cit.* note 54 at 217.

[69] Punch, K.F. *op. cit.* note 54 at 218-219.

[70] See Denzin, N.K. and Lincoln, Y.S. (eds.) *Handbook of Qualitative Research* 2nd Ed. (Thousand Oaks, California: Sage Publishing, 2000) at 509-535.

data for the purposes of the analysis. The next section considers documentary research methodology before considering whether documents may be used to generate data in a meaningful way for the purposes of a study of this kind.

2.2 Documentary Research

This study relies heavily on documentary sources to draw conclusions by constructing a theory about what messages the two professions send to their members about the appropriate professional approach to divorce clients and divorce matters. Documentary sources, other than primary legal sources such as cases and statutes, are relatively under utilised in socio-legal research, even though they provide a rich source of data to analyse. May notes that,

> Documents, as the sedimentations of social practices, have the potential to inform and structure the decisions which people make on a daily and longer-term basis; they also constitute particular readings of social events. They tell us about the aspirations and intentions of the period to which they refer and describe places and social relationships at a time when we may not have been born, or were simply not present.[71]

The reluctance of socio-legal researchers to use non-legal documents as sources of data may in part be explained by the many differing conceptions of what constitutes appropriate method and also what reliance may be placed on documents as sources of data. This section will consider some of these differing conceptions before explaining the documents that were employed in this research.

Firstly, to what extent may documents be used as a source of data? Documentary analysis has been criticised on a number of grounds, firstly that documents are not capable of scientific forensic analysis that will yield absolute truths. In addition, at the other end of the theoretical spectrum, they do not lend themselves well to abstract theories of research as the use of documents may be viewed as another form of empiricism, which such research theories reject. Further, May explains that documentary research has been under-utilised because of concerns about how to extract data from documents in a systematic fashion:

> Documentary research is, in comparison to the other methods we have covered so far, not a clear cut and well-recognized category, like survey research or participant observation ... It can hardly be regarded as constituting a method, since to say that one will use documents is to say nothing about **how** one will use them.[72]

This places documentary analysis in a difficult theoretical and methodological position. Another view of the research process is required.

---

[71] May, T. *Social Research: Issues, Methods and Practices* 2nd Ed. (Buckingham: Open University Press, 2001) at 157-158.

[72] Platt, J. 'Evidence and Proof in Documentary Research: 1 Some specific problems of documentary research' (1981) Vol. 29 No. 1 *Sociological Review* 31. For an analysis of Platt's point see May, T. *op. cit.* note 71 at 158.

To what extent can one draw conclusions for these documents? 'For some researchers a document represents a reflection of reality. It becomes a medium through which the researcher searches for a correspondence between its description and the events to which it refers.'[73] This once again tends towards a positivist approach if the researcher considers that the document contains an objective account of what actually occurred, in other words that there is objective truth to be gleaned from the document. An alternative view is that documents represent the practical requirements for which they were created, in other words that they reflect the purpose of the document. The third conception is that documents do not report social reality as such but they are a source of meanings, '...we now utilize our own cultural understanding in order to 'engage' with 'meanings' which are embedded in the document itself.'[74] This requires a researcher to make use of hermeneutics in order to make sense of the documents, juxtaposing their meanings within those found in the text, as well as the way in which the documents were produced and their social context. However, this can lead to the conclusion that there is no meaning outside the meaning of the document, in other words that the document represents nothing but the words and meanings within it.

May returns to consider the extent to which documents are considered to be a reflection of anything at all. He states, 'It is argued that a text must be approached in terms of the intentions of its author and the social context in which it was produced.'[75] He elaborates,

> Following from Gidden's ... approach, John Scott suggests that a researcher should approach a document in terms of three levels of meaning interpretation. First, the meanings that the author *intended* to produce. Second, the *received* meanings as constructed by the audience in differing social situations, and third, the *internal* meanings that semioticians exclusively concentrate upon. However, they cannot "know" these "independently of its reception by an audience"[76]

This method rejects a straight positivist approach to documentary analysis, by fusing 'elements of realism, critical theory, feminism, postmodernism and poststructuralism'.[77] It is important to remember that the authors of documents also wish to present a certain view of themselves and their organisation and thus this context may also be considered during the analysis of documentary sources.

Aside from what data or meaning may be derived from documents, how does a researcher establish whether this document or documents are appropriate for the purposes of a study? Documents are frequently classified into primary, secondary and tertiary documents, then into public and private documents and finally into

---

[73] May, T. *op. cit.* note 71 at 158.

[74] *Ibid.* at 163.

[75] *Ibid.* at 165.

[76] Scott, J. *A Matter of Record: Documentary Sources in Social Research* (Cambridge: Polity Press, 1990) at 34.

[77] For a discussion see May, T. *op. cit.* note 71 at 166.

unsolicited and solicited sources.[78] In this respect all the documents, which are the subject of analysis in this thesis, are primary sources, although Burgess notes that primary sources must always been seen in their social context.[79] To this extent, the sources in this study have been selected because their purposes are relatively clear - they are training, accreditation and best practice standards. By the second classification, all the documents considered here are public documents rather than private documents and further are considered to be open-published documents, widely available to the public, including to course providers and to nascent as well as experienced professionals. Finally, with reference to the final mode of classification, the documents that have been used are all solicited in that they were written with scrutiny in mind rather than for personal use.[80] However, these forms of classification say little about their reliability other than the fact that the documents are of a type that are written by the bodies themselves for the purposes of setting standards for training, accreditation and professional good practice, and they are open to scrutiny by professionals. What other criteria may be used to judge the reliability of the document?

Scott considers a researcher should approach a document's quality using four separate criteria: authenticity, credibility, representativeness and meaning.[81] Authenticity relates to whether the document was produced by the person or organisation that purports to have produced it. Credible documents contain '... evidence [that] is undistorted and sincere, free from error and evasion."[82] Thirdly, a document will be considered to be representative if it is considered to be typical of documents of this sort. Typicality is important, if a researcher intends to draw more general conclusions for a document, to extrapolate from a particular document to a level of generality. The document's meaning is the fourth criteria to consider in order to establish its quality as a research subject. The meaning of the document should be considered in relation to 'what is it, and what does it tell us?'[83] This, of course, is rather more difficult than those two questions would appear to suggest, however, without reference to the social context within which the document was written.

Punch refers to Finnegan's list of eight questions that should be considered in relation to documentary research, which are set out below for the sake of completeness, although not all are relevant for the purposes of this study:

    1.   'Has the researcher made use of the existing sources relevant and appropriate for his or her research topic?

---

[78] *Ibid.* at 161.

[79] See Burgess, R. *In the Field: An Introduction to Field Research* 4th Ed. (London: George Allen & Unwin, 1990) at 124. For a synopsis of this discussion see May, T. *op. cit.* note 71 at 161.

[80] *Ibid.* at 162.

[81] *Ibid.* at 169.

[82] Scott, J. *op. cit.* note 76 at 7.

[83] Scott, J. *op. cit.* note 76 at 8.

2.   How far has the researcher taken account of any 'twisting' or selection of the facts in the sources used?

3.   What kind of selection has the researcher made in her or his use of the sources, and on what principles?

4.   How far does a source which describes a particular incident or case reflect the general situation?

5.   Is the source concerned with recommendations, ideals or what ought to be done?

6.   How relevant is the context of the source?

7.   With statistical sources: what were the assumptions according to which the statistics were collected and presented?

8.   And, finally, having taken all the previous factors into account, do you consider that the researcher has reached a reasonable interpretation of the meaning of the sources?'[84]

The majority of these questions relate to the selection of sources to be analysed in the research rather than to the mode of analysis. Again, this falls in to the arena of sampling for the purposes of this study. In this instance, it would perhaps be useful to consider each of the questions in turn in relation to this research to consider why the sources that have been employed in this study are to be considered as relevant to the enquiry. Firstly, the documents that form the basis for this study are ones drawn from the professional bodies themselves, and are the core documents relating to training, to accreditation and to codes of conduct for solicitors who conduct divorce cases and family mediators who undertake divorce mediation. This study consider the cues that the two professional bodies give to their members and therefore the extent to which the professional bodies may twist their intentions through the publication of these documents is pertinent to study as regards the context of the documents. The sources selected in the study represent the totality of the official published policy documents on training, accreditation and codes of conduct, up to the end of 2006. These documents range from documents that set out best practice statements to those that set out mandatory requirements for the profession. Question seven asks whether statistical sources have been used and if so what were the assumptions according to which the statistics were collected and presented? Statistics have not formed part of this study and so are not relevant. Finally, the documents have been analysed using a grounded theory research method in order to develop a theory from the data contained within them. Other studies that have employed the grounded theory method have used documents as a source of data – this is certainly not a novel approach.[85]

---

[84] Finnegan, R. 'Using Documents' in Sapsford R. and Jupp V. (eds.) *Data Collection and Analysis* (London: Sage Publications Ltd, 1996) at 146-9. For Punch's discussion see Punch, K.F. *op. cit.* note 54 at 191.

[85] For further information see the Grounded Theory Institute for a discussion of studies that make use of documents to generate data using the grounded theory method. This can be accessed at www.groundedtheory.com/.

Content analysis is a favoured approach in documentary analysis. Scott considers meaning in terms of the document's intended meanings, its received meaning and its content meaning.[86] Even meaning needs to be further explained, as it is itself a value-ladened term. The theoretical frame adopted for this purpose is content analysis, which as May explains, may be divided into a three stages: 'stating the research problem, retrieving the text and employing sampling methods and interpretation and analysis.'[87] Content analysis considers the frequency that words are used in a document in order to explain the meaning of the document, on the basis that the more frequently a word or phrase is employed the more significant it is thought to be. After this the words or phrases are used to construct a theoretical framework from these words or phrases. This involves a quasi-quantitative mode of analysis. There are difficulties with this approach in that this measures what can be categorised and thus relies heavily on the sensitivity of the coding frame, in addition, as May notes, it also excludes information about the purpose of the document including the context within which it is written, its practical use and that the intended audience will analyse it in the same way as the researcher. This all runs contrary to Scott's view of a three stage analysis that considers what the author intended by producing the document, what meaning was given or was likely to be given by the audience before considering the third issue which is the meaning of the document (by content analysis or another form of analysis which considers the nature of the content).[88] Scott suggests a qualitative mode of content analysis that begins with the context of the document, with emphasis placed on the author and the audience the author seeks to address. The document is then analysed by the researcher in this context using a qualitative method, by using a process through which 'the analyst picks out what is relevant for analysis and pieces it together to create tendencies, sequences, patterns and orders. The process of deconstruction, interpretation, and reconstruction breaks down many of the assumptions dear to quantitative analysts.'[89] This provides a high degree of flexibility to the researcher; it requires the researcher to develop the process of analysis, to generate a theory and then to test it and to modify it from the document to the general understanding of its social context.[90] Scott notes that this allows for the document to have various meanings depending on the audience's interpretation.[91]

Content analysis may be compared rather interestingly with grounded theory. Qualitative content analysis requires that the document is looked at in the round, which traditional grounded theory may not, however, the mode of theory generation and refinement is similar in the two forms of qualitative analysis but for the fact that grounded theory offers a far more structured approach to the analysis of the data

---

[86] See Scott, J. *op. cit.* note 76. For a discussion of Scott see May, T. *op. cit.* note 71 at 171.

[87] *Id.*

[88] Scott, J. *op. cit.* note 76.

[89] See Ericson, R., Baranek, P. & Chan, J. *Representing Order: Crime, Law and Justice in the News Media* (Milton Keynes: Open University Press, 1991) at 55 as cited by May, T. *op. cit.* note 71 at 173.

[90] *Id.*

[91] Scott, J. *op. cit.* note 76.

generated from documents and other sources. Grounded theory requires that the document be considered in order to generate the data, rather than the document be positioned within its context as part of the data generation process. However, grounded theory, does require that thought be given to sampling of data sources, and the context of the document would have to be considered in order to decide whether the document was a relevant data source for the study. Context is important, but for different reasons. The sources used in the study are set out below, including the assumptions behind their selection and use.

2.3 The Literature Review

The study began with a review of the literature of the area, although the literature review phase extended in to analysis of documents' phase. Previous research shed light on the area of enquiry and stimulated thinking on the conceptual and theoretical categories that emerged from the documents. The literature review examined dispute settlement theories and the way in which family law solicitors and family mediators appeared to be allied to distinct and different dispute settlement theories or ideologies. This served as a basis for subsequent research and permitted an extended field of enquiry than would not have been possible by a simple examination of the divide between theory and practice, to encompass issues of ideology versus descriptive definitions of the process. This, in turn, led to a re-evaluation of the line between theory and process, and indeed to consider whether there was indeed a line between them at all. The review considered the literature on family solicitors and family mediation studies to date, including the skills that solicitors and family mediators use. Family mediator skills have been examined in the literature in detail and therefore these were compared and considered. Family solicitor skills have been the subject of few research studies in the UK, whereas generic solicitor skills have been the subject of more extensive research, therefore, the literature on both has been examined. Finally the literature review considered the role of professional bodies, their codes of practice and best practice statements to examine whether these have an impact on the way in which family solicitors and family mediators approach divorce. The literature review provided a starting point for an examination of the research and a reference point against which to compare tentative conceptual categories and theoretical categories that emerged from the documentary analysis phases of the research. Consequently, the literature review was not limited to the initial stages of the study.

2.4 Training for Entry into the Profession

The second tranche of the study was a grounded theory analysis of the training course requirements set by the solicitors' professional body: the Law Society of England and Wales and the family mediators professional body: the UK College of Family Mediators in order to allow individuals' admittance as initial or trainee members to the profession. The professional bodies control, at least in part, the content of initial training courses. They do not provide courses themselves; instead they accredit other course providers to run courses that meet the bodies' training standards. The training course requirements, including their length, the organisations that are permitted to offer courses, under what circumstances and to whom, as well as the content requirements of courses were open coded, then theoretically coded before the core theory was developed and refined. The training course requirements that were compared, were those developed for students who had a prior undergraduate degree. Both types of courses also permitted initial entry into the profession on successful completion, subject to further training and supervision requirements prior to full membership status. There was evidence in the literature, discussed in the next chapter, that training has an impact on the way in which professionals view their role and carry out their profession. Training is not, of course, the only influence, however, it is none-the-less a useful starting point to determine the messages or cues from the Law Society and the UK College of Family Mediators that may influence the professional approach of their members, whether that tends towards the adversarial or towards consensus. This has been considered in more detail in the literature review and in chapter four in which this part of the research has been reported.

It is admitted that there are difficulties with this method. Solicitors do not specialise prior to beginning legal practice and therefore generic courses for would-be solicitors have been considered alongside family specific courses for family mediators. This is not ideal, however there was no effective way of considering generic courses or specific courses for both professions, as there are no family specific courses for would-be solicitors. There are generic courses for mediators that are not restricted to family mediation; however, family mediators are not generally members of generic mediation bodies such as Centre for Effective Dispute Resolution of the Civil Mediation Council. They have tended to join the UK College of Family Mediators and to have undertaken family mediation training rather than generic training. The reality of professionally ascribed training, for those who enter legal and mediation practice in divorce matters, has been generalist in scope in the context of solicitors and subject specialist in the context of family mediators and this has been reflected in the study.

In addition, a number of other assumptions have been made. It has been assumed for the purposes of this study that those entering family mediation training and professional training to be a solicitor have already successfully obtained an undergraduate degree or equivalent other qualification. It is admitted that a large proportion of entrants into the solicitors' profession do so after completing an undergraduate LLB degree course rather than through the non-qualifying law degree route followed by the Graduate Diploma in Law (GDL) course (often known as the CPE course or the conversion course). The Law Society's Annual Statistical Review 2006 notes that the GDL route is the second most frequently adopted route into the professional, after the LLB route, in a list of seven possible routes. However, there is no equivalent subject specific degree programme for family mediators with which to compare a law degree programme. In addition, LLB degrees, while broadly similar in core content, may be extremely different in terms of options subjects offered, pedagogical approach, theoretical perspective and assessment. The most closely equivalent courses are those that generally require a degree level qualification to allow entry on to the initial training programme. Having said that, while successful completion of the initial training programme for family mediators permits entry into the profession, successful completion of the GDL does not permit entry as a trainee solicitor. Would-be solicitors must also successfully complete the Legal Practice Course (LPC). The requirements for LPC courses have therefore also been included for the purpose of this study.

The course requirements set by professional bodies have been considered rather than individual courses run by training providers. Different course providers commit different types of information to paper, some produce very detailed course handbooks, others provide hand-outs for each lecture, those with a training focus rather than an academic focus may provide a training pack, and others even provide some of their training on-line. It would have been tremendously difficult to compare courses for which different types of information and levels of information were available for scrutiny. Instead, courses have been examined at a macro level by considering the essentials of the courses as set by the professional bodies from their published course criteria. This does not provide as much detail as individual course content, it is accepted, however, with any analysis that seeks to consider two or more bodies, it is suggested, that it is important to be able to analyse similar data sources. In addition, individual courses may reflect the cues that the professions have sent to their members to a greater of lesser extent, whereas the training documentation issued by the professional body provides a primary source of data on this point. The analysis has focused on initial entry requirements and any further additional entry requirements over and above an undergraduate degree, the content of the course in terms of the subjects covered and where possible the number of hours that are attributed to each subject, the skills that are taught during the course, the balance between skills and substantive knowledge balance, the mode of assessment and the duration of the course.

2.5 Accreditation or Post-Entry Requirements for Full Membership of the Profession

The third tranche of the study was a grounded theory analysis of the accreditation requirements or the post-entry training and supervision requirements for full membership of the solicitors' profession (to reach 'solicitor of the Supreme Court of England and Wales' status) and of the family mediation profession (to reach full membership of the UK College of Family Mediators or practitioner members of the Family Mediation Panel of the Law Society of England and Wales). Once again, the underlying assumption for this method of analysis has been that mandatory professional requirements will have an impact on the way in which professionals approach their work. This assumption has been examined in the light of the literature in the next chapter, in which there is an examination of studies that have indicated that the way in which professionals have been introduced to professional practice has had an impact on their view of their professional approach and shape their professional identity.

Once again, trainee solicitors have not been required to specialise prior to full solicitor status and therefore the requirements have been drawn as generic requirements rather than family law specific ones. There are family law specific requirements that are considered, however, these requirements have been for a more specialised level of legal practice rather than for qualification as a solicitor and it is important to see those requirements in that light. The Law Society has not considered it to be necessary for to require any family law training prior to becoming a qualified solicitor, who would be entitled to practice in that area. The accreditation requirements have also been considered for solicitors who wish to be accredited as family law specialists by the Law Society. The UK College had set out its accreditation requirements for full membership of the College. These include further training, supervision and the number of hours of professional practice that must be undertaken prior to full status being granted. The Law Society also has requirements for practitioner status of the Family Mediation Panel. The accreditation or post-entry requirements have been analysed to consider what these reveal about professional approaches to divorce dispute settlement as were any further training programmes that must be undertaken in order to achieve full membership status. The analysis focused on the requirements set by the professional bodies for the content of additional educational and practical training to be undertaken including modes of assessment and once again followed the grounded theory approach to data analysis.

2.6 Codes of Conduct & Best Practice Statements

The fourth tranche of the study was a grounded theory analysis of the codes of practice and additional specialist codes for divorce solicitors and for family mediators. The assumption underlying this method was that codes of conduct and best practice statements would have an impact on the way in which professionals approach their work. This assumption has been considered in more detail in the literature review in the light of others' studies. In addition, the force of the codes by the Law Society and the UK College of Family Mediators were considered in view of the fact that enforcement itself may have an impact on the way in which the professions approach professional practice, for example whether codes are declaratory or whether they have a constraining effect.

All practicing solicitors are required to follow the solicitors' code of conduct, the *Guide to the Professional Conduct of Solicitors* and family mediators who apply for accredited family law status must comply with the *Protocol on Family Mediators Practice*. Solicitors who carry out family mediation are encouraged to meet the requirements of the voluntary code of conduct on family mediation, the *Code of Practice for Family Mediators*. Family mediators who are members of the UK College are required to meet the requirements of the College *Code of Practice for Family Mediators*. These codes have been open coded, theoretically coded and then the core concept has been developed and compared with those derived from the earlier data cycles including the documentary analyses and the literature review stages.

2.7 Conclusions

The study concluded by setting out the core theory that has been established in respect of the cues that the professional bodies send to their members about the professional approach and role to be adopted in divorce dispute settlement, as evidenced through their training and accreditation requirements and codes of conducts. The core concept has drawn together the categories developed through open coding and the linkages established through axial coding to reach a theoretical understanding of the approach that the professional bodies encourage their members to adopt in divorce matters. Each of the data tranches has been considered in turn, in the subsequent chapters, before the core theory is explained in the final chapter. The next chapter considers the literature reviewed during the study.

Chapter 3: Review of the Literature on Dispute Resolution

The previous research on this area is reviewed in this chapter, in particular the literature on approaches to divorce dispute settlement in respect of family mediators and divorce solicitors. The literature review was not limited to the early stages of the research, although an initial review of the literature was conducted to situate this study within previous academic work. It also ran alongside the grounded theory analysis of professional literature and, where appropriate, the academic literature has been used to assist in creating conceptual categories and theoretical categories derived from the professional counterparts. The conceptual categories and theoretical categories have not been displayed in tabular form, unlike in subsequent chapters, as, firstly, this did not appear to be an appropriate structure for the academic literature and secondly, the literature has been used to suggest concepts rather than as a stand alone data source. However, four empirical studies on divorce solicitors and research on family mediators have been discussed in detail, each in turn, to show the development of thinking.

The chapter begins with a brief explanation of the legal process of divorce and theoretical perspectives on adversarialism and alternative dispute resolution, to place divorce within its context. Secondly, the literature has been reviewed to consider evidence of the nature of solicitor participation in the divorce process and their approach in divorce matters and similarly the nature and approach of family mediation and family mediators. The chapter concludes with a tentative theory on the approach that divorce solicitors and family mediators adopt in divorce matters, which is developed later in the context of the research undertaken on the messages that the processional bodies send to their members through training, accreditation and codes of conduct.

3.1 Divorce: The Legal Process

Marriage is a recognised legal status with legal consequences although many couples would not view their wedding as the day on which they entered into a legal relationship. Divorce, on the other hand, is popularly understood to be a legal process, is associated with the courts and is also synonymous in the minds of many with solicitors. It is suggested that by far the majority of those who are going through a divorce seek third party assistance at some stage during that process, most usually from solicitors but some also from family mediators, even though this is not required by law.[92] Full court hearings were a feature of divorce in the earlier part of the twentieth century, however, by 1966 only a very small minority of divorces were defended (7%) and in 1989 only 285 defended divorces went on to a full court hearing.[93] Lowe considers that this figure may now be as low as fifty per year,

---

[92] Davis, G., Macleod, A. & Murch, M. 'Undefended Divorce: Should Section 41 of the Matrimonial Causes Act 1983 be Repealed?' (1983) Vol. 6 No. 2 *Modern Law Review* 121.

[93] As cited in Hoggett, H., Pearl D., Cooke E. & Bates P. in *The Family, Law and Society Cases and Materials* 4th Ed. (London, Edinburgh, Dublin: Butterworths, 1996) 225. Since then the annual figures appear to have stabilised at around 200, although there is little hard evidence upon which to judge this as indicated during the House of Lords debates at the time of the passage

although reliable figures are difficult to come by.[94] Elston, Fuller and Murch found that judicial hearings served little purpose in divorce cases in any event, as it was rare for judges to find the legal ground for divorce to be unproven.[95] With the extension of the 'special procedure' in 1977 to all undefended divorces, the dissolution of marriage relied less on court hearings.[96] Although few divorce cases are fully litigated, it is not unusual for an aspect of a case, whether it relates to child contact and residence, or financial or property issues, to appear before a judge at some point in the divorce process.[97] Legal assistance is still sought by the majority of couples at some stage during a divorce[98] although as solicitors are rarely seeking to prove that the grounds for the divorce are or are not met, they do not necessarily need to adopt an adversarial approach to the divorce. It is, however, generally understood that their role is a partisan one and that they are, with few exceptions, required to represent the interests of their client.

The history of the divorce process and the nature of partisanship go a long way to explaining why adversarialism has come to be associated with it. Divorce law has evolved from the paradigm of judicial adjudication and as adversarialism has generally been favoured over inquisition in the common law tradition, divorce has consequently been associated with adversarialism, legal process, and legal professionals. There are those who consider that adjudication is the most appropriate way for decisions to be taken when there is a dispute,[99] others consider that the couple are the best people to settle family issues,[100] either with the assistance of solicitors (although this is often still discussed as an extension of adversarialism)

---

of the Family Law Bill 1996.

[94] Lowe, N. *Grounds for Divorce and Maintenance Between Former Spouses, England and Wales*, October 2002 Law Department, University of Cardiff Wales at 6 available at: http://www2.law.uu.nl/priv/cefl/Reports/pdf/England02.pdf?

[95] Elston, E., Fuller, J. & Murch, M. 'Judicial Hearings of Undefended Divorce Petitions' (1975) Vol. 38 *Modern Law Review* 609.

[96] Divorce has not been removed from the court altogether, as a District Judge still considers the petition, supporting affidavits and evidence in order to be satisfied that the legal ground for granting a divorce has been met, prior to pronouncing the decree in open court. This is, however, far removed from an adversarial hearing before a judge. The judge must remove the case from the special procedure if he is not satisfied with the petition, although he may ask for further information or evidence prior to taking this step. For a full explanation of the special procedure see Appendix C of the Law Commission's Report *Family Law: The Ground for Divorce: The* Law Commission Number 192 (London: HMSO, 1990). For a discussion see Hoggett, H., Pearl D., Cooke E. & Bates P. *op. cit.* note 93 at 225.

[97] See note 8 for a breakdown of judicial statistics in relation to divorce in 2005. As the figures indicate, courts are not called upon to make orders on ancillary issues in the majority of divorce cases, and the largest category of the orders is consent orders Judicial Statistics 2005 (London: Department for Constitutional Affairs, 2006). The 2006 statistics were not available at the time or writing.

[98] Davis, G., Macleod, A. & Murch, M. *op. cit.* note 92 *cf.* Genn, H, *op. cit.* note 4.

[99] See the discussion of Fiss' and Twining's work later in the chapter.

[100] See the discussion of Finlay's work later in the chapter.

or with the help of family mediators.[101] The next section will consider the extent to which the literature supports or rejects the place of judicial decision-making on divorce.

3.2 Judicial Decision-Making: Justice or Fairness?

The mode of dispute determination will have an impact on the way in which professionals within the field will operate, and thus the approach that they are required to adopt. Solicitors operating within a paradigm of judicial determination may be more likely to look to precedent in divorce matters to assist in advising a client, if cases are likely to come before a judge, whereas they may be more likely to negotiate in a less legalistic manner if it is less likely that cases will proceed to judicial determination. There is strong support in some quarters for judicial determination of disputes, over private decision-making. Owen Fiss provides an interesting insight into the purpose of adjudication in his article 'Against Settlement'. To him, settlement is a decision to reach a peace rather than to reach justice and to suggest that adjudication is merely the public decision of a private dispute takes away the underlying public function of adjudication and its great strength.[102] He claims that the purpose of adjudication is not to maximise the parties' private interests, nor is it designed to settle a dispute. Instead, its purpose is to reinforce the values that are embodied in the law, to interpret the values and apply them within society. Private ordering undermines the duty of the law to perform these functions.[103]

It is further argued by Fiss that the move away from adjudication and towards private ordering through ADR mechanisms stems from the misunderstanding of adjudication as a formal process of settlement.[104] Fiss further explains,

> I do not believe that settlement as a generic practice is preferable to judgment.... It should be treated instead as a highly problematic technique for streamlining dockets. Settlement is for me the civil analogue of plea bargaining: Consent is often coerced; the bargain may be struck by someone without authority; the absence of a trial and judgment renders subsequent judicial involvement troublesome; and although dockets are trimmed, justice may not be done. Like plea bargaining, settlement is a capitulation to the conditions of a mass society and should be neither encouraged nor praised.[105]

---

[101] See the discussion of Roberts, S. & Roberts M.'s work later in the chapter.

[102] Fiss, O.M. 'Against Settlement' (1984) Vol. 93 *Yale Law Journal* 1073 at 1085.

[103] *Id.*

[104] This is of interest in civil procedure in Britain more generally as seen in the Civil Procedure Rules 1.4 in which the parties are encouraged to use an alternative dispute resolution procedure (CPR 1.4.(2) (c)) including the potential for cost penalties to be imposed on the parties by the court in the light of 'all the circumstances' including the 'conduct of the parties' including the 'efforts made, if any, before and during the proceedings in order to try to resolve the dispute' (CPR 44.5 (1) and (3) (a)(ii)).

[105] Fiss, O.M. *op. cit.* note 102 at 1075.

He criticises ADR supporters' assumptions of equality of bargaining power between the parties, and the opportunity to predict the courts' outcome and thus pre-empt it. He also claims that financial inequalities make settlement unequal as bargaining power is affected and this is at odds with 'justice' that is blind to financial status.[106] If settlement is privileged over adjudication, a plaintiff may be forced to settle for less than may be awarded by a court on grounds of financial exigency, rather than be compelled to wait for the court's pronouncement of what justice demands. Fiss' arguments turn the spotlight firmly on the cost of litigation and financial assistance for those on meagre resources, so as to prevent capitulation to an early settlement to avoid litigation costs.

ADR advocates would profoundly disagree with Fiss' conclusions, in part on the basis that cost reduction and time savings are not the aim of mediation, even if they may be a beneficial corollary. Equally, the effect of financial imbalance is not restricted to mediation and other forms of ADR; it may also be felt in the solicitor-client context. Fiss acknowledges that financial imbalance between the parties can have an effect on an adjudicated outcome, as this can affect the lawyers that one may hire and the presentation of the case, however, he claims the judge can seek to redress or at least reduce the impact where it appears to be prejudicial.[107] He does not believe that this is possible without adjudication, although one could suspect that he is considering ADR by solicitors in the guise of inter partes negotiations rather than family mediation as currently established in Britain. Family mediators could argue exactly this defence of family mediation over solicitor assisted negotiations as well, although perhaps only those who are more interventionist rather than facilitative would have us believe that this is the essence of family mediation. In other words, it is the lack of legal norms within the process that appears to trouble Fiss; settlement without recourse to norms is the power broker's charter.

Fiss' discussion about the absence of authoritative consent[108] is more relevant to organisations than individuals within a family relationship in the way that he draws the discussion, as it refers to organisational structure and who is empowered to make a decision. This is based, it seems, on settlement as contract - the ability to bind others within one's organisation through one's contract with the other party. Phrased differently however, his objection about the absence of authoritative consent within negotiations could be made relevant to family disputes and it has been argued elsewhere as an objection to settlement in some family mediation contexts where a settlement is reached on the basis of a lack of information about the financial position of the other party or of the family as a whole, of entitlements such as pension rights or equity in a house, or even of the true value of outstanding debts.[109] This objection is mitigated, if the parties each have a legal representative, as the solicitor would be expected to know the relevant legal provisions and legal consequences of settlement options. This cannot necessarily be argued for unrepresented clients in a family mediation session. Consequently the role of a family solicitor may not necessarily be

---

[106] Fiss, O.M. *op. cit.* note 102 at 1076.

[107] Fiss, O.M. *op. cit.* note 102 at 1077.

[108] Fiss, O.M. *op. cit.* note 102 at 1078-1082.

[109] See Webley, L.C. *op. cit* note 16 at 88-90.

one of partisan in the true tradition of adversarialism, but of champion with a set of prevailing legal norms established to ensure that no party is unduly disadvantaged by settlement. In other words this is not 'winner takes all', but a 'who can do slightly better' situation within a defined framework. If so, it may be less important to have a truly adversarial solicitor, but one that is a specialist in the legal norms as Fiss suggests in another context.

Fiss also argues that judgment is often not the end of the process, but merely the start, whereas settlement assumes that the bargain struck is the end and the dispute resolved. Fiss does not recognise the 'transformative' nature of a process like family mediation, where the parties may learn the skills they need to resolve further issues between themselves in the future, however, in the context of solicitor negotiation settlement he may be correct in assuming that settlements struck through this means must either be renegotiated or litigated if they are not performed as contracted. Thus litigation may be merely delayed rather than avoided and judicial intervention at this stage may be hampered by previous attempts at settlement. The court may not have been previously involved in the process and therefore may lack the necessary knowledge of the parties' situation to be able to vary a consent order reached behind closed doors and out of sight of court scrutiny. However, to what extent it may be asserted that the court ever knows that much about the basis for consent order on divorce is a moot point and this objection may be more relevant to civil non-family cases where a full trial has taken place and a complete court file is available for inspection. Genn in her study noted that respondents who reached an agreement concerning their divorce or separation arrangements were significantly more likely than others to think the agreement was to be unfair and to wish that they had handled their problem differently so that they could have achieved their objectives.[110] The question is whether settlement is seen as a compromise too far for some clients, unlike judgments which are accorded legitimacy as a result of the adjudication process. One wonders whether cases settled by solicitors who explicitly refer to legal norms and explain these to their clients, are considered in the same way.

O'Donovan, however, criticises the role of legal norms to settle divorce settlement, by considering who the legal norms are aimed to protect. She sets out some of the literature on the standpoint of law in the family context. She reiterates Naffine's view that law is the preserve of white middle class men that strengthens and supports the values that underpin this group. Quoting Naffine,

> although officially the legal subject is universal, in practice:[the] man of law is assumed to be a freestanding, autonomous creature, rationally self-interested and hard-headed; on the other hand he is a being who is assumed both to have and to need access to the values of Gemeinshaft, the family values, though he must not display them in his public, legal Gesellshcaft life.[111]

---

[110] Genn, H. *op. cit.* note 4 at 200, 208. For a discussion of these findings see Douglas, G. *op. cit.* note 5 at 2.

[111] Naffine, N. *Law and the Sexes: Exploration in Feminist* Jurisprudence (Sydney, Melbourne, Wellington & London: Allen & Unwin, 1990) at 148 as cited by O'Donovan, K. *op. cit.* note 12 at 32.

If one takes this view, then law is prioritising one conception of family over another. The privileging of this 'man of law' and his view of society has been attacked by these and other feminist critics as silencing and distancing women from legal discourse and thus from the legal recognition of their worth and needs in divorce. However, it could be argued that the *'freestanding, autonomous creature, rationally self-interested and hard-headed'* label could also be applied to facilitative family mediation. Family mediation may give a forum for the private realm to be explored, however, in the face of the public realm, the private may be subsumed unless the family mediator is able to redress the balance and reinforce the importance of the private. It could be argued that legal and family mediation routes to divorce settlement are both operating under similar assumptions. Autonomy of decision-making, detachment and rationality are all prized over emotion, dependence and subordination. This fails to account for the relationship between the parties, as there will be a measure of emotion, dependence and subordination within the marriage. The party who fits less neatly into the articulate, autonomous male role and more squarely into the emotional, dependent, subordinated role, is more likely to be disadvantaged by both forms of dispute settlement unless overt steps are taken to redress the balance. Fiss would argue that a judge is in the best position to do this, family mediators may argue that they are better placed as they have insight into the private world of the parties through exploration of it through the mediation process.

O'Donovan further argues that the public is privileged over the private by family law, and it could be argued if so that the professionals who are involved in the process of divorce from a legal standpoint, reinforce the public view of the family through the overt or covert application of legal norms,

> As regards the conduct of "domestic life", the rule is that Courts of Law should not intervene except upon occasion. It is far better that people should be left free (Re Agar Ellis, 1883:335). Home and refuge being, in the eyes of the law, identical, it is for the inhabitants to sort out their disagreements. "The parties themselves are advocates, judges, courts, sheriff's officers and reporter. In respect of these promises each house is a domain into which the King's writ does not seek to run, and to which its officers do not seek to be admitted" (Balfour v. Balfour, 1919).[112]

It is suggested that it is not just law that takes this stance. Even with a more modern, forward thinking outlook, professionals are loath to impose strictures on the family and require particular solutions to particular problems. The law appears to offer only generalised solutions; however, family mediation appears to offer no solutions at all. The former imposes a public domain view on the family when called upon to adjudicate, the latter imposes none and therefore risks the charge that the public domain view will prevail as little can be done to strengthen the private.

This should be viewed in the context of marriage itself. As O'Donovan discusses, marriage is a legal institution rather than a true contract into which adults may freely enter after freely negotiating the terms of the contract.[113] The law dictates who may

---

[112] O'Donovan, K. *Commenting on the court's role in the case of Balfour v. Balfour* [1919] All ER 800 in *Family Law Matters* (London: Pluto Press, 1993) at 41.

[113] O'Donovan, K. *ibid.* at 44.

and who may not marry, on what terms, what the legal consequences will be and how the institution may be terminated. The parties cannot easily challenge these predefined consequences, although, it could be argued that there are now ways of attempting to mitigate some of their effects by skilful use of the law, even though the legal restraints on eligibility to marry are still real and state imposed. The legal consequences do permeate all marriages and therefore the ethical underpinnings of law must have an effect on divorcing couples, whichever mode of dispute settlement they choose to adopt.

Not all scholars are in favour of the move towards alternative dispute resolution and the reduction in the importance of legal norms. Twining suggests that the move towards ADR, both by lawyers and by other professionals, is pragmatic rather than theoretically sound.[114] He claims that legal education and continuing legal education has itself promoted this drive towards ADR. He identifies three assumptions that underlie this move: the concern that the courts were becoming overburdened, a perceived need for private dispute fora particularly for commercial clients, and the idea that a system, overburdened, creaking under the weight of cases and stifled by delay and excessive cost, could not provide justice for all.[115] Twining argues that much of the literature on ADR is atheoretical, premised on assumptions about institutional modes of dispute settlement, assumptions about the desirability of ADR, and assumptions about the desirability of teaching lawyers to develop ADR skills. The exception to the atheoretical tag, Twining contends, is legal anthropological literature by Malinowski, Llewellyn, Hoebel, Gluckman, Gulliver and Nader.[116] There are those that suggest that there is a disjunction between the writing on ADR and mainstream American jurisprudence that focuses on the role of the court in the legal system. Twining argues that this may be due to the focus on doctrinal issues in mainstream legal education, focusing on the hard cases and the higher courts rather than the bulk of legal cases. Therein lies the problem, as ADR is predicated on the basis that it is alternative to litigation and yet few cases actually go through this route even in the world of non-alternative dispute resolution. Disputes are usually settled through negotiations and this along with mediation, Twining suggests, remain part of the legal process. Consequently mediation cannot be described as an alternative to litigation.[117] If it is an alternative to adjudication, then again it is a comparison with the atypical as few cases reach that stage. That is certainly true with regard to divorce cases. Consequently, the comparison may be better articulated as facilitated partisan and non-partisan negotiations.

Twining draws on Bentham's writings on 'rational adjudication and the 'Natural System of Procedure', to examine differences between adjudication and alternative

---

[114] Twining, W. 'Alternative to What? Theories of Litigation, Procedure and Dispute Settlement in Anglo-American Jurisprudence: Some Neglected Classics' (1993) Vol. 56 No. 3 *Modern Law Review* 380.

[115] Twining, W. *op. cit.* note 114 at 380.

[116] Twining, W. *op. cit.* note 114 at 381. See Snyder, F. 'Anthropology, Dispute Processes and Law: A Critical Introduction' (1981) 8 *British Journal of Law & Society* 141; and Roberts, S. *Order and Dispute: An Introduction to Legal Anthropology* (Harmondsworth: Penguin, 1979).

[117] Twining, W. *op. cit.* note 114 at 382.

dispute resolution.[118] He points to Bentham's view that reconciliation (not in the sense of marriage) was possible via the proper implementation of law consistent with his theory of utility. This could be achieved through adjudication using the natural system of procedure. However Bentham was against compromise as this leads to the parties sacrificing their rights for the object of expediency, usually cost and time, both of which are subordinate, secondary aims of the rules of procedure but not the reason for the system itself - the principal aim is to implement substantive laws. This is an interesting point in the context of both family mediation and inter partes negotiations, whether assisted or non-assisted, as both lead to compromise at the expense of the direct object of the system in order to meet the needs of the secondary objectives of the system. It may well be that there is a conflict in divorce cases between the primary objectives of the system and the evils of procedure that the natural system of procedure seeks to avoid. This does not obviate the need to apply the substantive law in individual cases; rather it is a call to reform procedural rules rather than move to alternative dispute settlement modes.

This may be considered alongside O'Donovan's analysis of family law more generally.[119] She suggests that family law has not been taken seriously by the legal establishment because it is subject to a distinct methodology; it is by its nature about individual situations rather than generalisations. Families are not legally defined. There is little coherence in a true positivist sense and it is difficult to apply rules dispassionately to such an amorphous state as 'the family'. Family law is operated informally by a wide range of professionals, few cases come to court for full adjudication and actors such as solicitors, barristers, social workers, court welfare officers and many more have an impact on the way in which individual family issues are decided. This further weakens the positivist conception of the application of legal rules to a given situation and provides weight to the case for genuine private ordering, although how this is to be achieved is unclear. Mediation seeks to facilitate this aim; however, whether process and approach are necessarily entwined has not yet been established.

3.3 Adversarialism: A Necessity?

The criticisms of legal decision-making have also been elided with the criticisms associated with adversarialism within the legal system, as adversarialism has been viewed as synonymous with legal practice. The obvious starting place is a definition of legal adversarialism. The classic definition of adversarialism in this area is Lord Brougham's, speaking of his role in opposing the petition to the House of Lords in 1820 brought to permit George IV to divorce his wife as a result of her 'unbecoming and degrading liaison allegedly adulterous', with a courtier,

> An advocate, by the sacred duty which he owes his clients, knows in the
> discharge of that office but one person in the world, that client and none

---

[118] As discussed by Twining *op. cit.* note 114 at 384-385. See Fiss O.M., *op. cit.* note 102 who is against settlement for very different reasons, and Stuart Hampshire who is strongly in favour of compromise in *Innocence and Experience* (London: Allen Lane, 1989) cited by Twining, W. *op. cit.* note 114.

[119] O'Donovan, K. *op. cit.* note 12 see 'Chapter 2: The Producers of Family Law' at 10-29.

other. To save that client by all expedient means, to protect that client at all hazards and costs, to all others, and among others to himself, it is the highest and most unquestioned of his duties; and he must not regard the alarm, the suffering, the torment, the destruction which he may bring upon any other. Nay, separating even the duties of a patriot from those of an advocate, and casting them, if need be, to the wind, he must go on reckless of the consequences, if his fate it should unhappily be to involve his country in confusion for his clients' protection.'[120]

A more extreme statement of pure partisanship, it would be harder to find, and melded in to the partisanship is also the use to which that partisanship is to be put – adversarialism in the interests of justice. It is both a definition of role and an approach to that role.

One of the main justifications made in favour of adversarialism relates to the nature of the lawyer-client relationship. If the lawyer only chooses cases because she thinks that the person is innocent, then the client has been judged by the lawyer on the basis of partial information gained prior to a court hearing and has been tired pre-court, undermining the whole trial system. Rhode posits that, if advocates see themselves principally as representing society, then clients may be unwilling to confide in their counsel, thus making counsel's task of representing her client even more difficult. Rhode cites Casper's study of criminal public defender clients, eighty per cent of whom did not believe that their lawyer was on their side.[121] Mann's study found clients unwilling to disclose information even to their private counsel due to concern about the lawyer's professional focus.[122] These considerations may apply to family cases as to criminal ones, although to a lesser extent in many cases, especially in circumstances where there is general agreement between the parties that they would like to divorce and where allegations of fault are being kept to a minimum. This may not be the case where there is serious disagreement about child residence and the upbringing on the children, as allegations may be made by one partner against the other to discredit the parenting skills of the parent to bolster their own case. This is, however, frowned upon and is certainly not considered to be a good practice approach to child cases by Resolution and specialist accreditation schemes such as the Law Society's own accreditation for family solicitors. The lawyer-client relationship may not require an adversarial approach in family law on traditional grounds, even though there may be a perception that this is how divorce cases are conducted.[123]

---

[120] *Report of the Proceedings Before the House of Lords on a Bill of Pains and Penalties Against Her Majesty, Caroline Amelia Elizabeth, ed. J. Nightingale*, 1-3 (London 1821) as cited by Rhode D.L. 'An Adversarial Exchange on Adversarial Ethics: Text, Subtext, and Context.' (1991) Vol. 41 No. 1 *Journal of Legal Education* 21 at 30, note 1.

[121] Casper, J.D. *American Criminal Justice: The Defendant's Perspective* (Englewood Cliffs, N.J.: Prentice Hall, 1972) at 105-06; and Casper, J.D. 'Did You Have A Lawyer When You Went to Court? No, I Had A Public Defender.' (1971) 7 *Yale Review of Law & Social Action* 4.

[122] Mann, K. *Defending White-Collar Crime: A Portrait of Attorney's at Work* (New Haven, Yale University Press, 1985) 37-55, 103-123 as cited by Rhode, D.L. *op. cit.* note 120 at 32.

[123] Policy statements during the passage of the Family Law Bill suggest that it is a perception in

Adversarialism in the form of zealous representation is also applauded in criminal cases to encourage proper investigations by the prosecuting authorities and police, especially in an atmosphere in which few cases are tried on the facts. It is argued that zealous advocacy in those few cases that do go to court can have profound effects on the way in which the police investigate all cases which have the potential to go to court.[124] In family cases, of course, there is no equivalent of trial by jury with the prosecutor being called to account. However, few family cases do go on to court and the point could equally be made that lawyers operating for the 'other side', when required to put their case to test before a judge, may be influenced by the need to produce evidence for some of their assertions for a small number of cases and therefore more circumspect in relation to allegations that they make during the course of out of court negotiations, in all cases.

There are inherent difficulties in taking Lord Brougham's statement at face value, however. Rhode, asked to critique the ethic of zealous advocacy (as adversarialism is termed in the United States), considered how Lord Brougham conducted the celebrated case and his motivations for doing so. She concluded that his justifications masked an expert strategy which, whilst claiming that to find against his client would turn the country upside down, in fact sought to advance his client's position rather than loyally representing her in a way which might lead to civil war and the destruction of the current social order: 'For Brougham, the good of the client and of the country coincided in Queen Caroline's case.'[125] She went so far as to cite a letter Brougham wrote after the trial to William Forsyth, '[t]he real truth is, that the statement was anything rather than a deliberate and well-considered opinion, it was a menace, and it was addressed chiefly to George IV, but also to wiser men ... I am confident it would have prevented them from pressing the Bill beyond a certain point.'[126] Rhode expressed concern that adversarialism is underpinned by the principle that all advocates are equal in their abilities to represent their clients, that they have similar incentives and motivations to do so, and that all of society is represented by the law and can pay for representation. Where this is not the case, adversarialism may disadvantage some clients rather than protect them, which is the obverse of its stated aim.

Adversarialism as an approach, may not achieve the results that it claims are inherent to its success. Indeed, adversarialism may have an actively negative affect on the legal process rather than an actively positive one. Rhode provides civil law examples of cases in which zealous advocacy appears to be not only inappropriate but also unethical, for example cases in which lawyers for manufacturers were, she claims,

---

England and Wales that family solicitors approach divorce cases in an adversarial manner.

[124] See Rhode, D.L. *op. cit.* note 102 at 32-33. There are none-the-less arguments against adversarialism in a wider context, posed by those who prefer mutualism with its different philosophical underpinning. Adversarialism and mutualism are compared briefly in chapter 7.

[125] Forsyth, W. *Hortensious: An Historical Essay on the Office and Duties of an Advocate,* 3rd Ed. (London 1879) 389 at note 1 quoted in Elliot E. Cheatham (ed.) *Cases and Other Materials on the Legal Profession* 227 (Chicago: University of Chicago Press, 1938) and cited by Rhode, D.L. *op. cit.* note 120 at 35.

[126] *Id.*

complicit in the continued production and distribution of asbestos without including warnings of the potential health hazards.[127] Whilst these examples are compelling and indeed good evidence for the case against adversarialism, they would not be typical of the kinds of situations that regularly occur within family cases. The cases cited are high watermark cases which indicate not only the difficulties of zealous advocacy but also of lawyers working for big business for clients that wield strong power and influence not only over the public, but also their legal teams due to the financial might. Equally, this suggest that zealous advocacy provides an untrammelled licence to withhold significant evidence that may need to be disclosed in the public interest, which may would consider to be unconscionable. Rhode makes the distinction between advocacy ethics for criminal cases and for civil ones on the basis of the potential consequences of a verdict for the defendant in a criminal case, when compared with that of a civil trial.[128] It may also be true to say that family cases are distinct again from many other forms of civil case, when continuing relationships between the parties may make zealous advocacy inappropriate as a starting point for continuing future contact between the parties with regards to children.

If some consider adversarialism to be inappropriate in family cases, what are the alternatives? Legal process, litigation and adversarialism often appear to be considered to be part of the same concept rather then distinct entities. Finlay considers that mediation offers a worthwhile alternative to resolving family disputes through litigation and claims that one of the reasons why litigation is favoured by some is that it offers a public element to the process – outcomes are open to public scrutiny and consideration.[129] He counters one of the principal criticisms of mediation, the lack of public scrutiny of mediated settlements[130], on the basis that the

---

[127] Brodeur, P. *Outrageous Misconduct: The Asbestos Industry on Trial* (New York: Pantheon Books, 1985) as cited by Rhode, D.L. *op. cit.* note 120 at 36.

[128] Rhode, D.L. *op. cit.* note 120 at 37. Consider too Tur's view of zealous advocacy in a US context 'Yet lawyers are often perceived to aggravate conflict by identifying themselves too closely with their clients' interests. Richard Tur, for example, writes: "In the ordinary run of cases, where lawyers zealously pursue the conflicting interests of their clients. Very considerable costs may be run up without either lawyer deserving reproof. Indeed, each lawyer could point to a professional ethical duty zealously to pursue the interests of each client.' ['Family Lawyering and Legal Ethics' in Parker, S. & Sampford, C. (eds.) *Legal Ethics and Legal Practice: Contemporary Issues* (Oxford: Clarendon Press, 1995) at 150] in Eekelaar, J., Maclean, M. & Beinart, S. *op. cit.* note 34 at 89-90. Scholars have argued that there has been a distinct move away from adversarialism in the civil law context in England and Wales, and that this in part may be due to a feminization of the legal process. This is discussed in more detail in chapter 7. For a consideration of the shift see Mulcahy, L. 'Feminist Fever? Cultures of Adversarialism in the Aftermath of the Woolf Reforms' Holder, J. & O'Cinneide, C. (eds.) *Current Legal Problems 2005* (Oxford: Oxford University Press, 2006).

[129] Finlay, H.A. 'Family Mediation and the Adversary Process' (1993) Vol. 7 *Australian Journal of Family Law* 63.

[130] Although is should be remembered that there are few family law settlements that are open to full public scrutiny as there are few reported family law cases and family courts are generally closed to the public. However, judges do see many divorce settlements if asked to turn a settlement in a consent order.

law is designed to serve the people and people are not there to serve the interest of the law; public scrutiny serves the law rather than individuals who are involved in the case. The criticism of the need for public scrutiny of the operation of the law in family cases, is as relevant to solicitor negotiated agreements that do not lead on to a consent order, as it is to mediated ones that do not lead on to such an order. It is not the type of negotiations that affect public transparency of the outcome, but whether the court is involved at any stage in final decision-making process- through adjudication or a consent order. For Finlay, process and approach appear to be elided. He is concerned that the adversarial system and therefore solicitors' approach to divorce cases is detrimental to parties. He views the professional role as follows,

> While counsel cannot ethically suppress evidence merely because it is damaging, the line between mere reticence in volunteering information on the one hand, and the knowing concealment of relevant facts on the other is, at times, a very fine one indeed. One obviously does not have to make one's opponent's case for them by leading evidence that may be damaging to one's own client.[131]

Further it is argued that the role and purpose of a solicitor to be a partisan one. That the process of constructing a case, telling a partisan story and supporting this with evidence distorts the situation in front of the judge to the extent that the parties are reinforced in their views or are required to take on the fiction of story that has been constructed on their behalf.[132] The question is perhaps whether this is what the parties do themselves or whether this is something that solicitors instil in their clients.

Cross-examination is viewed as a particularly destructive part of the adversarial process in respect of personal relations between the parties, although this assumes that full scale cross-examination does indeed go on and in a more zealous way than would otherwise take place between the parties, if they were to attempt to deal with the dispute between themselves. It is suggested that the attempts to discredit witnesses are particularly damaging, although whether it is then easier for the parties to blame the advocates for this behaviour and therefore walk away from some of the more hurtful allegations at a later date, rather than take them as personal insults between the parties, is not explored. Instead these tactics are considered to be devastating for the parties themselves. Finlay's view of the role of cross examination does not meet the reality of cross examination within the setting of a county court in chambers hearing, nor the operation of round table meetings between the parties and their solicitors that seek to reach a negotiated settlement.[133] Admittedly this may accurately reflect practice at the time in Australia rather than current practice in England and Wales. However he does add that,

> The worst aspect of this kind of questioning is that the subject matter of the questions may not advance the case that is sought to be made out one iota. Indeed it could well be argued that arousing suspicions or inflaming hostile

---

[131] Finlay, H.A. *op. cit.* note 129 at 65.

[132] *Id.*

[133] Finlay, H.A. *op. cit.* note 129 at 66.

emotions retards and ultimately obstructs the ascertainment of objective truth, if indeed that is the object of the exercise. It is naïve, then, to ask whether that is always the case.[134]

He quotes Lord Denning who states that this is the only way in which the witnesses' evidence can be tested, at odds with Lord Devlin's view quoting Lord Mackenna who doubts that this type of questioning actually adds much to the assessment of a witness' credibility. Lord Devlin instead is quoted as favouring the inquisitorial system. However, could it not be argued that the questions being posed by the judge prior to the trial could be seen as 'hurtful' to the parties themselves in a different but nonetheless authoritative way to those posed by advocates for the parties, especially in a family case where full cross-examination of witnesses is rare in any event? It is argued that,

> [I]t is not uncommon to hear disappointed or disgusted litigants coming away from the court expressing their surprise and disgust at the duplicity and hostility of the other party. They have had to listen to their opponent or their opponent's lawyers make highly disparaging statements or utter lies about themselves and the matters in issue, often in strongly partisan and inflammatory terms.[135]

It is true to say that a judge's approach will be somewhat different from that of one of the advocates as the judge is not performing a partisan role. This does not remove the hurt that the parties may feel at being asked to provide very personal information about their marriage nor the fact that their views of events may be diametrically opposed thus making 'fact-finding' difficult. If these are to be aired in the court, whether by the judge in the dossier or in front of the parties then they may be framed in less inflammatory terms but will contain the fault-based allegations made by either party. Finlay is arguing, rather, against a fault based divorce culture rather than the adversarial process.

There is evidence of long standing damage being caused to the parties' relationship that results from stated the need to construct a partisan view of their situations. Finlay states that this is,

> The negative feelings engendered towards one's opponent may also carry over to a perception of one's opponent's lawyer. The personal detachment from litigation which lawyers practice or believe they practice does not form part of the average client's perception of what the legal profession is about. Few lay persons are able to appreciate the subtleties of the distinction between an advocate voicing his own views and acting merely as the mouthpiece of his client.[136]

It could be added that if the lawyer is acting as the client's mouthpiece then a move from the courtroom to the mediation room will not in itself prevent such venting of hostility between the parties unless the mediation is firmly controlled by the

[134] *Ibid.* at 67.

[135] *Ibid.* at 68.

[136] *Ibid.* at 68-69.

mediator. Hostility deflected from one party to that party's lawyer may actually be a good thing rather than a negative, if it reduces future bitterness between the parties, although it may have the negative result of bringing the profession into disrepute rather than bolstering its image as an ethical and honourable vocation. Once again, Finlay's experience of divorce practice is focused on a court-based process through which the evidence is tested and the cases for both sides considered for merit and inconsistencies. It is a long way away from negotiated settlements and round table discussions. Solicitors, adversarialism and the court have once again been inextricably linked.

The view that adversarialism is at the heart of legal practice, and that this tied into aggression, and the lawyers' personal needs to vent their aggression, is not limited to Finlay's work. Milne suggests that,

> Lawyers who pride themselves in aggressively representing their clients may be fighting more for their own needs than for those of their clients. The attorney who wants to put on a good show for his or her client may introduce conflict where it did not exist before... the conflict spreads from the divorcing parties to a personal battle between the lawyers. At this point, the attorneys are driving the conflict; the parties may be too intimidated by the professional aura of their attorneys to pull in the reins.[137]

Milne's observations relate to the United States' context rather than to the situation in England and Wales and yet Milne's understanding of the US system is not that dissimilar to many of the criticisms levelled at the UK system during the passage of the Family Law Bill in the mid 1990s. These criticisms of the US divorce arena were not entirely borne out by Felstiner and Sarat's research, which found that lawyers adopt different approaches to divorce matters depending on the situations they find themselves facing, rather than that lawyers use more aggressive or conciliatory styles.[138] However, there was some evidence of the approach outlined by Milne. Indeed, Resolution within the UK has campaigned for many years for more conciliatory modes of practice and a movement away from adversarial aggressive lawyering in divorce cases. It is admitted that full-scale cross-examination would do a tremendous amount of damage as between the parties, with very little obvious benefit, but few cases in England and Wales result in a full trial with cross-examination to lead to such a negative situation. However, the spectre of a court 'battle' has been seen by some commentators as a way to put pressure on clients to talk to each other and try to reach a settlement without the need for a court order. Sarat and Felstiner suggest that lawyers may not themselves be adversarial, even if the legal process is structured in that way. Conciliatory approaches may be possible

---

[137] Milne, A. 'The Nature of Divorce Disputes' in Folberg, J. & Milne, A. *Divorce Mediation, Theory and Practice* (New York: The Guildford Press, 1988) 27.

[138] Felstiner, W.L.F. & Sarat, A. 'Chapter 2 – Negotiation between Lawyer and Client in an American Divorce' in Dingwall, R. & Eekelaar, J. (eds.) *Divorce Mediation and the Legal Process* (New York, Oxford: Oxford University Press 1998). See further Sarat, A. & Felstiner, W.L.F. *Divorce Lawyers and Their Clients: Power and Meaning in the Legal Process* (New York, Oxford: Oxford University Press, 1995).

within the adversarial system and likewise lawyers may adopt an adversarial approach in a divorce context, even where a case is not being put to the test in court.

The next section considers the evidence of solicitors' approach to divorce matters.

3.4 Solicitors and the Divorce Process: Evidence of Approach

This section considers four key empirical studies that have examined the work of solicitors in divorce cases. The first was carried out by Davis, Cretney and Collins, the second by Sarat and Felstiner, the third by Ingelby and the final one by Eekelaar, Maclean and Beinhart. Three examine the context in England and Wales, and Felstiner and Sarat's examines the situation in the United States. The four studies, when taken together, provide an insight into the approach adopted by solicitors on divorce.

The first study considers the interaction between solicitors and their clients in divorce matters. In this first study Davis notes that the power relationship that is played out between the couple during their marriage, and the way in which they negotiated with each other, will have an impact on the way in which they deal with the separation and the issues that it raises.[139] While this may appear self-evident, it is important to bear this in mind, as the client-dynamic will have an impact on the way in which professionals respond to and participate in the dispute settlement process. Solicitors do not start with a clean sheet upon which they impose their views of settlement without let or hindrance and mediators do not open the mediation with a tried and tested client dynamic.

The nature of the dynamics between the former couple will not only affect the way in which they approach the divorce. Davis found that there was a disjunction between the way in which the parties considered their financial position, their spouse's financial position and the prevailing attitudes of the law, lawyers and court decisions, in part as a result of folk myths around what happens when a couple divorces.[140] Apparent myths that clients laboured under ranged from: the man's belief that it is his money because he earned it, the presumption of an equal division (50/50), that wife and children would be provided for by the State and therefore the man was reluctant to pay, and that conduct should be taken into account in the financial settlement. These financial presumptions were not shared in common by the couple, it was clear that men tended to have a less than realistic view about what they could expect and that women tended to undersell themselves. Thus clients' perceptions of settlement may vary widely, as will their power relationships. Both of these may have an impact on solicitor approach.

In addition, the couple did not share a common view of the negotiation process making it difficult for them to negotiate at all, as they had little shared understanding from which to begin. In part, this is evidenced by Davis *et al.*'s findings that the husband's wish to negotiate directly with the wife, contrasted with her desire to

---

[139] Davis, G., Cretney, S.M. & Collins, J. *Simple Quarrels: Negotiations and Adjudication in Divorce* (New York: Oxford University Press, 1994). See 'Chapter 3: The Parties Views of Justice' at 46.

[140] Davis, G., Cretney, S.M. & Collins, J. *ibid.* at 47-52.

negotiate financial matters through a solicitor.[141] It is not clear whether some men favour this approach because they feel they can exert more pressure on their wife's than their wife's solicitor. Solicitors have knowledge of legal norms; these tend to favour the wife by comparison with the myths, whereas women may not be as aware of their entitlement nor even the financial position of the family. Solicitors viewed their role in part as managing the expectations of the parties to reach a 'reasonable' settlement. As Davis *et al.* put it,

> [T]he courts are loath to adopt a historical perspective. The parties' sense of justice is based on their knowledge and interpretation of events over time, including events occurring before, during, and after their marriage. The refusal of lawyers and courts to take 'conduct' into account negates the historical perspective upon which many people construct their understanding of the relative merits of their case. In contrast, lawyers and courts focused only upon the circumstances, needs, and resources pertaining at the time of divorce. The legal construction is thus in the nature of a 'snapshot' view of justice, lacking any historical or relationship dimension.[142]

Thus, a key finding was that solicitors manage the expectations of their clients in an effort to broker, what they consider to be, a fair outcome for the divorcing couple. This runs contrary to an adversarial approach, which would suggest that solicitors would fight as hard as they could to reach a good settlement for their client at the expense, if necessary, of their client's former spouse. The other studies of solicitors in England and Wales found similar behaviour as discussed below.

It is considered a rare case when a solicitor makes a spouse's conduct an issue in the divorce. Solicitors and the court view this as inappropriate in all but the most exceptional cases.[143] This can lead to tension between solicitor and client and create the impression that the solicitor is not acting in their client's best interests at all. This can pervade any settlement achieved, even if the client feels that the outcome was appropriate, in other words the solicitor ended up with the right result but for the wrong reasons.[144] This is an inherent problem within the system for some clients who cannot achieve catharsis. It may explain, at least in part, divorce clients' dissatisfaction with their solicitors. It is arguable that certain approaches to mediation would mitigate this tendency, if they permitted views on conduct to be aired in the mediation. On the other hand, the feeling of a lack of catharsis may be a product of the commonly held view that if you go to law you get justice, there is a hearing, you will be publicly vindicated, which clearly is not the case in divorce cases, if at all in the vast majority of cases.[145] Negotiating through a solicitor does not provide, as Davis puts it, that rite of passage through which clients may feel that they have moved from being married to being divorced. Mediation may provide that, but

---

[141] *Ibid.* at 60-61.

[142] *Ibid.* at 53.

[143] Davis, G., Cretney, S.M. & Collins, J. *op. cit.* note 139 at 54 and their discussion of *Wachtel v Wachtel* [1973] Fam. 72, CA in support of the courts' view.

[144] *Ibid.* at 55.

[145] Discussed in more detail by Davis, G. *et al. ibid.* at 64.

not in a public sense. Perhaps it is the need to have one's pain publicly acknowledged that is important in the end? Davis did find that for the parties to be able to separate with some feeling of self and mutual respect, they had to achieve this themselves outside of the formal negotiations between their solicitors.[146] It did not come as a natural result of the process. This, once again, suggests that solicitors are not using all the weapons in their arsenal, as one would suggest in the context of a partisan and adversarial approach to divorce.

Having said that, Davis *et al.* found that the cases examined in their research were ones in which the couple had difficulty negotiating between themselves, and therefore these may be the couples that would traditionally turn to solicitors rather than to a family mediator. The particular issues which seemed to make it more difficult to negotiate were: physical separation, new relationships being formed, financial difficulties and power issues between husband and wife within the lifetime of the marriage.[147] Solicitors and therefore also mediators are faced with couples who have very different views about what would be fair in the circumstances. It is claimed that solicitors attempt to come to a reasonable financial settlement, whereas mediators attempt to facilitate the couple in reaching their own reasonable solution. Both models have to contend with differing perspectives on entitlement and also a desire to achieve fairness in the light of the history of the relationship. Davis *et al.*'s research discredits the view that any eventual settlement is merely the solicitors' view of what the court would order at adjudication. They suggest that an important factor is the extent to which each party is benefiting from the position remaining unresolved, in other words the party that needs the settlement will be in a weaker position than the one who can hold out, classic negotiation tactics.[148] The research also found varying degrees of lawyer involvement in the financial settlement. This ranged from virtually no involvement by solicitors, to the provision of information and advice leading to the parties' own settlement, to settlements negotiated by the solicitors without much input from the parties. In some cases solicitors managed their clients' expectations heavily to either empower their client, to show the woman (usually) that she was entitled to much more than she was prepared to accept at the outset, or to challenge the man (usually) to make what the solicitor considered to be a more appropriate settlement. In the latter cases, the solicitor was actively damping down male expectations rather than inflating them, something that critics of solicitors would have you believe was never possible.[149]

Felstiner and Sarat in their work in the United States in the 1980s, and their subsequent development of this work in the 1990s,[150] noted that it is difficult to answer questions on lawyer-client relationships and therefore the role of lawyers in the divorce process without the reference to lawyer-client communication. Felstiner and Sarat observed divorces cases in Massachusetts and in California over nearly

---

[146] *Ibid.* at 65.

[147] *Ibid.* at 56.

[148] *Ibid.* at 57.

[149] *Ibid.* at 67.

[150] Felstiner, W.L.F. & Sarat, A. *op. cit.* note 138.

three years. They had access to one side rather than both parties to the divorce, forty cases in total were observed. They taped the sessions between the lawyer and the client as well as observing them. They also attended court hearings, mediation sessions and the trials and interviewed the lawyer and the client about these. Their findings revealed lawyer client interaction on divorce and the way in which negotiation play a part in reaching a conclusion to the divorce case. It is true that their research reflects a United States' perspective; however, the themes identified do have a degree of universality that transposes well to England and Wales.

Felstiner and Sarat indicate that a theme that emerged in lawyer-client discourse was the client's need for justice through the legal system via the lawyer. The client wishes to be vindicated by the legal system and the lawyer attempted to temper this by damping down expectations of what can be expected from the system, similar to Davis' findings discussed above. An example given in the research is as follows:

> Client: But as you say, if you want justice in this society, you look somewhere other than court. I believe that's what you were saying to Bob [her financial consultant].
>
> Lawyer: Yeah, that's what I said. Ultimate justice, that is.[151]

Felstiner and Sarat concluded that the central discussion in the lawyer-client relationship is whether lawyers should attempt to negotiate with the other side or insist on court adjudication. This can be raised for each issue, or for the whole case. They state that,

> While many clients think of the legal process as an arena for a full adversarial context, most divorce disputes are not resolved in this manner. Although not all lawyers are equally dedicated to reaching negotiated agreements, most of those we observed advised their clients to try to settle the full range of issues in this case. This is not to say that these divorces were free of conflict, for the negotiations themselves were often quite contentious.[152]

They noted that 'occasionally' lawyers did suggest that clients make larger claims than they had asked for, or that they refused offers or demands by the other side, however most seemed to believe that it was better to settle issues through negotiation rather than through the courts.[153] Therefore, the lawyer-client relationship appears to be premised on the lawyer attempting to manage the client's expectations of the system, and then to manage their expectations about the terms of settlement, rather than a court based fight in the traditional sense of adversarialism.

That is not to say that lawyers do not act as partisans for their clients, Felstiner and Sarat did find strong evidence of partisanship in negotiations, however, this is against a backdrop of lawyers' views of a reasonable settlement for their client, with their eyes on what a court would be likely to order given adjudication:

---

[151] Felstiner, W.L.F. & Sarat, A. 'Negotiation between Lawyer and Client in an American Divorce' *op. cit.* note 138 at 26.

[152] *Ibid.* at 27.

[153] *Id.*

Lawyer: Okay, What I would like your permission to do then is to meet with [spouse's lawyer], see if I can come up with or negotiate a settlement with him that... he says, we've got something here that I can recommend to my client, and I can say, I've got something here that I can recommend to my client. My feeling is ... that if we reach that point ... if either of the clients ... find something terribly disagreeable with the proposal that we have.. come to between [o]urselves, then the case just either can't be settled or it's not ripe for settlement.[154]

In other words the lawyers asked for permission to reach the settlement they consider to be reasonable, while suggesting that clients retained the right of veto in the knowledge that this may lead to adjudication, which may or may not yield a better outcome for the clients. This is an interesting interaction as it gives moral validity to the lawyers' role as negotiator, and the lawyers' view of reasonableness is to be preferred over that of the courts' in some senses.

They found, too, that while the lawyers appeared to endorse adversarialism through litigation, and to reflect back the client's perceived desire to litigate, they also stepped back from litigation by stressing its negative effects.[155] Interestingly this is allied with a refocusing of the client's attention to the issue that the lawyers felt were important in the case, rather than the issues that the clients felt they wanted to discuss. This could be perceived as the lawyers attempting to legalise the case, which is after all their role, or lawyers attempting to take a long view rather than become embattled in the short term issues that threaten to derail the settlement of the dispute. In fact, Felstiner and Sarat go as far as to state,

> Most of those [lawyers] we observed, construct an image of the appropriate mode of disposition of a case that is at odds with the conventional view in which lawyers are alleged to induce competition and hostility, transform non-contentious clients into combatants, and promulgate a 'fight through of justice.[156]

And further,

> To maintain this balance the lawyer acknowledges the difficulty of separating emotional and property issues, but continually reminds the client of the necessity of going to reach what he calls a 'satisfactory disposition' of the case.... [This] tends to exclude the part of the client's personality that is angry or frustrated.[157]

The responsibility for the settlement is placed on the client and the client is encouraged to be 'reasonable' in a legal and therefore non-emotional sense. A point that O'Donovan would argue is evidence for the proposition that family law privileges the public over the private. On the other hand, the client sees the property and emotional issues as linked, intertwined and impossible to separate as the

---

[154] *Ibid.* at 28.

[155] *Ibid.* at 29.

[156] *Ibid.* at 30.

[157] *Ibid.* at 35.

marriage and consequent divorce are not just about property and finance. In the long term the financial and property issues may be more important to the client's future than the emotional side of the divorce, it is suggested, and so the lawyer may be acting in the client's best interests in focusing on those issues rather than the ones that appear more immediately relevant. It also makes the process less difficult for lawyers who do not feel able to engage in raw human emotion. However, if lawyers wanted to adopt a truly adversarial approach to divorce disputes, one would expect them to exploit emotion within negotiations to maximise their client's settlement.

Having said that lawyers appear to manage their client's expectations, interaction of this nature does not operate in just one direction. Clients do appear to place demands on lawyers about what issues are raised, how frequently they are raised and how lawyers are required to deal with them with the other party. Ultimately they also have the power to veto any recommended settlement and to demur from decisions that the lawyers believe to have been reached and settled along the way. Lawyers are forced to justify settlement over litigation, they are forced to justify why settlement recommendations should be respected as fair and they are required to concede to the client's need to discuss their feelings about the process they are undertaking. These findings could be argued to indicate that clients require their lawyers to mediate on their behalf. This vision of the indispensable lawyer, the down-playing of the client's emotional needs and the lack of respect to be accorded to the legal system, would appear to strengthen the case for family mediation as a consensus based, empowering decision-making tool. However, as discussed later, the reality may not be quite as high-vaulted as the mediation conceptualist school would suggest.

Ingelby has also examined the role of the solicitor as mediator in divorce cases in England and Wales.[158] He begins his discussion with,

> Advocates of mediation have often characterised lawyers' behaviour in divorce cases as adversarial and disputatious. But studies of legal dispute processing over a wide variety of areas suggest that litigation tends to be a last resort rather than the norm... and empirical evidence to support the notion that divorce lawyers are routinely adversarial is notably lacking.[159]

Ingelby even quotes Parkinson, a well known and well respected family mediation advocate, stating that studies of divorce lawyers have shown that: '...solicitors do not necessarily take a sharply adversarial stance in matrimonial proceedings... they often restrain their clients from litigation.'[160] Consequently, even family mediators consider that divorce solicitors may restrain rather than encourage litigation, and yet this does not appear to be the general perception of the approach that solicitors adopt in divorce matters.

Ingelby reports on his research, a longitudinal year long study of the management of sixty divorce cases drawn equally from five solicitors' practices in one English city.

---

[158] Ingelby, R. 'Chapter 3 – The Solicitor as Intermediary' in Dingwall, R. & Eekelaar, J. (eds.) *op. cit.* note 138.

[159] Ingelby, R. *ibid.* at 43.

[160] Parkinson, L. *Conciliation in Separation and Divorce* (London: Croom Helm, 1986) at 25.

Ingelby argues that he found evidence that solicitors preferred conciliatory representation over adversarialism and that the nature of English divorces makes this a preferred mode of dispute resolution by comparison with family mediation. Ingelby found that solicitors were reluctant to overturn agreements that had already been reached between the couple prior to arriving at the solicitor's. [161] This conforms to the Solicitors Family Law Association (SFLA) guidelines (now Resolution), at the time, although only one of the solicitors in the sample was an SFLA member, even though others were considering membership. Ingelby noted that in some cases solicitors commented to their clients that the spouse had made a generous offer, apparently strengthening rather than seeking to undermine the basis of the privately negotiated agreement. This tends to argue against an adversarial approach.

Adjudication was a rarity in all respects in Ingelby's sample. The threat of a court application was made in only three cases and then always with a statement that it would be desirable for the matter to be dealt with by agreement instead. Only one of these cases resulted in an application being made, and even then an agreement was made just outside the court and translated into a consent order.[162] Even when the court is in sight, and there was every incentive for the solicitors to resort to a litigious (often referred to as an adversarial) approach, an agreement was negotiated to prevent it. Ingelby's view is that while solicitors do not embrace adversarialism, quite the contrary, the availability of the court is an important weapon in getting clients to reach an agreement. Its role should not be underestimated, even though it is not used frequently. Interestingly this is not a weapon only open to solicitors, and Dingwall also makes reference to it as a factor that mediators can and do use.[163] The divorcing couple also have the option of court adjudication, if their negotiations in mediation prove fruitless. The process is available in both instances, it may not be encouraged by family mediators, but nor does it appear to have been by solicitors either.

Ingelby concludes that there are strategic and economic advantages to solicitors operating non-adversarially in situations where the parties have more similar bargaining power and where there is likely to be a continuing relationship between the parties.[164] Litigation costs are more likely to go to barristers rather than to solicitors and where legal aid is being used as part of the case there are few incentives to prolong a case unnecessarily when rates of pay are so low. In addition, it could be suggested that there may be a continuing relationship between the client and the solicitor, if there is a need to renegotiate aspects of the agreement as children grow up and the family's personal circumstances change. Ingelby also suggests that solicitors view negotiated agreements as more likely to subsist over time that those imposed by the courts and therefore they favour negotiation over litigation. He

---

[161] Ingelby, R. *op. cit.* note 138 at 44.

[162] *Ibid.* at 45.

[163] As cited by Ingelby, R. *op. cit.* note 158 at 46.

[164] Ingelby, R. *op. cit.* note 158 at 47. He contrasts this with the economic and strategic advantages of adversarial behaviour in personal injury claims as found by Ross H.L. *Settled Out of Court: The Social Process of Insurance Claims* (Chicago: Aldine, 1970) and Genn, H. *Hard Bargaining* (Oxford: Oxford University Press, 1987).

suggests that but for partiality, solicitors are acting as conciliators in all but name according to Parkinson's definition of conciliation,

> A structured process in which both parties meet voluntarily with one or more impartial third parties (conciliators) to help them to explore possibilities of reaching agreements, without having the power to impose a settlement on them or the responsibility to advise either party individually.[165]

Galanter considers that all negotiations, regardless of forum, are only one step removed from litigation, coining the phrase litigotiation.[166] Ingelby suggests that family mediation and inter partes negotiation through divorce solicitors are part of this phenomenon and that family mediation is not an alternative mode of dispute resolution. In addition, through both forms of dispute settlement there will be other parties that have a part to play in the decision-making, particularly public authorities where there are benefits issues or local authority housing issues and their legal requirements may place the decision-making of the couple within a legal sphere, limiting their agreement opportunities. The state of knowledge of the parties will increase and their views may fluctuate on the outcome with which they feel most comfortable.[167] This is true in both solicitor assisted divorce and in family mediation. Consequently, the divorce settlement process may be different as may professional focus, but professional approach may not.

If it is suggested that professional approach may not be that different between solicitors and family mediators, then what is the difference between the roles that they play? Ingelby considers that there are 'advantages to partiality and formalism'[168] in divorce negotiations. Negotiations through solicitors can allow time for the parties to adjust to their new situations and to assist in more long-term solutions - studies by Wallerstein and Kelly and Hart bear this out.[169] It also permits more fact-finding. It is suggested that physical separation may be important in cases of spousal violence but in others it may also take some of the bitterness out of the discussions. Negotiations through solicitors may reduce rather than increase tensions and emotion between the parties. This suggests that partisanship may serve a useful purpose. Ingelby also attacks the notion that all family mediators are impartial rather than partisan. This will be discussed later elsewhere, but suffice to say that Ingelby views overt partiality as preferable for clients, and considers it particularly necessary where the bargaining power between the spouses is unequal to begin with.

---

[165] As cited by Ingelby, R. op. cit. note 158 at 48.

[166] Galanter, M. 'World of Deals: Using Negotiation To Talk About Legal Process' (1984) Vol. 34 *Journal of Legal Education* 368 at 368.

[167] These three 'changeable facts' are identified by Ingelby as being peculiar to matrimonial matters and having a bearing on the way in which decision-making operates. op. cit. note 158 at 50-51.

[168] Ingelby, R. *ibid.* at 53.

[169] Wallerstein, J.S. & Kelly, J.B. *Surviving the Break-Up: How Children and Parents Cope With Divorce* (London: Grant-McIntyre, 1980) and Hart, N. *When Marriage Ends: A Study in Status Passage* (London: Tavistock, 1976).

Formalism and partisanship by solicitors also provide a way of requiring disclosure and a method through which negotiations can take place with third parties such as the Benefits Agency. This is not adversarialism, Ingelby argues, it is simply partisanship at a time when the parties need to negotiate a myriad of new relationships, not just with their former spouse and family members but with other agencies and authorities. An adversarial approach may not be evidenced by partisan representation. The two may be distinctive phenomena.

The benefits of partisanship may extend even further. Some clients wanted solicitors to agree a settlement and take away the need for them to make a final decision, this was in the context of conciliation in divorce survey in the Bristol court.[170] It appears that some clients would like a professional adviser to take responsibility for decision-making on sensitive issues such as finances and property matters, providing a person to blame if they later feel disappointed with the settlement. Davis reported one woman as saying,

> I don't agree with it [mediation]. It's an effort to put your opinion across. Ideally it should have gone to the solicitors and been left at that... You're under pressure of time and a tremendous pressure to reach a decision – which you do, and it's only after that you wonder it if was the right decision. And because you're given the impression that it's your decision you have to live with your guilt. That's another aspect of it. You already have enough guilt without having more to add to it. I suppose, really, you need a scapegoat. If you have solicitors, you can always turn round and blame them [171] ....

It may be that the solicitor performs an important function as 'scapegoat' for the parties' emotional upheaval, guilt and hurt on their divorce, and that this is part of the process of coming to terms with uncoupling and moving forward.

The need for less apparent empowerment rather than more empowerment was evident in the woman's views, perhaps because she felt the couple had reached a point when a solicitor or a court was in a position to make a better decision that them. Interestingly she was not calling for greater partisanship, for her solicitor to represent her side more forcefully, but rather for her solicitor to act as her delegated representative to reach a decision on her behalf without the need for her to make that decision. Another interviewee noted that, 'I didn't feel that he [solicitor] was forceful enough; I felt that he was backing down a bit. And at the end, my opinion was that all they [solicitor and welfare officer] wanted was it sorted out and out of the way — they wanted an ending to it all.'[172] Again, this sentiment was expressed about solicitors involved in conciliation appointments; however, the clients obviously felt that there was a bias towards consensus rather than adversarialism. Davis found that

---

[170] Davis, G. 'Chapter 6-The Halls of Justice and Justice in the Halls' in Dingwall, R. & Eekelaar, J. (eds.) *op. cit.* note 138 at 97. The research findings quoted resulted from research conducted in the Department of Social Administration, University of Bristol 1979-1981, directed by Murch, M. and sponsored by the Joseph Rowntree Memorial Trust.

[171] *Ibid.* at 101.

[172] *Ibid.* at 102.

the most frequent criticism about solicitors was the fact that they did not sufficiently back-up their clients.[173] This is not the image of the adversarial solicitor that we are used to hearing. Nor does it suggest that all solicitors are *that* partisan in client negotiations.

It appeared too, that that criticism was also expressed, to a lesser extent, about the courts. The courts appeared to be settlement orientated rather than willing to impose their opinion. There were criticisms in this survey that the courts were attempting to promote consensus rather than making a decision themselves and ending the uncertainty. Davis comments that, '... the Special Procedure has taken us into the realm of 'administrative divorce' ... what we now appear to be observing is an attempt to apply a cloak of consensus even to contested legal applications, so that courts seek to respond in administrative rather than judicial terms."[174] Davis expressed that 'justice' becomes little more than accepted bargaining practices and that clients may not have the opportunity to air their views before a court because they are pressed to reach their own agreements outside the door of the court.[175] However, this was against a back-drop of what appeared to be a generally accepted set of norms about what was and was not a reasonable settlement in a divorce case, as explained by the solicitor, 'Solicitors to me have got blinkers on and they just look one way. I think in divorce, custody, and children, you can't do that. It's too personal, too emotional. You've got to look at each case individually. I just think it's too standardized really'.[176] Interestingly, the pressure to reach a consensus is really a consensus within a given range of acceptable solutions. The parties are then expected to take responsibility for that decision, even though some of them felt under tremendous pressure to settle, and without the backing of their solicitor acting as their champion.

Research conducted by Eekelaar, Maclean and Beinart examined the divorce work of solicitors to discover what solicitors actually do in divorce cases. They carried out a two fold methodology. In the first instance they observed ten partner level solicitors at work for a day (fourteen days observation in total as two researchers observed in some instances), recording what they did. They explained that, 'The purpose of this exercise was to acquire evidence of the business context in which the lawyers operated, how they prioritised and responded to issues as they arose, and the details of their interaction with clients.'[177] These solicitors were members of the SFLA (now Resolution) and firms were geographically spread. The second mode of data collection was to interview forty solicitors, to get the solicitor to talk through selected cases from the beginning of the case to the present position. These solicitors were selected from four regions in England and Wales and were randomly selected from solicitors offering family work from the Law Society Regional Directories.[178]

---

[173] *Ibid.* at 103.

[174] *Ibid.* at 102.

[175] *Ibid.* at 103.

[176] *Ibid.* at 104.

[177] Eekelaar, J., Maclean, M. & Beinart, S., *op. cit.* note 34 at 31.

[178] *Ibid.* at 34.

The researchers asked the solicitor to pull out the file prior to the interview and to talk through the case. After the pilot the researchers drew up a list of prompts they could use with the solicitor to ensure that key information was not missed from the case.[179] This method was used to find out the characteristics of how solicitors undertook their case work.'[180] The observational data revealed some interesting results. The research team found two extreme positions, that of the legal aid practitioner providing a service as regards all aspects of the client's life, legal and non-legal, juxtaposed against the private practice model of high monetary value cases for which the solicitor took instructions and acted more as an adversarial champion than did other divorce solicitors. The mid-point, the private practice solicitor carrying out non-legal aid, non-high value cases, tended to have a client that had views on what they wanted but who was also there to be advised. The clients of these solicitors were able to negotiate with their spouse and could perhaps also be helped by mediation. Eekelaar et al. noted that the legal aid clients were by far the most numerous and were also the ones who had the few others from whom they could seek help.[181] These clients' cases were not handled in an adversarial manner, far from it.

The key finding in this research was that the lawyers did try to resolve clients' matters with reference to legal norms in the great majority of cases. Occasionally they departed from the legal norms but this was on the advice of their clients.[182] The team noted that, 'The greater problem which lawyers have encountered is the perception that, by the very fact that they do operate within the legal framework, they have a deleterious effect on all affected by the issue by inflaming conflict and running up unnecessary costs.'[183] It is interesting to consider that the perception of adversarialism was just that, a perception. The research examined this in the light of assumptions made by government policy makers that were considered by Lewis[184] in his work. The assumptions suggested that communication through solicitors via letters did much to inflame already simmering tensions between the parties, and yet the researchers came across only two cases in which there was any evidence of 'point scoring' between one or both of the solicitors and this appeared to be driven by the clients rather than originating from the solicitors. Instead they found a plethora of examples of solicitors providing practical support, guidance, assistance with third parties, assistance over and above the view of a solicitor as adviser and champion in the adversarial paradigm. Solicitors tried to encourage the clients to negotiate between themselves in relation to the children and to household issues and items rather than encouraging a complete break in communication, so that the professional advisers could 'handle' the case in all respects.[185]

---

[179] Ibid. at 32.

[180] Ibid. at 34.

[181] Ibid. at 79.

[182] Ibid. at 182.

[183] Ibid. at 183.

[184] Lewis, P.S.C. op. cit. note 27 at 6-7.

[185] Eekelaar, J., Maclean, M. & Beinart, S. op. cit. note 34 at 184.

The team did find that, if anything, solicitors tried to take measures to reduce tension between the couple rather than increase it. They did not see tension as an effective tool to resolve disputes between the parties in a divorce context. In addition, on the basis of this research, there is evidence to suggest that solicitors do not attempt to maximise the outcome for their clients at the expense of the other party and other interested parties, other than in accordance with legal norms. In others words, they do not seek to stretch the norms to a point that the other party was unlikely to accept nor to an extent that would not succeed, if it were to go to court.[186] Solicitors were not keen on clients coming to informal arrangements without having sought advice on them first, but the research concluded that they were also unwilling to unpick agreements unless they felt them to be unreasonable. The researchers found that the other party often had a great feeling of bitterness where such informal agreements were reneged on after a client sought advice. Thus there was little evidence of an adversarial approach, or the encouragement of an adversarial approach

Eekelaar, Maclean and Beinart also make another important point in the context of challenges made against the profession as being adversarial. They state that, 'The pejorative connotation which the expression adversarial has attracted conjures the image of the troublesome, selfish, individual, unwilling to settle for what the existing dispensation delivers. Yet it can sometimes be only by challenging that dispensation that justice is promoted.'[187] This is an important point as without the difficult cases on the margins that challenge the status quo, there would be no legal or social development. Adversarialism in some cases may reduce the need for others to fight for what they believe to be right, as norms develop to accept social change. Solicitors are well placed to take on this role on a case-by-case basis where they are required to do so, but to attempt to negotiate a settlement within the normative tradition for other more straight forward cases. This underlies the conceptual difficulty of the role of the law in divorce. Eekelaar *et al.* make the point well,

> The very concept of divorce itself has been a battleground between the pursuit of individual self-interest and the interests of other parties and communal values. Parents' rights v. children's rights (or welfare); family autonomy v. state supervision; short-term v. long term; clean break v. continuing obligation: all these dichotomies reflect the inherent conflict between the individualistic values of the contemporary Western world and an aspiration for protection and cultivation of the benefits if caring, co-operation and communality. It is therefore quite wrong to present the conflict only, or even primarily, as one between law, rights, or legal processes on the one hand and non-legal discourses, duties or 'alternative' resolution processes. There are tensions within the law itself.'[188]

The researchers felt that these dichotomies were found within the working life of solicitors and the outcomes they achieved with their clients. They are there to pursue the interests of their clients but within legal norms that are designed to keep a balance between the interests of the couple, children and other interested parties.

---

[186] *Ibid.* at 185.

[187] *Ibid.* at 185.

[188] *Ibid.* at 187.

If divorce solicitors do not appear to be acting for the most part as true adversarial champions, how does their role differ from that of a family mediator? As observed above, it could not be said that they are acting as independent, impartial third party facilitators between the parties, but if the solicitors for both parties are putting pressure on the parties to settle within the legal norms and are giving their view on a reasonable settlement, nor can it be said that they are acting as true partisans. Is it simply a case of two professional heads being better than one: are they acting as adjudicators together in the way a judge would, are they cajoling the parties into making their own settlement and giving advice on possible settlement options, are they facilitating negotiations at arms length? How does their apparent behaviour fit within the theoretical paradigm?

Thus it appears that adversarialism as a concept is linked to litigation and adversarialism has been linked to family legal practice within policy statements leading up to the Family Law Act 1996. There is evidence of partisan behaviour as one would expect, although the partisanship may be the outward expression of the solicitor's role, while the inward expression to the client may be one of expectation management – of refocusing the client's view of what is an appropriate settlement. There is evidence that partisanship is based on the legal norms established by the common law and Parliament and interpreted by the courts through the hard cases that are litigated, and yet that solicitors do not feel totally bound by legal norms and in some cases do not appear to refer to them to any great extent. And yet few divorces reach a litigated conclusion and there is little evidence to support either widespread use of adversarial techniques or an adversarial approach to force low settlement by the other spouse.

3.5 Family Mediation: An Alternative Process & Approach?

Family mediation, as stated earlier, is cited as the watchword in consensual decision-making by the couple; it has been referred to as an alternative to solicitor assisted decision-making in divorce matters,[189] and one of the reasons that it has been held up as an effective alternative is that family mediation is viewed as an alterative to adversarialism through the promotion of consensus based settlements by the parties with the aid of a family mediation professional. Thus, family mediators have been viewed as promoting a consensus based professional approach in contrast to some solicitor critics who consider solicitors as adopting an adversarial approach to divorce matters. This section will begin with a consideration of the definitions of family mediation in order to consider the essence of the process. A definition of the process is important as fewer people have been through the process of family mediation or have seen an accurate (or in some cases inaccurate) depiction of family mediation via the media – unlike its litigation counterpart. This section will then consider the extent to which there is evidence that family mediators adopt a consensus based approach to dispute settlement.

Family mediation has been given a range of definitions, although attempts at providing a precise definition have been resisted on the basis that family mediation aims to be responsive to the needs of the individuals involved in the process, rather than imposing a process on the individuals. This was underlined in the White Paper

---

[189] See Finlay's work, *op. cit.* 129, as well as statements made during the passage of the Family Law Bill *op. cit.* and the discussion later on in this chapter.

on divorce reform which preceded the Family Law Act 1996: 'Mediation is a flexible process which can take into account the different needs of the families, and the differing attitude and positions of the parties.'[190] This definition tells us little about the nature of mediation, other than its ethos. Many practising mediators and academics have nonetheless searched for a concise yet accurate definition of mediation in an attempt to show, in many cases, what mediation is not, to distinguish it from other processes and approaches to dispute settlement. Richards, a mediator, trainer and mediator supervisor, has defined mediation as a process by which a mediator encourages clients to think differently about their needs and conflict in order for them to reach a decision between themselves.[191] The mediator has no solution to the problem as she does not have a professional view of an ideal solution that the parties should work towards. Instead the mediator takes the parties[192] through a process, which permits them to attempt to find their own settlement terms for the issues they have identified.

Boulle and Nesic have taken this a stage further by identifying differing approaches to mediation, the conceptualist approach and the descriptive approach.[193] They outline the conceptualist definitions as ones based on ideology, in many ways aspirational, which attempt to show how mediation ought to be practiced. They use Folberg and Taylor's definition as an example of this: '[T]he process by which the participants, together with the assistance of a neutral person or persons, systematically isolate disputed issues in order to develop options, consider alternatives, and reach a consensual settlement that will accommodate their needs.'[194] Note the word consensual in there, the bedrock of conceptualist approaches to mediation that distinguishes mediation, it is claimed, from other forms of dispute settlement. This is not an unusual definition, in fact it could be argued that more commentators have tended towards a conceptualist definition in the terms set out by Boulle and Nesic,

---

[190] Lord Chancellor's Department *Looking To The Future: Mediation And The Ground For Divorce* The Government's Proposals (London: HMSO, 1995).

[191] Richards, C. 'The Expertise of Mediating' (1997) *Family Law* 52.

[192] It is admitted that the term 'party' is rather more appropriate to a legal context in which those who are involved in the process are referred to as 'the parties', however, it is difficult to find a neutral term that explains those individuals that are directly involved in the decision-making related to their divorce. 'Individuals to the process' was considered as an alterative, but then ran in to difficulties as this appeared to suggest that decision-making was purely individualistic and did not have to take account of the family as a unit or units (including the best interests of the children). 'The couple' was considered but it was obviously problematic in the context of divorce. The 'former couple' appeared to be too negative and a little long winded, as well as difficult in that during the divorce process they are considered to be a legal couple at the beginning and not a couple in law by the end. 'Each side' was rejected as too dichotomous and against the spirit of family mediation and family law practice. In the end the decision was taken to continue with the use of 'parties' while acknowledging that this is not a neutral term and tends towards the legal rather than the non-legal paradigm.

[193] Boulle, L. & Nesic, M., *op. cit.* note 25 at 4-6.

[194] Folberg, J. & Taylor, A. *Mediation: a Comprehensive Guide to Resolving Conflict Without Litigation* (San Francisco: Jossey-Bass, 1984).

than a descriptive one, particularly in the realm of family mediation.[195] The descriptive definition draws upon the practice of mediation rather than its aspirations.

Marion Roberts has also developed a descriptive definition: '... a process of dispute resolution in which the disputants meet with the mediator to talk over and then attempt to settle their differences.'[196] This is different from the usual understanding of the 'professional' role in which a professional has the knowledge and the facility to analyse the problem and propose and activate a solution, at the end of a set of logical and accepted steps. In this definition, a mediator's function is processual and the parties' role is a decision-making one. Thus, 'the subjective standards of the parties are as important, if not more important, than external standards of fairness, such as the law; the quality of the process and satisfaction of the parties is more important than reaching an agreement for the sake of settlement.'[197] This purely facilitative interpretation of mediator function is underpinned by the rationale that the parties are in the best position to make decisions about their lives and those of their children. The private world of the parties is given emphasis over public perceptions of what it ought to be.

The mediator's role is to allow the decision-making to take place by encouraging effective communication between both of the parties. This is at the heart of the 'art' as it involves,

> ... effective communication, fully informed decision-making, empowerment of the autonomy of each individual, mutual recognition of each party's needs and interests, and the management of conflict and power imbalances; an orientation toward structuring the present and future rather than focusing on recriminations about the past; and a search for mutual gain and a mutually satisfactory resolution.[198]

This underlying approach is assumed to a greater or lesser extent by all family mediator organisations and bodies.[199] This distinguishes mediation from other forms of dispute resolution such as party and party negotiations carried out by solicitors on behalf of, or with, their clients, and arbitration. Inter partes, or party and party negotiations are characterised by lack of disclosure, partisan fencing between the

---

[195] Boulle, L. & Nesic, M. *op. cit.* note 25 at 5. See Davis G. & Roberts, M.'s definitions in *Access to Agreement: A Consumer Study of Mediation in Family Disputes* (Milton Keynes: Open University Press, 1998), also work by Karl Mackie on this point including *A Handbook on Dispute Resolution* (London: Routledge, 1991), CEDR's definitions in *Model Mediation Procedure Guidance Notes* and Lord Woolf's *Access to Justice Interim Report* (London: Lord Chancellor's Department, 1995).

[196] Roberts, M. 'System of Selves? Some Ethical Issues in Family Mediation' (1992) Vol. 10 *Mediation Quarterly* 11.

[197] *Id.*

[198] Foster, N.J. and Kelly, J.B. 'Divorce Mediators; Who Should Be Certified?' (1996) Vol. 30 *University of San Francisco Law Review* 667.

[199] See, for example, the definition used by the Academy of Family Mediators in the US. Academy of Family Mediators, *Standards of Practice for Family and Divorce Mediation*, 1998.

two sides moving towards possible mid-point solutions.[200] Arbitration relies on the decision of a third party nominated by the parties after hearing evidence presented, rather than as a result of the parties' decision-making. Adjudication is a further step removed from the parties, in which a judge decides the case on the basis of the evidence brought before the court according to the rules of law and procedure laid down by the court and by Parliament. These understandings may be less accurate than these statements would suggests, however, mediation is nonetheless defined as an alternative to them on the basis that it seeks to assist the parties to reach a consensus using their own normative framework.

These distinctions may be clearer in the abstract than they are in practice. In mediation, the extent of the decision-making between the parties and the mediator will depend on the approach that the mediator adopts during the sessions. By directing the process, the mediator imposes a framework in the sessions and takes the process out of the parties' control. This distinguishes mediation from pure bilateral negotiations, because the parties have agreed to adopt someone else's conception of how the negotiations should be played out.[201] If the mediator intervenes in the discussions to help the parties towards an agreement, then the mediator is also imposing a perception of the couple's situation on to the session. This imposition may be a minimal one, and it may be one that the parties are happy to accept, however, any form of intervention is a reframing of the parties' focus. The greater the intervention, the more mediation is removed from being a process that allows the couple to set the parameters, discuss the issues that are the most pertinent to their understanding of their situation and to reach a decision themselves based on their own understanding. The parties may reach consensus, but that does not mean that they have reached a decision based purely on the basis of their own norms.

Differences of mediation approach consequently have an impact on the autonomy of the parties and the involvement of the mediator in decision-making. This flexibility may be a great strength within the context of private ordering, that is to say within the context of a process that allows the parties to have the freedom to choose the way the dispute is talked through and settled. This is only true, however, if it is the parties themselves who have the final say on the role that the mediator adopts and the extent to which they both permit the mediator to intervene in the process in respect of discussions about settlement. This also assumes an equality of power, knowledge and integrity as between the parties, which many would suggest does not exist at the point of relationship breakdown. This would require mediators to possess a wide range of skills and an understanding of their appropriate use, in order to respond to the needs of the parties. It certainly requires a high degree of flexibility on the part of the mediator.

Simon Roberts believes, however, that the process cannot be entirely flexible. He defines the conditions that must be met in order for meaningful negotiations to take place without partisans appearing with or for the parties.[202] This limits the scope of

---

[200] See Fisher, R. & Ury, W. *Getting to Yes: Negotiating Agreement Without Giving In*, 2nd Ed. (London: Hutchinson, 1982).

[201] See Roberts, S.A. 'Mediation in Family Disputes' (1983) Vol. 46 No. 5 *Modern Law Review* 537.

[202] Roberts S.A. 'The Path of Negotiations' (1996) Vol. 49 *Current Legal Practice* 108.

the mediator and the parties to set the terms of reference for the mediation. Roberts states that the parties need to be able to exchange information that is relevant to the negotiations and to have the information on which to make a decision. There must be a common intention between the parties that they wish to reach an agreement that is acceptable to both of them. There must also be at least a semblance of power balance so that each can bargain freely, as the mediator may find it difficult to fulfil the role of power broker without appearing to be partial. Roberts is of the view that if these elements are not present then it may be better to use a litigation route towards dispute solution rather than mediation. If, however, the only obstacle to the mediation is one of power imbalance, then it may be redressed sufficiently successfully for negotiations to take place where partisans, such as solicitors, accompany the parties. This is an interesting insight, as it highlights that mediation is a process of decision-making above all else, and suggests that its importance lies in the fact that the parties themselves have to negotiate. It does not, however, suggest that the lack of legal norms is in itself a difficulty, nor the presence of partisans as advisers, albeit used as a support rather than a replacement for personal decision-making. If this is the case, then the distinction between solicitor facilitated and mediator facilitated negotiations does not relate to the presence or absence of legal norms, or to the nature of the decision that is reached, but rather to the extent to which parties negotiate personally rather than through their representatives.

There are alternative methods of structuring mediation within these constraints, which may be more appropriate to match the needs of the couple attending the session. These will be influenced by cost restrictions on the parties and the competence of the mediator to offer each of the models of mediation. Dominant models of mediation practice are set out in the UK College of Family Mediators Directory and Handbook,[203] although these categorisations do mask many variations found in practice. Two main forms of mediation are recognised: sole mediation and co-mediation; plus different mediation processes described as face-to-face or caucusing. An added categorisation relates to the subjects that are under discussion within the mediation - children and parenting issues, finance and property, or all issues. These all have an impact on the process of family mediation, which may in turn affect the approach adopted by the family mediator.

A mediator may see the parties simultaneously or individually and consecutively within the sole or co-mediation models, by sitting with the parties face-to-face or shuttling between them. Caucusing or shuttle mediation is a practice that is used more often in commercial or neighbourhood mediation rather than family cases, to enable the parties to be kept apart. The mediator moves between the parties to assist with the negotiations, and may never bring the parties together during the process. This may have a certain appeal in family cases, where domestic violence is considered to be an issue, although it does have the flavour of assisted negotiations rather than mediation, as the mediator will in some senses reframe the parties' comments before transmitting them to the other side. It may also provide a strained basis for future continuing parenting arrangements in cases involving children, as the parties may not have the benefit of a partisan to put their case for them. Nor may they have the

---

[203] UK College of Family Mediators *Directory & Handbook 1997-98* (Glasgow: FT Law & Tax, 1997).

opportunity to put their own case in a face-to-face mediation. This may not, however, be that dissimilar from the way in which settlements are made at the door of the court in family cases, where the parties' solicitors fulfil this function even within their partisan role. Nor may it be that different to the way in which solicitors operate during bi-partisan negotiations, who shuttle back and forth between themselves and the parties to explain what each side is prepared to offer and accept.

The difference between bi-partisan negotiations and shuttle mediation may relate to the extent to which the offers are developed by the individuals themselves rather than by the professionals involved. The absence or presence of legal norms may also be a difference, but probably less so when solicitors are advising their clients in shuttle mediation, rather than where the parties are both present in the same room and are not being supported by legal advisers.

Each of the models of mediation mentioned above, with the exception of lawyer assisted mediation, in which lawyers are involved in the process to assist or to represent their clients, involves the mediator in the use of similar skills, although it could be argued that different emphasis will be put on each depending on the model adopted. Typologies of mediator skills have been developed for use in non-subject specific mediator training, others exclusively for family mediation, but all focus on a few basic skills. These rely heavily on negotiation skills within the framework of an impartial setting. It would be difficult to distinguish the skills typologies from negotiation skills but for the requirements that the mediator must remain neutral as opposed to taking a partisan stance for their client. However, although all mediators are expected to make adept use of their skills there is not the same expectation in relation to specific knowledge such as legal norms. All branches of family mediation, other than those practised by lawyer mediators, consider that knowledge of legal norms may be desirable so as to provide basic legal information, but specific and detailed knowledge of legal norms is not relevant to the family mediator's role. This may limit the extent to which legal norms are overtly present in the legal context, but they may be present covertly if one or more of the parties has sought legal advice in relation to the divorce and related issues. Equally myths about legal norms may be present during the mediation, and these may affect decision-making and may not be countered during the process. The question is, does this matter, as long as the parties have reached a genuine and personal consensus in relation to the settlement?

This perhaps depends on two issues: whether the parties have reached a genuine consensus with which they would remain content, even if they were later to find that a solicitor negotiated settlement of a court adjudicated one were to have favoured them more. Secondly, whether the decision that they have reached is one that they have reached on the basis of their own norms, or whether this has been heavily influenced on the basis of the mediators. It is admitted that the second issue is pertinent to solicitor negotiated settlements as well, because, as discussed earlier in this chapter, it is not clear that solicitors always suggest settlements based exclusively on legal entitlement derived from legal norms.

Extensive research has been carried out on what family mediators do in family matters: research such as that documented by Boulle and Nesic in their book *Mediation,*[204] as well

---

[204] Boulle, L. & Nesic, M. *op. cit.* note 25.

as that carried out by Honeyman and the Test Design Project.[205] However, much of the research has focused on the process values of family mediators, which obliquely provides evidence about the professional approach they are considered to adopt, namely they encourage a genuine consensus between the parties. However, many of these studies have considered family mediation at an intellectual level rather than examining family mediation sessions through empirical studies. The results of the process studies are set out below before consideration of the few empirical findings on family mediation that have been published.

Gulliver[206] identified six styles of mediation, which he characterises by the role assumed by the mediator. In effect, he suggests that mediation is a fluid process, open to interpretation by the mediator and the clients as their relationship and needs develop. The six roles are as follows: a) the chairperson: the mediator actively encourages the parties to focus their attention on one aspect of the discussions; b) The passive mediator: the presence of the mediator is sufficient to encourage the parties to interact; c) The enunciator: the mediator provides the rules and any further information relevant to the topic of discussion; d) The prompter: the mediator makes a more positive contribution by making suggestions to the parties, although he does not express his opinion; e) The leader: the mediator is directly involved in the negotiations, puts forward his opinions and evaluates the parties' opinions; f) The go-between: the mediator controls the flow of information between the parties. These reflect the range of mediation styles or approaches.

Process and approach are distinctive for each of these six styles of family mediation, just as they are for solicitors involved in divorce matters. The process that is adopted does not necessarily require the professional to adopt a particular professional approach, however the first two roles suggest that the mediator is facilitating a process to aid the parties to come to their own consensus, the role of enunciator begins an approach that requires some level of intervention in the decision-making of the parties, providing some information on norms that are not particular to the individuals, and thereafter exterior norms become increasingly important. The further through the list of roles that one reads, the closer the mediator appears to risk becoming a partisan rather than a neutral. At that point when a mediator begins to offer suggestions as to possible settlement, it is difficult to distinguish a mediator from a solicitor, other than whether the norms are based in legal or other perceptions. It is true to say that the mediator may not be taking on a partisan role, he may be remaining as a neutral, but as we have seen previously, some solicitors appear to adopt a more neutral approach as between the parties to the divorce, by reframing their own client's perceptions of entitled to bring their client closer to a position that is considered to be acceptable to the other party. Consequently, in these instances consensus based approaches appear to mean reframing clients expectations so as to promote settlement. If so, then there is evidence to suggest that solicitors as well as mediators adopt this approach, although the reframing may be done in different ways and may be based more or less on legal or other norms.

---

[205] Test Design Project *Performance-Based Assessment: A Methodology for Use in Selecting, Training and Evaluating Mediators* (National Institute for Dispute Resolution, 1995). This is non-family law specific, however.

[206] Gulliver, P. 'On Mediators' in Hamnett, I. (ed.) *Social Anthropology and Law* (London: Academic Press, 1977) at 26-31.

Roberts defines the role of a family mediator in different terms. He identifies four tasks, which underlie mediation, and three further roles that he believes to be fundamental to the process.[207] The four main tasks consist of: a) establishing and maintaining contact between the parties; b) providing a place for the parties to meet; c) providing a neutral place for negotiation in terms of both physical environment and in terms of atmosphere; d) stimulating the exchange of views between the parties. The three further roles are: a) providing some rules which act as a foundation for the whole process; b) helping the parties to express their views; c) identifying the options open to the parties. Roberts proposes a minimal form of family mediation, which allows the couple to remain responsible for any decisions they reach in the course of a mediation session. However, his tasks for this model do not suggest how the mediator is to assist the parties towards a settlement. Roberts does not rule out two other conceptions of family mediation which he identifies as 'directive intervention' which joins advice-giving with joint decision-making, and 'therapeutic intervention' which aims to examine the reasons behind the relationship breakdown, to allow views to be aired before decision-making is undertaken.[208] The approach adopted by the family mediators may, once again, vary according to the model of family mediation that is adopted, but the model does not presuppose a particular approach even though it may incline a professional towards a particular one. Equally, while it may be true to say that the mediators may be adopting a consensus based approach because they are seeking to promote a settlement between the parties, this does not in itself distinguish mediation from inter partes solicitor negotiations. The primary difference in approach appears to be the extent to which the parties are required to suggest their own solutions rather than to consider solutions that are put to them by outsiders. This too is a less obvious distinction where direct intervention is used as a tool by a mediator.

Opposition to a minimal role of mediation has been voiced by many commentators, principally in relation to inequality of bargaining positions between the parties. The question of impartiality has been further raised by Ingelby in research relating to solicitors as intermediaries.[209] He notes that an impartial mediator can reinforce the power imbalance between the couple and therefore result in an unequal settlement between them. He suggests that mediators have yet to find a way to combat this problem without resorting to blatant interventionism. McEwen suggests that power imbalance is inherent in any mediation as a result of the relationship between the parties, their personalities and experiences. He prefers an approach that attempts to counteract this problem by introducing ground-rules to the process, and even the participation of legal representatives in the mediation, instead of suggesting that a skilful mediator redresses any imbalance unilaterally.[210] Alternatively, Haynes suggests that 'real' negotiations can only take place if the mediator is willing to counteract any power

---

[207] Roberts, S.A. 'Towards A Minimal Form of Alternative Intervention, International Developments in Divorce Mediation' (1986) Vol. 11 *Mediation Quarterly* 30.

[208] Roberts, S.A. 'Three Models of Family Mediation' in Dingwall, R. & Eekelaar, J. (eds.) *op. cit.* note 158 at 144.

[209] Ingelby, R. 'The Solicitor as Intermediary' in Dingwall, R. & Eekelaar, J. (eds.) *op. cit.* note 158 at 53.

[210] McEwen, C. 'Competence And Quality' (1993) *Negotiation Journal* 313.

imbalance that may exist between the parties.[211] Dingwall even asserts that in consequence, mediation can include an element of 'enforcement' where a settlement is considered to be morally desirable.[212] If so, then the accepted 'facilitating' role of a mediator requires some rethinking. This debate illustrates that the role a mediator assumes will also dictate the skills that are required and the family mediator's approach to divorce matters. An 'element of enforcement' by the family mediators would appear to run contrary to a consensus based facilitative model of family mediation, that is so often used as the distinguishing feature between family mediation and inter partes solicitor negotiations.

More evidence of the role and function of family mediation and of family mediators is provided by the Council of Europe,[213] which has sought to set out the essentials of family mediation: its voluntary nature, consensual decision-making by the parties (as it is suggested that this will lead to more durable settlements), an impartial, neutral mediator, equality of bargaining positions by the parties, privacy and confidentiality guaranteed for the parties, and there be appropriate procedures for the selection and training of mediators to ensure that they are adequately trained for the role. When one considers the differing models of mediation, this is hardly surprising, as the mediator is left with a difficult and demanding role in the face of emotional issues and little support from colleagues in the mediation room as discussed below.

The role of the mediator, mediator in this instance being non-family issue specific, has also been the subject of an in depth study by a commission chartered by the Society of Professionals in Dispute Resolution. Two different approaches to mediation are identified, the 'settlement-oriented approach' and the 'transformative approach'.[214] These have also been described as the 'narrow focus' and the 'broad focus' approaches[215] and even 'facilitative' and 'evaluative' styles of mediation.[216] Put simply a narrow focus approach is one which focuses on the problem which the parties feel they need to settle,

---

[211] Haynes, J. *op. cit.* note 1 at 62-63.

[212] Dingwall, R. 'Empowerment or Enforcement?' in Dingwall, R. and Eekelaar, J. (eds.) *op. cit.* note 158 at 151; Greatbatch, D. & Dingwall, R. 'Selective Facilitation: Some Observations on a Strategy used by Divorce Mediators' (1989) Vol. 23 *Law and Society Review* 613; Taylor, A. 'Concepts of Neutrality in Family Mediation: Contexts, Ethics, Influence and Transformative Process' (1997) Vol. 14 *Mediation Quarterly* 215. See too in another mediation context – community mediation – in which Mulcahy observed partiality rather than pure mediator neutrality. Mulcahy, L. 'The Possibility and Desirability of Mediator Neutrality: Towards an Ethic of Partiality' (2001) Vol. 10 *Social and Legal Studies* 505. Consider too Astor's research in which she considers a new theory of mediation which removed the fiction of neutrality but reinforces consensuality: Astor, H. 'Mediator Neutrality: Making Sense of Theory and Practice' (2007) Vol. 16 *Social and Legal Studies* 221.

[213] *Council of Ministers Recommendation R(98)1* as cited by Bartsch, H.-J. *Council of Europe-Legal Co-operation in 1998-9* (Council of Europe, 1999) at 540.

[214] Test Design Project *op. cit.* note 205 4-6.

[215] Riskin, L.L. 'Understanding Mediator Orientations, Strategies and Techniques: A Grid for the Perplexed.' (1996) Vol. 1 *Harvard Negotiation Law Review* 7.

[216] Riskin, L.L. *id.*

a broad focus goes beyond this to attempt to help the parties with the wider issues surrounding the dispute. Therefore the 'settlement-oriented approach' is closely identified with the 'narrow focus', as are the 'transformative approach' with the 'broad focus' approach.[217] The terms 'evaluative' and 'facilitative' may describe subtly similar distinctions. However an evaluative mediator is identified as a mediator who provides the party with options for settlement and guidance on the merits of those options, whereas a facilitator provides the conditions necessary to allow effective communication between the parties so that they can reach their own decisions.[218] This may be a function of mediation in general terms, rather than family mediation specifically, although Haynes considers family mediators to have an evaluative role. [219] Where evaluation is used, the potential distinction between the professional approaches adopted by solicitors and mediators become increasingly blurred and in some instances virtually indistinguishable.

A further study on divorce mediation conducted in the US by Pearson and Thoeness shows that the stance the mediator takes has a direct effect on whether a settlement can be reached, and suggests that 'the mediator's ability to facilitate communication' is of prime importance.[220] They found that their research results were in agreement with those conducted by Donohue et al.[221] in a study of audio tapes of ten successful and ten unsuccessful mediation sessions. The most successful divorce sessions were characterised by a structured approach to the discussions, and the mediator's 'reframing' of any verbal attacks made by one side to the other. This suggests that a degree of interventionism may be desirable in order to diffuse potentially explosive situations, and facilitate negotiation. With this in mind, and as part of the overview on mediation, the skills literature by Lewis-Ruttley[222] in relation to arbitrators and their role in reaching settlements has also been examined. Although at first glance this would seem to be at odds with the spirit of mediation, there is a considerable overlap between the skills needed by arbitrators and mediators, if the mediator is taking a very active role in the mediation process. If the mediator is to take an active role in the decision-making process, for example acting as a chairperson,[223] then there will be an overlap between the skills of mediator and arbitrator.[224] If such an overlap does exist then family mediation

---

[217] Honeyman, C. 'A Consensus on Mediators' Qualifications' (1993) *Negotiation Journal* 289.

[218] The Test Design Project, *op. cit.* note 205 at 5.

[219] For a review of Haynes' approach to mediation see *The Fundamentals of Family Mediation, op. cit.* note 1.

[220] Pearson, J. & Thoeness, N. 'Divorce Mediation: An American Picture' in Dingwall, R. & Eekelaar, J. (eds.) *op. cit.* note 158 at 212.

[221] Donohue, W.A., Drake, L. & Roberto, A.J. 'Mediator Issue Intervention Strategies: A Replication and Some Conclusions' (1994) Vol. 11 *Mediation Quarterly* 261.

[222] 'Arbitrator Competence Skills Analysis' Handout for the Divorce Mediation & Arbitration Centre 10/5/1995, now contained in Skills for Legal Functions 1: Deciding Disputes, IALS, Legal Skills Working Papers.

[223] Gulliver, P.H. *op. cit.* note 206 at 26-31.

[224] The skills for arbitrators which may be relevant to mediators, following the model developed by Lewis-Ruttley, are: 1. Management skills – (a) ability to design and maintain

may at times appear to be more adjudicatory than facilitative and less consensual and more closely allied to a single normative framework without the legal norms there to act as a backdrop for adjudication.

Slaughter has taken the analysis of marriage and the difficulty surrounding negotiations on divorce a stage further and has identified the underlying assumptions behind negotiation and game theory in divorce situations.[225] Slaughter considers economic modes of the family (common preference models, and challenges to Becker's model of the family as unit), bargaining models including threat points, extramarital factors and intramarital factors and behavioural factors including credible exit threats, sense of entitlement, endowment effects and risk aversion. Retaliation factors are also considered and it is this that is pertinent to the context of adversarialism and consensus. The former assist in explaining why couples reach the settlements they reach, or their solicitors reach those settlements, however retaliation factors go to the heart of the adversarial/consensus dichotomy true or imagined. The discussion of retaliation factors encompasses the tension between co-operation and game theory. Slaughter argues that marriage as an institution favours men and therefore that divorce bargaining also favours men, as women are the ones who have lost out comparatively in the labour market and once more have more to lose through divorce. They will also find it more difficult to remarry with children than their former spouses will. Women it is argued are also more inclined towards co-operation.[226]

The resulting inequality of bargaining power between men and women and the desire by women to co-operate rather than fight would appear to suggest that consensus based negotiating strategies with little or no partisan involvement would appear to favour men to the detriment of women. Without support and an adviser raising a wife's expectations, would not she be at risk of settling too low? Slaughter suggests that the complexity of private ordering results from the need to find an individual

---

office systems; (b) ability to allocate time, effort and other resources effectively; (c) ability to work according to systems or rules governing the handling of cases; (d) ability to bring the file to completion. 2. Procedural steps – The ability to conduct matters using fair, flexible and effective procedures. The details of the procedure would be specific to mediation, and therefore are not covered by the *Skills Analysis* for arbitrators. 3. Decision making skills – The ability to reach a reasoned decision on the basis of the arguments presented to the mediator. The scope of this skill will very much depend on the role of the mediator as a decision maker. 4. Award writing skills – This is translated into the skill of drafting any agreement that is reached between the parties, and consequently is far removed from the skill of reaching a decision on an award, substantiating it, and conveying it to the parties. 5. Interpersonal skills – The skills outlined under this heading in relation to arbitrators appear also to be of equal value to mediators. (a) ability to maintain a good relationship with the parties; (b) ability to remain impartial and independent; (c) ability to maintain legitimacy; (d) ability to listen actively; (e) ability to speak effectively; (f) ability to maintain a civil atmosphere at the hearing.

[225] See Slaughter M.M. 'Chapter 3 – Martial Bargaining: Implications for Legal Policy' Maclean, M. (ed.) *op. cit.* note 40.

[226] Rose, C.M. 'Women and property: gaining and losing ground' (1992) Vol. 78 *Virginia Law Review* 421. See further the discussion in Slaughter M.M. 'Chapter 3 – Martial Bargaining: Implications for Legal Policy' in Maclean, M. (ed.) *op. cit.* note 40.

solution to a collective problem.[227]   One solution to the collective problem is for women to insist on premarital agreements; however, Slaughter argues that this in itself does not solve the issue of inequality of bargaining power. It may be true that pre marriage bargaining is more equal, however, the retaliation strategy would be unappealing to many, the refusal to marry is an extreme solution, especially as without mass support from women the retaliation is at best sporadic and more likely useless.

Legislation is the most likely solution to the inequality of bargaining power and the concern that women will be disenfranchised on marriage and on divorce, however that is the role the law claims to perform currently. Unless the law is enforced, and can be seen to be enforced, in an open and transparent fashion, Slaughter's worries are likely to persist. Mediation as a process does not permit analysis of divorce settlements as there are no public records of settlement that are scrutinised by a judge, unless private settlements become consent orders, however, this is also true for solicitor negotiated divorce. The difference, one could argue, is that solicitor negotiate settlements should have some passing reference to the law, whereas the ideology of true private ordering is that law is not the main point of reference for divorcing couples. Finlay suggests that there are situations when a mediator should insist that a party seeks legal advice because, if one party is represented and the other is not then the power imbalance is so great that this may make mediation close to impossible.[228] Although cost consideration may be prohibitive and even if they can be afforded the cost will come out of the family purse together and therefore has a knock-on effect on both parties. Finlay suggests that mediation need not be a bargain struck in a legal vacuum, but should be one that is based on consensus rather than on confrontation, otherwise considered to be adversarialism.[229] In fact, Finlay can see a role for lawyers as mediators 'in the conjoint team model, the roles of the attorney and therapist are defined as mediators, neutral facilitators, problem solvers, and resource people. Neither team member is functioning in a traditional role, and this must be made clear to the clients'.[230] Legal information may be a bridge between the two forms of dispute resolution that allows the parties to access to legal services and therefore legal advice with an understanding of the way in which the system operates and knowledge of how a lawyer may and may not assist them.[231] However, the greater the legal input into the family mediation process, the less it can be set to be a form of private ordering. If legal norms become dominant, and if Slaughter's theory of the threat posed to women through a private decision-making is correct, then partisan negotiations may appear to reach the least coerced decision. The distinction between family mediators' and solicitors' approaches becomes less evident as the need for mediator intervention to promote equality increases.

---

[227] Slaughter M.M. *op. cit.* note 40 at 44.

[228] Finlay, H.A. *op. cit.* note 129 at 70.

[229] Finlay, H.A. *op. cit.* note 129 at 71.

[230] See Gold, L. 'Lawyer and Therapist Team Mediation.' in Milne A., & Folberg, J. (eds.) *Divorce Mediation: Theory and Practice* (New York: Guildford Press, 1988) at 210.

[231] Finlay, H.A. *op. cit.* note 129 at 74.

3.6 Conclusions

The literature throws up many themes. Some commentators retain the view that solicitors either intentionally or subconsciously adopt an adversarial approach to divorce, diagnosing it as a legal problem that needs to be battled out by two partisans representing their clients. These same commentators look to family mediation as a process that places power back in the hands of the couple, to permit them to reach a consensus that may or may not be formalised in a binding legal agreement. In addition, they point to pluralism, participation and transformation as benefits provided to a greater of lesser extent by the process. Others argue that solicitors have been misjudged and claim that the adversarial litigation process is a different entity from partisanship, and partisanship may be distinct from the adversarial approach to divorce. They claim that true litigation is virtually absent in divorce matters and where present is more a function of client demand than of professional preference approach. They claim that the difference between mediated and solicitor negotiated agreements is the absence or presence of bargaining within legal norms. They point to the protection afforded by the law, particularly for the less powerful party. They consider that solicitors act in the interests of the client within the protection afforded to the family as a whole. Academics and policy makers are split on the appropriate role for solicitors and family mediators in divorce matters and on the way in which they operate. However, recent empirical studies in England and Wales challenge the traditional association between solicitors and adversarialism and mediators and client driven consensus.

The research reviewed does not show a consistent picture of adversarial solicitors and consensus based facilitative family mediation. It appears that professionals adapt their approaches to meet the needs of the couple or the client and may attempt to coax the parties to reach their own settlement, give options to assist them to reach a settlement or may frame what they consider to be an appropriate settlement, if necessary. Solicitors have more scope for this, but there does appear to be some evidence to suggest that some family mediators may fall back on this option in an attempt to settle the issues. However, how the professional decides upon an 'appropriate' settlement is an interesting point. It appears that the real distinction in this instance is the reference to or absence of legal norms within the decision-making process. In the next chapter the thesis considers what the training undertaken by solicitors and family mediators indicates about what the professional bodies consider their roles and approach to be.

Chapter 4: Adversarialism & Consensus? What Do the Professions Train their Professionals to Do?

This chapter examines the training requirements set by the professional bodies for divorce solicitors and family mediators, to consider what these indicate about the professions' approach to divorce dispute settlement. The chapter begins by developing the background of solicitor and family mediator training. Abel argues that the legal profession sets entry requirements to create a barrier to restrict the number of solicitors who reach full professional status in order to restrict supply of legal services and drive up prices.[232] He notes that the profession justifies this, as do other professions, by claiming that this ensures the quality as do other professions, by claiming that this ensures the quality and competence of members of the profession although there is little hard empirical evidence to justify this claim. Both the UK College and the Law Society have set entry and training standards that must be met by individuals wishing to enter the profession. It considers whether training requirements give an indication of professional approach, before focusing on the requirements for initial (or foundation training) of both the professional bodies.

The research in this chapter is centred on the policy and regulatory documents produced by the Law Society of England and Wales and the UK College of Family Mediators in respect of training. Training has been defined here as the course or courses and periods of supervised training to be undertaken before being permitted to practice as a qualified professional member of the Society or College. The Law Society of England and Wales has mandatory *Training Regulations 1990* (as amended)[233] for all course providers and training establishments who wish to train students to gain the legal qualifications that allow students to enter the profession and to practice law.[234] In addition it also has the *Common Professional Examinations Rules Joint Academic Stage Board*;[235] the *Legal Practice Course Written Standards*;[236] and the *Professional Skills Course Guidelines*.[237] The UK College of Family Mediators has mandatory training

---

[232] Abel, R.L. 'Taking Professionalism Seriously' (1989) *Annual Survey of American Law* 41 at 44.

[233] The Law Society of England and Wales *The Training Regulations 1990* version 1 (London: The Law Society, August 2004) – still in force. The detailed training provisions are set out in the *Authorisation Guide*, which has also been considered, as has *Training Trainee Solicitors – The Law Society Requirements* (version 7 July 2007).

[234] The Law Society of England and Wales and the Bar Council of England and Wales are responsible for laying down the training requirements for solicitors and for barristers for entry into the profession by virtue of the *Courts and Legal Services Act 1990* (as amended).

[235] Version 2 was considered in this research. Version three has since been published as at 24th August 2007, although these do not make substantial changes that affect this study.

[236] The Law Society of England and Wales *The Legal Practice Course Written Standards* Version 10, (London: The Law Society, September 2004) – still in force.

[237] The Law Society of England and Wales *Professional Skills Course; Course Structure, Provider Information and Course Accreditation* Version 3 (London: The Law Society, August 2005) – still in

requirements as set out in the following policy and regulatory documents: *Requirements for Providers of Foundation Training;*[238] *Recommended and Required Curriculum and Teaching Methods for Foundation Training Courses;*[239] *Requirements for the Registration of Mediators;*[240] *and Competence Assessment for Family Mediators*[241] in order for family mediators to be recognised as having the qualifications necessary to join the professional body and to practice as a family mediator member of the UK College as well as *Requirements for Providers of Professional Practice Consultancy.*[242] As yet there is no legal requirement that family mediators must be accredited members of the College and consequently, while mandatory for joining the College, the training requirements do not have the same force as those set by the Law Society, who set the requirements for and maintain the legal roll of all solicitors.[243] The Law Society also has *Family Mediation Accreditation Scheme;*[244] and the *Standards of Competence for the Assessment of Family Mediators*[245] for solicitors who train as family mediators through a Law Society approved family mediation training body. These are of a similar status to the UK College family mediation standards; there is no statutory requirement that a Law Society approved course be taken in order for a solicitor to become a family mediator.

---

force.

[238] UK College of Family Mediators *Requirements for the Providers of Foundation Training – and the Guidelines to the Requirements for Providers of Foundation Training* Amended by the College Board of Governors June 2005 – still in force.

[239] UK College of Family Mediators *Recommended and Required Curriculum and Teaching Methods for Foundation Training* Courses Reconfirmed (without substantive amendment) by the College Board of Governors April 2003 – still in force.

[240] UK College of Family Mediators *Requirements for the Registration of Mediators* Minor Amendments Board of Governors October 2005 – still in force.

[241] UK College of Family Mediators *Competence Assessment for Family Mediators: Portfolio Guidelines, Specification and Template* as amended with minor amendments November 2005 – still in force.

[242] UK College of Family Mediators *Requirements for Providers of Professional Practice Consultancy – and Guidelines as to the Requirements of Professional Practice Consultancy* Approved by the College Board of Governors April 2003 – still in force. This is coupled with the College's *Professional Practice Consultancy for Family Mediators: A Guide to Roles and Responsibilities* June 2003 – still in force.

[243] The requirements are different for fully qualified foreign lawyers who seek the right to practice in the UK.

[244] The Law Society of England and Wales *Family Mediation Accreditation Scheme: Criteria and Guidance Notes* Version 1. This has been reissued in 2007 as a result of the inception of the Solicitors Regulatory Authority although no substantial changes have been made. All Law Society accreditation schemes are currently under review. The Law Society of England and Wales *Family Mediation Training Standards* Version 1.

[245] The Law Society of England and Wales *The Standards of Competence for the Accreditation of Family Mediators* Version 1, draft date now showing as 1st January 2007 as a result of the change over to the Solicitors Regulatory Authority, although it is the original version 1 from 2004 that is still in force.

4.1 Solicitors' & Family Mediators' Training: Background

There is no one route to becoming a solicitor, nor is there a discrete group of family solicitors who are required to undertake specific family law training. Instead, all solicitors follow seven core subjects either through an undergraduate qualifying law degree route, which is usually referred to as a Batchelor of Laws (LLB) or the Graduate Diploma in Law route (GDL) after successfully completing another recognised undergraduate degree. The training comparator selected for the purposes of this study is the GDL route to qualification as a solicitor, including the subsequent Legal Practice Course (LPC), training contract and Professional Skills Courses (PSC), with mandatory foundation training for family mediators with professional practice consultancy, also known in some Law Society documentation as family mediation consultancy. That is not to say that the majority of solicitors follow this route (many will do a law degree instead of the GDL), however, this appears to be the most appropriate comparison.[246] Individuals who have a non-law degree may 'convert' to law by undertaking the one year full-time or two year part-time GDL course, which contains the core subject the Law Society requires for conversion from a non-law degree background. These core subjects also form the basis of all LLB or qualifying law degree programmes. On successful completion students will then move on to their one year full-time or two years part-time LPC course, to finish their pre-training contract training followed by the two-year training contract, which must include successful completion of the PSC. It has been argued by family mediators that family mediator training tends to be post-graduate study and not undergraduate study, more akin to the GDL.[247] Family mediators have argued that trainee mediators will be admitted on to a course, if they have a relevant degree qualification or sufficient experience in a related field to be considered as equivalent. This is discussed further below. As a result, it would appear to be a fairer comparison between the GDL/LPC and family mediation training than a comparison between the undergraduate law degree /LPC and family mediation training. The GDL is the minimum training in law necessary to qualify as a solicitor and that training is relatively standardised.

It is possible for a divorce solicitor to practice in the area of divorce law without having studied family law either on the GDL or the LPC. Family law is an optional subject in the curriculum rather than a core, although most undergraduate programmes would consider family law as a staple subject although it is not a compulsory subject. Academic family law is also difficult to define as family law courses vary considerably from law school to law school and cover a wide range of public and private law issues.[248] Family law would not generally be offered on the GDL as the timetable is dominated by the compulsory modules. Many LPC courses

---

[246] The rationale for this comparison is explained in chapter two.

[247] See Webley, L.C. *op. cit.* note 16 for further details.

[248] See Burton, F. Martin Clement, N., Standley, K. and Williams, C. *Teaching and Learning Manuals: Teaching Family Law* (Warwick: National Centre for Legal Education, 1999). The authors suggest that family law is a relatively new subject as far as the undergraduate curriculum is concerned, with the introduction of the first textbook in 1957 by Peter Bromley. Having said that they also point to the Faculty of Law King's College centenary of family law collection of essay in 1957, which may counter this view. See p. 27 for details.

do offer family law as an optional subject, and solicitors who were planning to practice in this area on completion of the LPC would normally be expected by their destination firm to have family law on their curriculum vitae. That does not prevent solicitors from entering the profession without family law qualifications or experience.[249] It could be argued that the general legal principles that they will use within family law practice will be similar to other areas of law that they have studied, as is argued in relation to transferable skills teaching elsewhere.[250] Others have argued that family law is distinctive, and must be taught in a distinctive way that takes in to account the difficulty of applying generalised law to highly individualised and personal situations.[251] Either way, all solicitors will have studied the seven foundations of legal knowledge and will have followed the core elements of the LPC and PSC.[252] These core subjects will be compared, as the solicitor training, against those for family mediators, as will family law or family mediation based options where extant.

Family mediation is not currently a profession defined by statute, thus the UK College of Family Mediators, the professional body which has gained credence within the profession after a period of fragmented leadership, does not have the power to regulate entry into the profession in the same way as the Law Society has for solicitors.[253] As Wilensky states,

---

[249] The Law Society does have an accreditation scheme for family solicitors through the Family Law Panel. This is discussed in chapter 5 as the level of entry related to a solicitor with post qualification experience rather than at trainee solicitor or recently qualified solicitor level, which is the subject of this chapter.

[250] This is certainly the argument put forward by the QAA as regards general transferable skills in their benchmarking standards. See *Law-Subject Specific Benchmark Standards* (Gloucester: Quality Assurance Agency for Higher Education, 2000).

[251] For a discussion of training and family lawyer behaviour see Fritze-Shanks, A. 'Some Models of Professional Behaviour for Family Lawyers and an Examination of the Strengths and Weaknesses of those Models' (1989) Vol. 3 *Australian Journal of Family Law* 202.

[252] With a limited number of exceptions, for example for fully qualified foreign lawyers.

[253] On this basis there is an argument about the extent to which the UKCFM is a professional body regulating a profession (family mediation). For a discussion of professionalisation and the development of professions, see Wilensky, H.L. 'The Professionalization of Everyone?' (1964) Vol. LXX No. 2 *American Journal of Sociology* 137. See further Friedson, E. *Professionalism Reborn. Theory, Prophecy and Policy* (Cambridge: Polity Press, 1994). For an applied discussion in relation to solicitors and family mediation see Brain, P.E. 'Reclaiming Professionalism: The Lawyer's Role in Divorce Mediation' (1994) Vol. 28 *Family Law Quarterly* 193; and in respect of the professionalisation of family mediation in the US see Barrett, R. 'Mediators Certification: Should California Enact Legislation?' (1996) Vol. 30 *University of San Francisco Law Review* 617; Carey, T.V. 'Credentialing for Mediators – To Be or Not to Be?' (1996) Vol. 30 *University of San Francisco Law Review* 635; Harper, B.N. 'Mediator Qualifications: The Trend Toward Professionalization' (1997) *Brigham Young University Law Review* 687; Russell, N.R. 'Mediation: The Need and a Plan for Voluntary Certification' (1996) Vol. 30 *University of San Francisco Law Review* 613; Spiegelman, P.J. 'Certifying Mediators: Using Selection Criteria to Include the Qualified – lessons from the San Diego Experience' (1996) Vol. 30 *University of San Francisco Law Review* 677. For a discussion of the market in privately funded family mediation in England and

Any occupation wishing to exercise professional authority must find a technical basis for it, assert an exclusive jurisdiction, link both skill and jurisdiction to standards of training, and convince the public that its services are uniquely trustworthy. While this traditional model or professionalism, based mainly on the "free" professions of medicine and law, misses some aspects of the mixed forms of control now emerging among salaried professionals, it still captures a distinction important for the organisation of work and for public policy.[254]

Using Wilensky's model the UK College is well on the way to becoming a fully fledged professional body, although it will have to claim either an exclusive jurisdiction or exclusive jurisdiction along with related bodies. The UK College does set entry requirements for family mediators who want to claim UK College accreditation. Training providers who wish to provide training that leads to accreditation must adhere to their standards and training framework. The UK College does not itself provide training; instead it accredits others to provide training for them. Trainers range from private training organisations to academic educational establishments that provide some vocational training.

Family mediation has developed within individual professional bodies to meet the needs of their members and their professional ethos, as different bodies have traditionally had distinctive identities. Consequently there had been little attempt to standardise and regulate training programmes and qualifications until the advent of the UK College of Family Mediators. The College is now performing this function; however, some of the previous bodies' practices have been continued in the criteria that have been developed by the College. Other bodies are free to set their own standards for qualification, and offer their own mediation training programmes, although they must meet the minimum UK College or Law Society family mediator training requirements, if they are to provide their students with equivalent status. Richards suggests that most initial mediation programmes consist of forty hours of training leading to a mediation certificate, although there is a wide diversity of training programmes.[255] These reflect affiliations with the Law Society and the UK College, in order that their trainees may attain accredited status from one or both of these bodies.

This chapter focuses on the training that would be required for a student who had a first degree in a non-law/mediation subject, in order to permit as clear a comparison as possible. The rationale is set out below. The research has focused on the training regulations and requirements, including the content of the courses as set by the two

---

Wales see Head, A., Head, M. & England, H. *Privately Funded Work in Family Mediation: Calculating the Volume of Privately Funded Family Mediation Cases:* A report prepared for the UK College of Family Mediators (London: UKCFM, December 2006) at 8. For a discussion of publicly funded work see National Audit Office & Legal Services Commission *Legal Aid and Mediation for People Involved in Family Breakdown* HC 256 Session 2006-2007 (London: The Stationery Office, 2007).

[254] Wilensky, H.L. *ibid.* at 138.

[255] Richards, C. 'A Knighthood or an Entry Pass? – What Does It Mean To Have Mediation Training?' (1997) *Family Law* 204.

bodies; the open coding analysis provided a wide range of concepts which in turn have produced theoretical concepts which link them together for legal and family mediation practice. They go to the heart of the adversarial and consensus based approach to divorce dispute settlement. The chapter groups the concepts together in tabular form and provides an analysis of what the data have revealed about the nature of solicitor and family mediator training. Finally the chapter concludes by drawing out the core concept in relation to the professional approach that the bodies encourage their members to adopt in divorce matters.

4.2 Training Requirements: Do They Provide an Indication of Appropriate Professional Approach?

Thus far the assumption has been that the training requirements set by the two professional bodies will provide an indication about appropriate professional approaches in divorce matters to nascent professionals. Training is a vital part of the professional project, a way to provide substantive knowledge, develop skills and shape the approach that new professionals will adopt in their practice. Training is obviously not determinative of behaviour; however, it does provide an insight into the issues that the profession currently considers to be important to its members. There is certainly a literature on the role that legal education plays in shaping students' attitudes to the law and to legal practice, and by allusion it is possible to draw the conclusion that the professional bodies' training requirements must provide an indication to students about professional approach.[256] Abel goes further to state:

> The ideology of professionalism developed by service occupations and endorsed by social scientists offers a simple solution to these disturbing problems [social control of technical expertise; ensuring that specialists use their skills properly]. If producers are left alone (by both the state and consumers), they will spontaneously develop a sense of community and a service ethic, which will ensure technical quality and teleological rectitude.[257]

However, he goes further to argue that the reality is more complex that this, even if professionals forming a grouping will seek to control and regulate their practice.[258] Training course regulations, therefore, provide a good indication of what the professions consider to be appropriate roles, approaches and skills for their members. These in turn shape the way in which professionals see themselves, practice their craft and interact with clients in the divorce context. As Cavenagh *et al.* note,

> A key dimension in becoming professional is the process of socialization... part of this socialization experience is the acquisition of a set of attitudes pertinent to the profession, and the aim of professional training is to achieve

---

[256] For a discussion see Menkel-Meadow, C. 'Can a Law Teacher Avoid Teaching Legal Ethics?" (1991) Vol. 41 *Journal of Legal Education* 3.

[257] Abel, R.L. *op. cit.* note 232 at 43.

[258] See further Larson, M. 'The Rise of Professionalism; A Sociological Analysis (Berkeley: University of California Press, 1977) and Abel, R.L. 'The Rise of Professionalism' (1979) Vol. 6 *British Journal of Law and Society* 82.

not only necessary knowledge and skills but to indoctrinate with the appropriate values and attitudes.[259]

Pre-entry training and pre-qualification training have been considered in detail here, as a way to examine the professions' approaches to professional practice on divorce. There are difficulties, however, in considering training for solicitors and for family mediators for a number of reasons. The two 'professions' are not easily comparable as discussed in chapter two. Secondly, practitioners may be members of both professions, there is no bar on a solicitor being a mediator, or a mediator being a solicitor, and this cross fertilisation makes it difficult to talk in absolute terms about professional approach, although this is less of an issue at a macro level than a micro level. Cross-fertilisation of professional identity and approach at a micro level may in time affect the professional bodies' views of professional approach (indeed it may have done so already through the links between the SFLA/Resolution and family mediators). As borders are made up of members who shape the organisation, the more regularly members work with different professionals, the more likely they are to be influenced by their professional approaches. However, it does not change the validity of findings about the messages sent by the professions to their members. Thirdly there are also issues about the term 'profession' being applied to family mediators. This has been discussed in chapter three; the arguments shall not be rehearsed here. It is argued that an analysis such as this will provide insight, even if it does not provide a dichotomous comparison between two professions at similar points during their development.

The impact of legal education and training is discussed in the literature with regard to the inculcation of professional values of ethics and the socialisation of would-be professionals. Menkel-Meadow observes that traditional law teaching techniques in the US

> foster adversarialness, argumentiveness, and zealotry, along with the view that lawyers are only the means through which clients accomplish their ends – what is 'right' is whatever works for this particular client or this particular case. We extol loyalty to the clients above all and neglect the responsibility of the lawyer to counsel the client about moral and other concerns.[260]

In addition she states that the case by-case method of teaching and of looking at legal principles leads to moral relativism, placing a premium on individualism rather than responsibility towards others. This encourages the view that lawyering is about zealous advocacy, she claims. This is an interesting discussion in respect of family law and the practice of family law. Those family solicitors who first studied for a law degree or even those who attended a GDL course will have studied a whole range of legal subjects, many taught on a case-by-case basis rather than through critical legal approaches or other theoretically underpinned syllabi. They will have picked up, if

---

[259] Cavenagh, P., Dewberry, C. & Jones, P. 'Becoming Professional; When and How Does it Start? A Comparative Study of First-Year Medical and Law Students in the UK.' (2000) Vol. 34 *Medical Education* 897.

[260] Menkel-Meadow at 7; Menkel-Meadow draws the reader's attention to the Model Code of Professional Responsibility EC7-7 & EC 7-8 (1986).

not through the study of family law, these images. It is interesting to refer to Cramton's examination of the underlying principles of legal education in the late 1970s:

> [a] moral relativism tending towards nihilism, a pragmatism tending toward an amoral instrumentalism, a realism tending toward cynicism, an individualism tending toward atomism, and a faith in reason and democratic processes tending toward mere credulity and idolatry'[261]

Thus there is a school of thought that legal education in the US fits students for a pragmatic, morally relativistic, adversarial professional approach to legal practice. It is not argued that education and training have no impact on students, and that the content of courses and their mode of teaching are irrelevant to the way in which students come to see their discipline and their role.

In addition Menkel-Meadow suggests that through studying law, students will learn from many law teachers that they care more about ideas than about the people and thus they will learn to divorce the practice of law from emotion.[262] In support of this she cites the 'hidden bodies' case to indicate that once law students have learnt the 'rules' they are likely to answer questions relating to what they would do in that situation very differently from how they did prior to learning the 'rules'.[263] However, the 'black letter' approach to legal education has been criticised in the UK, and although some law academics remain wedded to this form of teaching, the skills movement,[264] the critical legal education,[265] and the socio-legal[266] approaches have all sought to develop a reflective approach to education which may in turn produce

---

[261] Cramton, R. 'The Ordinary Religion of the Law School Classroom' (1978) Vol. 29 *Journal of Legal Education* 247 at 262. See further Menkel-Meadow, C. *op. cit.* note 256.

[262] Menkel-Meadow, C. *op. cit.* note 256 at 7.

[263] Menkel-Meadow, C. *op. cit.* note 256 at 8. At note 27 she states, 'In People v. Belge (376 N.Y.S.2d 771, 50 A.D.2d 188 (1975)) two criminal defense lawyers failed to disclose the whereabouts of two dead and long-missing adolescent girls, thought to be murdered by their client. Even though the bodies were not at issue in the case, the lawyers would not provide the information to the parents of the missing children because the information was obtained through confidential communications with the client. For a full account of the case and the lawyers' professional and personal dilemmas, see Tom Alibrandi & Frank H. Armani, Privileged Information (New York, 1984).'

[264] See, for example, the development of the Legal Skills Research Group at the Institute of Advanced Legal Studies. For a discussion see Duncan, N. 'The Skills of Learning: Implications of the ACLEC First Report for Teaching Skills on Undergraduate Law Courses' (1997) Vol. 5 *Web Journal Current Legal Issues*. See further Maughan C. & Webb, J. *Lawyering Skills and the Legal Process* 2nd Ed. (Cambridge: Cambridge University Press, 2005) for an example of skills teaching in context.

[265] See Kennedy, D. (ed.) *Legal Education and the Reproduction of Hierarchy. A Polemic Against the System: A Critical Edition* (New York: New York University Press, 2004).

[266] See Friedman, L.M. 'The Law and Society Movement' (1986) Vol. 38 *Stanford Law Review* 763 for a US example. For a UK discussion see Cotterrel, R. 'Why Must Legal Ideas be Interpreted Sociologically?' (1998) Vol. 25 No. 2 *Journal of Law and Society* 171.

reflective practitioners who do not automatically adopt an adversarial approach to all legal issues.[267] Many law schools now claim to teach law with a 'liberal legal education' curriculum and counter the charge of content heavy 'black letter' law teaching by pointing to the emphasis now placed on skills teaching and on developing student reflection within the curriculum. Again, the reasoning behind these pedagogical developments is that the way one teaches and what one teaches, has a profound impact on the student experience, and further on what the student knows and how he or she uses and relates to that knowledge.

A 'liberal legal education' was promoted by a sector of legal academia and given some weight by the Lord Chancellor's Advisory Committee on Legal Education and Conduct in a review of legal education in England and Wales in 1996.[268] A 'liberal legal education' is an undergraduate or postgraduate curriculum that contains some critical reflection on the role of the law in society (as well as some skills teaching to allow students to make use of their substantive knowledge).[269] It also seeks to provide a broader educational experience by positioning the law within its context. It has gone hand in hand with more novel assessment techniques and has, in some cases, also included an element of clinical legal education, although this is a distinct mode of teaching and learning rather than a distinct type of legal curriculum.[270] None-the-less the foundation subjects must still include an examination of legislation and case law, and case law is by definition the product of an adversarial process.[271] There is far less time within a concentrated course like the GDL to position law within its context and to consider the theoretical debates in any detail. The legal skills movement was being discussed in the context of law teaching,[272] before law schools began to engage with the general transferable skills movement which has now been enshrined in publications like the Dearing report.[273] Transferable skills are

---

[267] See Sherr, A. 'Legal Education, Legal Competence and Little Bo Peep' *Inaugural Lecture by Professor Avrom Sherr as Woolf Chair in Legal Education at the Institute of Advanced Legal Studies* (London: IALS, 2001) accessible at sas-space.sas.ac.uk/dspace/bilstream/ 10065/246/1/AS_Woolf_Inaugural.pdf.

[268] *First Report on Legal Education and Training* (London: ACLEC, 1996).

[269] See for example Johnstone, G. 'Liberal Ideals and Vocational Aims in University Legal Education.' (1999) Vol. 3 *Web Journal of Current Legal Issues*; Bradney, A. 'Liberalising Legal Education' In Cownie, F. (ed.) *The Law School* (Aldershot: Ashgate, 1999) and Brownsword, R. 'ACLEC and the Idea of Liberal Legal Education' In Cownie F. *id*.

[270] For a discussion of law school curricula and skills, what they say they do and what the research discovered see Law Discipline Network: *Report on General Transferable Skills* 1998 which can be accessed via the UK Centre for Legal Education at www.ukcle.ac.uk/resources/ldn/skills.html (as at 2nd August 2004).

[271] This is all currently under review by the Training Framework Review Group of the Law Society. See further Boon, A., Webb, J. and Flood, J. 'Postmodern Professions? The Fragmentation of Legal Education and the Legal Profession' (2005) Vol. 32 No. 3 *Journal of Law and Society* 473.

[272] See Duncan, N. *op. cit. note 264* and Sherr A. *op. cit. note 267*.

[273] The Dearing Report: *The National Committee of Inquiry into Higher Education: Higher Education in the Learning Society* (Norwich: HMSO, 1997).

now seen as the key to future employment.[274] Legal skills are now a mainstream part of the legal curriculum although less evident in the GDL, perhaps, than at undergraduate level. As a result it may be assumed that the GDL remains closer to the (adversarial) case-by-case based curriculum than the undergraduate programme is currently, although there is little research evidence on this point.

Family mediation training is heavily influenced by skills teaching methods. Family mediation is taught as a series of skills, within their theoretical context. Training is relatively brief at approximately forty hours of training (six days) at the initial foundation stage with an additional two days of professional practice consultancy, however, it should be noted that many students will have undertaken previous academic and professional training in other disciplines prior to training as a family mediator. Reflection by the student on his or her performance is also now seen as an important part of skills development,

> Reflective practice is important to the development of all professionals because it enables us to learn from experience. Although we all learn from experience, more and more experience does not guarantee more and more learning... There are many times when our normal reaction to events are insufficient themselves to encourage reflection. We should not rely solely on our natural process of reflecting on experience, but actively seek ways to ensure that reflection itself becomes a habit, ensuring our continuing development.[275]

This quote is taken from teaching and learning to be a teacher, rather than a legal professional or family mediator training, but is discussed as a central tenet of good teaching and learning practice by the Higher Education Academy (formerly the Institute of Learning and Teaching in Higher Education). Reflective practice is included in the law school curriculum and is also being encouraged by the solicitors' profession and in the family mediators' profession through their professional practice consultancy, as discussed later. Reflective practice requires a professional to consider their role in context and this too should include one's approach as a professional. Interestingly, both professions ask their members to consider skills, attributes, role, function and approach. Legal education and mediation education have a part to play in challenging students to consider their role and the interests at stake for clients.

4.3 Professional Bodies' Requirements for Initial or Foundation Training

The professional bodies keep a watching brief on the content of the training programmes that provide the knowledge and skills they consider as a minimum requirement for entry into the profession. In a sense, the professional bodies act as gatekeepers of professional knowledge and skills in that they either directly or indirectly set the curriculum that all members of the professional must be exposed to, and in some cases tested on, in order to be admitted into the profession. The UK College of Family Mediators sets requirements for the foundation training course

---

[274] See Law Discipline Network 'Why should law school focus on general transferable skills?' *Report on General Transferable Skills* 1998 *op. cit.* 270.

[275] Sherr, A. 'The Value of Experience in Legal Competence' (2002) Vol. 7 No. 2 *International Journal of the Legal Profession* 95.

that prospective family mediators must undertake prior to applying to the UK College for 'associate' professional status. There were five organisations that provided UK College of Family Mediators accredited courses: National Family Mediation, Family Mediation Scotland, Solicitors Family Law Association, ADR Family Mediation Training, and Family Mediators Association, at the time of the research.[276] The tables below sets out the Law Society and UK College requirements for legal education and training and family mediation training by these accredited or approved institutions.

The Law Society of England and Wales (along with the Bar Council for barristers) sets the parameters of training for prospective solicitors. It approves legal education providers of the GDL (the academic stage of training). There were forty accredited institutions; the content of their courses is governed by the Law Society and Bar Council's Joint Academic Stage Board CPE/GDL Rules. The Law Society accredited thirty-three institutions to provide the Legal Practice Course.[277] Of these twenty-six are university based courses and a further seven branches are non-University course providers.[278] Eight institutions had been accredited by the Law Society to provide the Professional Skills Course as well.[279] Consequently, there are multiple course providers that are all governed by the training requirements set by the Law Society.

The Law Society also sets the training parameters for their family mediators. The Family Mediation Training Standards are set as competencies rather than as content based requirements. The training is structured to follow three stages of mediation, before, during and after the mediation and is broken down into the elements that make up each of these stages and the skills and knowledge requirements for each. The training standards are expressed in a 'students will be able to' form, in other words, they are outcome based. Commentary is provided to enumerate the issues and the theories that students should be aware of and understand. The training standards are extremely detailed in terms of the content and outcomes, but do not explain how the material is to be delivered or how the student mediators are to be assessed. This stands in stark contrast to the UK College of Family Mediators' best practice for training courses. These standards set out the issues that must be dealt with in the curriculum and how the training is to be conducted in terms of quality

---

[276] Subsequently, this has changed to two approved foundations courses: Hertfordshire Family Mediation and Key Mediation; and recognition has been granted to courses by ADR Group, National Family Mediation and Resolution.

[277] The figures have subsequently changed as at 15th October 2007 to twenty-eight institutions providing course in thirty-five LPC locations; twenty-five of these are University based: see www.lawsociety.org.uk/becomingasolicitor/qualifying/legalpracticecourse/courseproviders.law.

[278] The Law Society *LPC Provider Introduction* at www.lawsoc.org.uk/dcs/fourth_tier.asp?section_id=4543

[279] The PSC provider figures have also changed slightly since the time of the research. As at 8th November 2007, there were seven institutions providing the PSC, in fifty-nine locations: www.lawsociety.org.uk/documents/downloads/becomingpscexternalproviders.pdf, version 26 February 2007 Education and Training Unit, The Law Society 2007.

assurance requirements for the trainers, however, it is not expressed in an outcome orientated manner and is not as detailed as that for the Law Society. The Law Society has accredited five bodies to provide their accredited training, some of them providing Law Society and UK College training: the Solicitors Family Law Association, the Family Mediators Association and the ADR Group (Family). Other approved providers were only accredited initially up to either the end of March 2000 or the end of July 2001 and have not had their accredited status renewed. These are: Professional Development Training, Lawgroup UK and LawNet Centre. The training provided by ADR group (family) may be similar in content for the two professional bodies as they provide training that is accredited by both the Law Society and the UK College. The accreditation scheme is under review and may be subject to amendment in 2008.

4.4 Method

This chapter sets out the findings of the open and axial coding phases of the professional bodies' training documentation, and provides a theoretical perspective as regards the cues that the professional bodies send to their members through their training requirements. The training documentation analysed was all documentation extant during 2003, 2004 and 2005, although the documentation has been reviewed subsequently so that it is up-to-date as far as publicly available documentation is concerned up to 31st December 2006. It would perhaps be useful to explain how this was undertaken in more concrete terms than was discussed in chapter two. Each document has been analysed using the grounded theory approach and it can at times be difficult to demonstrate how this process has been undertaken and to provide evidence in support of the theory. To this end, each of the conceptual categories that have been developed from the data has been displayed in a separate table, with a summary of the principal data that led to the development of the conceptual category. It is quite difficult to display the whole data analysis process in grounded theory without providing the reader with all of the memos that led to the conceptual categories and the core theory. I considered the best way to approach this for some time, and decided to adopt a half way house approach - to set out each of the conceptual categories and to provide an illustration of the principal material (in summary form) that led to their development. This is by no means perfect, as it requires the reader, in part, to accept that the summaries that I have provided in the tables are representative of the wording and the totality of the documents considered in the research. However, the alternative, which was to type up the documents and my memo notes and provide those in an appendix, appeared to be too cumbersome, rather dry and extremely voluminous. The tables set out the academic teaching and training requirements for solicitors and solicitor family mediators as set by the Law Society and family mediation by the UK College of Family Mediators. Academic training has been defined for the purposes of the research as teaching or training that takes place predominantly in a classroom or in a simulated setting. By contrast, vocational training has been defined as training that take places predominantly in the work place or a training course that takes place alongside work based training.

This open coding phase is similar to descriptive ordering and labelling of data, the difference being that it is not possible to finalise the conceptual categorises until the researcher is assured that there are not others to be elicited from the data, and that the categories that have been developed are fully evidenced in the documents, rather than being isolated occurrences. As Strauss and Corbin explain 'The first step in building theory is *conceptualizing*. A concept is a labeled phenomenon. It is an abstract representation of an event, object, or action/ interaction that a researcher identifies as being significant in the data.'[280] Each document was taken in turn and was analysed line by line; any tentative concepts were noted and described. As more documents were analysed, some of the earlier concepts were refined and their nature and extent delineated. Others were rejected as they did not appear to hold good as the data cycle continued. Labelling the data is insufficient, however, to enable to researcher to consider possible relationships between concepts and later to use these to develop theory. It is necessary to consider the properties or characteristics of the concept, and their extent, as well as any sub-categorising that develops – a process of conceptual categorisation. This analysis is set out in each of the tables – the detail in the tables illustrates the data that led to developing the conceptual categories.

Axial coding is the process through which the conceptual categories and related to each other, as described in chapter two. This task begins during open coding, as the phases are not linear ones. Strauss and Corbin explain this task thus, 'In axial coding, our goal is to systematically develop and relate categories. This step of analysis is important because we are building theory.'[281] Further they explain that this process is a fluid one. Relationships between the conceptual categories are discussed where relevant during the chapter, and are explained in more detail in the conclusions. The theory generation phase also took place in cycles. This is not discussed here, but is set out in the conclusions chapter.

4.5 The Data & Findings

The content of the education and training regulations for the three training regimes has revealed the following conceptual categories:

Firstly, professional gate-keeping and the maintenance of standards, by which the professional bodies seek to regulate their members and thus send cues about appropriate professional practice. This may be explained as: **Potential ability followed by benchmarked level of competence in law and skills** (solicitor); **solicitor qualification & inclination to mediate** (Law Society family mediator); **appropriate family mediator beliefs & values** (UK College family mediator).

Secondly, the professional's role, skills and knowledge, which as the title suggests reveals the knowledge and skills required of their members in order to perform their professional role, which are analysed further to consider evidence of adversarial or consensus based models of practice. The concept may be explained as follows: **Active partisan problem-solver** (solicitor); **actively informed consensus solution-facilitator** (Law Society family mediator); **active consensus solution-facilitator** (UK College family mediator).

Thirdly, the role of the professional in decision-making, which may be described as: **Partisan, protector & problem-solver** (solicitor); **actively impartial non-directive**

---

[280] Strauss, A. & Corbin, J. *op. cit.* note 64 at 103.

[281] *Ibid.* at 142.

facilitator (Law Society family mediator); **passively impartial & fair facilitator** (UK College family mediator).

Fourthly, 'the role of legal and non-legal norms in decision-making' and how these should be used to reach a settlement or determine an appropriate order. This may be reduced to the label: *The* **framework or the legal back-stop** (solicitor and Law Society family mediator); **one possible framework** (UK College family mediator).

Finally, 'assessed attributes' through which the professional bodies seek to ensure that members meet their professional criteria and therefore conduct themselves in a professional, competent manner. This is described as: **A legally knowledgeable, informed, problem-solving, communicator with business & financial acumen** (solicitor); **a family law expert, competent, fair, legally acceptable consensual solution-facilitator** (Law Society family mediator); **a competent, fair, impartial, consensual solution-facilitator** (UK College family mediator).

The nature and extent of the conceptual categories are out in tables later in this chapter, in some detail. Many of these concepts are susceptible to further subdivision, as indicated in the tables that contain summaries of the information contained within the professional documentation, indicating what led to the adoption of the concepts. Each concept is explained in detail after the relevant table, to examine the evidence for the concept, its nature and importance as well as the relationships that developed between categories and sub-categories and what these indicate by way of theoretical concepts. There are important overlaps as well as differences between the professional groupings as discussed in the sections that follow the illustrative tables.

Table 4.1: Gate-keeping & Maintenance of Professional Standards:

Potential ability followed by benchmarked level of competence in law (solicitor); solicitor qualification & inclination (Law Society family mediator); appropriate family mediator beliefs & values (UK College family mediator).

Solicitors Law Society of England and Wales (GDL Route)

Entry Standards

- *GDL*: standard entry qualifications are an undergraduate degree from a UK or Irish University. Non-standard includes a degree from an overseas University or certain legal professional qualifications or degree equivalent qualifications (a Certificate of Academic Standing is required by the Law Society). Students must also have a good command of English. Students who have not obtained a degree in English as the official first language must satisfy an English competency standard.
- *LPC:* A student must be enrolled as a student member of the Law Society and must have been granted a certificate of completion of the academic stage of legal training (either having been awarded a Qualifying Law Degree or a GDL).
- *Training contract:* be accepted by a law firm or other authorised training contract venue to undertake a training contract and have that registered with the Law Society. Successful completion of the training contract including the PSC fulfils the requirements for admission to the roll of solicitors.

Assessment Mechanisms

- *GDL*: Assessment by written work: exams and/or coursework.
- *LPC:* Assessment by written work: exams and/or coursework and practical assessment of skills including oral assessment.
- *PSC:* Assessment by written work including exams and practical assessment of skills (may include oral assessment).
- Training contract: Assessment through supervision by a more senior member of the profession.

Duration

- *GDL:* normally one year full-time.
- *LPC:* normally one year full-time.
- *Trainee Solicitor:* Training contract is two years full-time with Professional Skills Course (PSC) passed during the training contract. PSC involves face to face tuition as follows: advocacy and communication skills-eighteen hours; financial & business skills-eighteen hours; client care and professional standards -twelve hours & elective(s) of at least 24 hours, of which up to twelve hours on elective topics may be undertaken on a 'suitably supervised or assessed' distance learning basis. IT, Business Awareness and Commercial Awareness must also form a pervasive part of the course.

Quality of Teaching/ Training/ Assessment

- *GDL*: through academic routes such as external examiners, University procedures and committees and Quality Assurance Agency/HEFCE requirements.
- *LPC & PSC:* courses are accredited and monitored by the professional body.

Family Mediators Law Society of England and Wales

Entry Standards:

- Stage I – Met all the requirements to become a solicitor.

- Stage 2 - Family mediation training: No mention of entry requirements for family mediators training courses, although family mediators must first have met the academic requirements to be a solicitor. Complete family mediation consultancy stage of the training course: no entry requirements once on training course.
- Stage 3 - After foundation course completed (including family mediation consultancy stage of course) apply for General Member Panel status. Must be a qualified solicitor who has practised for at least three years and held a practising certificate through-out. Hold an unconditional practising certificate.
- Stage 4 - Apply for practitioner member status having met the requirements as evidenced by one of three routes (described below) which in general terms includes 90 hours of mediation practice over 2 years.

Assessment Mechanisms
- Stage I - As for solicitors.
- Stage 2- Assessment on family mediation foundation course: assessment by written work and practical assessment of skills. Assessment through family mediation consultancy – details not set out in the documentation.
- Stage 3 - Assessment of general membership status: Must supply evidence of successful completion of a family mediation training course approved by the Law Society or details of one that has not been so approved for consideration.
- Stage 4 - Assessment of practitioner membership:
    - Passported Route- successfully complete the LSC's family mediation competence assessment and have been recognised as fully competent in all issues; or
    - Practitioner Member Developmental Route: Be a General Member of the Panel; undertake at least 90 hours of mediation practice during general membership (max period of two years) & successfully complete the written assessment and include four summarises of cases that the mediator has mediated.; or
    - Practitioner Member Direct Route: competed foundation training course of at least 40 hours that complies with the Law Society's requirements and undertaken at least 90 hours of mediation practice during the two years preceding the application, according to the requirements below; & successfully completed the written assessment and include four summarises of cases that the mediator has mediated.

90 hours to be made up as follows: at least five mediations comprising at least 25 hours of mediation in total, CPD of at least eleven hours for each year of general membership, consultancy of eleven hours (2.5 hours must be face to face and 2.5 hours must be joint face to face). The remainder through providing training, practice and development, CPD or consultancy, drafting summaries of outcomes, writing articles of appropriate reading.

Duration
- *Family mediation training.* Minimum of 40 contact hours plus family mediation consultancy. This appears to be usually taught over six days in three blocks with additional consultancy time, often over two days.
- *General membership:* no duration period *per se.*
- *Practitioner membership:* 90 hours of mediation practice as set out above (unless undertake the LSC's competence assessment), which must be undertaken over no more than two years.

Quality of Teaching/ Training/ Assessment
- Family mediation courses are accredited and monitored by the professional body.

Family Mediators UK College of Family Mediators
Entry Standards
- Stage 1: Family mediation training. Trainers to set and use tests to assess potential mediators for aptitude for mediation (personal qualities, interpersonal skills, intellectual capacity, professional ethical behaviour), and ensure that candidates have a commitment to professional development. Candidates must also

demonstrate professional and other relevant qualifications and experience, although the nature of the qualifications is not set out in the policy documents.

- Stage 2 - Apply for Associate Member of UKCFM: Must have completed foundation course and be practising as a mediator, and be undertaking professional practice consultancy as per requirements.
- Stage 3: Apply for General Membership status through 1 of 2 routes either the Panel assessment route having completed at least 30 hours of practice in receipt of consultancy (PPC); or competence assessment route having completed foundation training, professional practice consultancy and a portfolio of assessment of completed mediation summarises reviewed with a Professional Practice Consultant (PCCt) assigned by professional body.

Assessment Mechanisms

- Stage 1 - Assessment by written work and practical assessment of skills including trainer and trainee evaluation and peer assessment. Professional practice consultancy – details set out in a subsequent table.
- Stage 2 – Associate Member status assessment through professional practice consultancy. PPC of at least four hours individual consultancy per year or 10% of time spent in face to fact mediation, whichever is greater to a max of twelve hours. At least one hour must be on an individual face to face basis.
- Stage 3 – General Member status.
  - ○ Either: Panel Assessment Route to membership which includes mediators in training to complete 30 hours of practice in receipt of consultancy in addition to an approved foundation training course, then presentation to the approved body for Panel assessment.
  - ○ Or: Competence Assessment route. Foundation training, practice in receipt of PPC followed by a candidate presenting to the College a detailed portfolio for assessment based on a minimum number of five cases, including a witness testimony by the PCCt recommending the mediator for practice, a PPCt being assigned by the College and then at least three meetings with the PPCt to assess how much assistance the mediator needs to complete the portfolio successfully; to discuss progress and competence against the standards. Once the PPCt believes the candidate is ready for assessment, the PPCt will complete the witness testimony and give a recommendation to practice. That is submitted with the completed portfolio to the UKCFM for assessment.

Duration

- A programme approved by the College must be a minimum of 40 contact hours. Training must include or be followed by a minimum of ten hours mediation practice in receipt of professional practice consultancy within twelve months of taught non-practising component, with consultancy by a College approved consultant, in a quality assured setting. This appears to be usually taught over six days in three blocks with additional consultancy time, often over two days.

Quality of Teaching/ Training/ Assessment

- Courses are accredited and are monitored by the professional body.

Potential ability followed by benchmarked level of competence in law and skills (solicitor); solicitor qualification & inclination to mediate (Law Society family mediator); appropriate family mediator beliefs & values (UK College family mediator).

Both professional bodies set entry requirements for entry into their professions, minimum skills competencies and knowledge levels, provide some indication of acceptable teaching and assessment methods and operate a monitoring programme for all accredited trainers. Both professional bodies act as gate-keepers to their professions. In short, there are few quality assurance differences at face value in respect of their programmes – the Law Society and the UK College of Family Mediators both appear to take the training of their future professionals seriously. They accredit teaching and/or training providers to provide courses providing recognised qualifications; both appear to keep the training needs of their professionals under review.

It is at the level of principles and values that differences begin to emerge between the professions. Some interesting theoretical concepts become apparent when comparing cues sent by the profession to their students through training requirements. Solicitors are selected on the basis of academic qualifications, if they wish to undertake the GDL and the LPC. Students should normally have achieved a degree qualification or to have been awarded a certificate of academic standing of equivalent level. Academic training in the UK does include an assessment of skills standards and all students who attain at least a pass in an undergraduate degree must meet the general transferable skills requirements set through the Quality Assurance Agency in Higher Education. Thus, the profession demands an undergraduate degree level of education including a minimum skills attainment. The skills that are required will include a core set of academic skills, plus a set of discipline specific skills. The Law Society cannot guarantee that all graduates have law disciplinary specific skills, as not all will have undertaken a law degree. They address this through the LPC course.

Family mediation training is predicated on a different basis. The Law Society family mediation training entry requirements do not set out a required academic standard because all students of initial family mediation courses have already qualified as a solicitor. Consequently the Law Society does not need to rehearse that. The UK College of Family Mediators (UKCFM) operates a values based policy, which is to say that it requires family mediation trainers to demonstrate that they have policies to ensure access to information and entry to courses for people from diverse backgrounds. The UKCFM also require training providers to select students based on their aptitude for mediation, which can be assessed considering the potential mediator's personal qualities, interpersonal skills, intellectual capacity and professional ethical behaviour. They must also ensure that candidates are committed to professional development. There is a requirement that candidates show evidence of professional and other relevant qualifications and experience but specific academic standards are not set. It appears that training to be a mediator is more about the type of person one is, than the level of academic achievement attained. Does this indicate a difference in approach for solicitors and for family mediators? Perhaps, although selection for a place on the GDL is in part based on qualifications, part based on life experience and the way in which a student presents him or herself through a personal statement on a UCAS form. However, the UKCFM's requirements suggest selection on the basis of values and potential for skills development rather than on the basis of academic attainment as evidenced by qualifications. While one can guess at the nature of the personal qualities, interpersonal skills, intellectual capacity and professional ethical behaviour, little guidance is given on what these should be within the policy documents.

Would be solicitors are also given cues on appropriate behaviour and interpersonal skills during the LPC training. While potential solicitors are not selected overtly on the basis of these attributes, they form an important part of the LPC, taught as they are through the skills of interviewing and advising and advocacy. These are skills that require the student to interact in particular ways with clients and to take on the mantle of professional solicitor. These are left until the second phase of training, the Legal Practice Course, in which students are put through their paces as solicitors in a classroom setting. Students are also taught the ethical context of legal practice including professional conduct and client care and all parts of the course must be passed in order to achieve the LPC. Consequently, selection for the profession may not be overtly based on personal attributes and values, but students are assessed on these and thus the professional body has a hand in shaping the way in which solicitors view their role and the way in which they should approach legal practice. This happens later on in the process, academic knowledge comes first and skills development comes later, however, it is still controlled by the profession. Skills and attributes are controlled by the solicitors' profession, but more covertly than by the UKCFM, who state up front that potential mediators must have particular attributes and qualities and the potential to develop certain skills.

Entry standards and ongoing competence are measured more by an assessment of aptitude for family mediation students, including an assessment of individual traits and values backed up through professional practice consultancy, than through more traditional modes of academic achievement. The UKCFM appears to consider that academic knowledge is relevant as an indicator of capability to mediate, but it is not as clearly defined for family mediators as it is for solicitors. It is weighed alongside other indicators. It appears that the UKCFM selects candidates on the basis of their aptitude to be a good family mediator and their possession of the core values necessary for that professional role. The Law Society uses academic standards, evidenced over a prolonged period of study as a proxy for aptitude. There is no apparent assessment of ethics or personal qualities in the early stages of training (although professional ethics forms part of the later stages) other than those ascribed to an academic context by virtue of academic achievement. It appears that the Law Society works on the principle that as long as the candidate has reached a sufficient level of academic achievement, it will be able to inculcate the necessary values and provide sufficient skills training during the LPC. Whereas the UKCFM, with its shorter training period, cannot rely on such a strategy and thus selects candidates on the basis that they already have the essentials required to make a good family mediator. The difference is one of values and aptitude versus academic foundation.

To conclude, potential solicitors are selected for legal study on the basis of aptitude for the academic arena. They are assessed against benchmarked legal skills and knowledge requirements. Law Society family mediators are selected for training on the basis of being solicitors along with an inclination to mediate. Potential UK College family mediators are selected for training on the basis of their beliefs and values and the extent to which these are in accordance with the principles and values of the College and its perception of family mediation. On this basis, the conceptual label applied to the professional groupings is: potential ability followed by benchmarked level of competence in law and skills (solicitor); solicitor qualification and inclination to mediation (Law Society family mediator); and appropriate family mediator beliefs and values for Law Society family mediators.

Table 4.2: Professional Role, Skills & Knowledge Associated with Skills & Role:

Active partisan problem-solver (solicitor); **actively informed consensus solution-facilitator** (Law Society family mediator); **active consensus solution-facilitator** (UK College family mediator).

Solicitors Law Society of England and Wales (GDL Route)

Context
- GDL: *Implied context is adversarial as situated within precedent based approach to law.*
- LPC: *operates with a partisan legal tradition, with a litigation angle, although transactional work is also taught.*
- Skills development through pre-GLD undergraduate degree benchmark general transferable skills, (no GDL skills standards), LPC, PSC, and training contract skills requirements.

Professional-client Relationships
- *LPC:* The solicitor-client retainer; the role of the solicitor in the professional relationship.
- *Training Contract and PSC:* Client care and professional standards.

Professional Skills
- *LPC:* Advocacy; interviewing; advising skills; writing and drafting; practical legal research skills. Negotiation skills were once compulsory, however, these have now been given the status of optional skills to be assessed and taught, until the training contract when they become a compulsory element.
- *PSC:* Financial and business skills; advocacy and communication skills; client care and professional standards.
- *Training Contact:* Identify client's goals; identify and analyse relevant factual and legal issues; summarise strengths and weakness of each party's case; plan how to present the case; outline facts in a simple narrative form; formulate a coherent submission in a structured, concise and persuasive manner. The trainee should be assisted with the skills of working effectively with others, with harnessing development opportunities and developing their personal qualities. Trainees must demonstrate they have skills in respect of: case and transaction management; client care and practice support; communication; dispute resolution; drafting; interviewing and advising; legal research; negotiation.

Knowledge Associated with Skills
- *GDL:* Substantive legal knowledge of Contract, Tort, Public, EU, Land, Crime & Equity & Trusts Law.
- *LPC:* Theory associated with skills set: interviewing and advising (not necessarily adversarial); advocacy skills (adversarial); drafting skills (generally consensual); the knowledge associated with the legal process.
- *Training Contract:* Must include 'proper training and experience' in at least 3 distinct substantive areas of English law.

Communication and Relating Skills
- *LPC:* Advocacy; Interviewing; advising.
- *PSC:* Advocacy and communication skills.
- *Training Contract:* Advocacy; oral presentation skills; identify client's goals; outline facts in a simple narrative form; formulate a coherent submission based upon the facts, general principles and legal authority in a structured, concise and persuasive manner. In addition a trainee should be assisted with the skills of working effectively with others

Professional Relationship Skills
- *LPC:* The role of the solicitor in the professional relationship.
- Training Contract: *In addition a trainee should be assisted with the skills of working effectively with others.*

Technological Skills
- *Pre-GDL:* IT skills including email and WWW use.

Other
- *PSC Electives:* There are illustrative electives for matrimonial practitioners: mediation; drafting pleadings; negotiation skills; FDR workshop; estimating litigation costs; selecting and instructing experts. NB: The ADR workshop is part of electives for commercial litigators rather than within the matrimonial elective.

Family Mediators Law Society of England and Wales

Context
- ***Based on the use of skills to reach consensus but also when inappropriate to do so (overtly stated in the literature).***
- ***Skills development through initial training and family mediation consultancy.***

Professional-client(s) Relationships
- *Initial Training:* Legal information provision (not advice).

Professional Skills
- *Initial Training:* How to draw relevant information for the parties; how to establish a secure and effective working environment; how to consider and analyse that information; the skills to mediate (questioning techniques; summarising; acknowledging; listening; observing non-verbal communications; mutualising; reframing; normalising); how to deal creatively and flexibly with problems and people; legal information provision; ability to manage the mediation process effectively; drafting.
- *Family Mediation Consultancy:* Reflection and professional development.

Knowledge Associated with Skills
- *Initial Training:* Knowledge of the mediation process; communication theory; an awareness of the principles of co-mediation; knowledge of the mediation process (practice and theory); awareness of systems theory and the place of mediation within the different systems; understanding when mediation is inappropriate (including the FLA 1996); understanding of negotiation theories, practice and approaches; understanding of impasse and its causes, and effective strategies to deal with it; knowledge of how to bring negotiations to a close; drafting including knowledge of how to draft appropriate records of agreement; settlement including knowledge of settlement implementation including relevant court formalities, and post-termination requirements.

Communication and Relating Skills
- *Initial Training:* Appropriate different methods of communication; how to draw relevant information for the parties; questioning techniques; summarising; acknowledging; listening; observing non-verbal communications; mutualising; reframing; normalising; an understanding of how to manage the expression of emotions; an understanding of how to put the parties at ease and to help them to communicate; how to deal sensitively with the issues, concerns and aspirations of each party; an empathetic approach without forming alliances.

Professional Relationship Skills
- *Initial Training:* An awareness of the practice of co-mediation; other professionals: ability to communicate and work with the parties' lawyers as necessary; understanding of how to involve effectively other professional advisors.

Technological Skills

- *Initial Training:* None explicit although benchmarking skills will be a requirement for recent graduates.

Family Mediators UK College of Family Mediators

Context
- *Based on the use of skills to reach consensus.*
- *Skills development through foundation training and supervision via professional practice consultancy.*

Professional-client(s) relationships
- *Foundation Training:* Ensuring informed participation; consulting with children; recognising domestic abuse; being aware of cultural diversity.
- *Professional Practice Consultancy:* The consultant must help the mediator with ethics.

Professional skills
- *Foundation Training:* Option development; drafting; co-mediating where appropriate; consulting with children; recognising domestic abuse; managing the process; managing conflict; facilitating the exchange of information; being aware of cultural diversity.
- *Professional Practice Consultancy:* Consultants assist with the development of the application of core family mediation skills; reflection and professional development; the positive use of consultancy; professional practice consultancy; professional mediation practice; procedures.

Knowledge associated with skills
- *Foundation Training:* Being aware of cultural diversity; mediation theory; negotiation theory; conflict theory and management; communication theory; family transition & psychological and social processes of separation and divorce; availability at all stages of separation and divorce; non-discrimination.
- *Professional Practice Consultancy:* Consultants assist with the development of the acquisition and application of core family mediation knowledge; the understanding of family mediation principles and values; the ability to cope with a range of family mediation issues.

Communication and relating skills
- *Foundation Training:* Ensuring informed participation; listening; acknowledging; managing the process; managing conflict; questioning; summarising; communicating clearly; power balancing; facilitating the exchange of information; consulting with children.

Professional relationship skills
- *Foundation Training:* Co-mediating where appropriate.
- *Professional Practice Consultancy:* May include co-mediation with an experienced mediator.

Technological skills
- *Foundation Training:* None explicit.

Active partisan problem-solver (solicitor); **actively informed consensus solution-facilitator** (Law Society family mediator); **active consensus solution-facilitator** (UK College family mediator).

What are the skills and attributes that the solicitors' profession encourages in those training to become solicitors? The professional literature reveals that there is still a strong association with 'hard law', with the basic tenets of professional knowledge – the seven foundations of legal knowledge. These must be taught and assessed in relatively traditional academic modes and there is still a strong association between professional expertise and the need for knowledge retention, academic rigour and broad spectrum knowledge, within the context of law. However, the LPC provides an insight into the type of values the solicitors' profession wishes to encourage. The LPC presupposes that legal practice will take place within a business context, that is to say that a solicitor will operate within a profit-making law firm – business skills are taught whereas skills associated with public sector lawyering are not (although there is now a legal aid LPC offered by the College of Law: The Public Legal Service Legal Practice Course, which is guided by a public service ethos although it is still required to meet the Law Society requirements). Secondly it also reinforces the concept of professionalism, that solicitors are members of a profession with a very particular role in relation to the client. Client care and professional conduct are high on the list of prerequisites for any course, but financial probity also plays an important role in this context.

The skills that form an essential part of legal practice training are process-based skills, in other words they are the skills required to get the job of a solicitor done effectively. These include skills such as putting the client at ease during the interview process and ways of eliciting information from the client. They do not include explicit facilitation skills to allow the solicitor to help the client to help him or herself. Instead, the solicitor is seen as the 'fixer', the person who diagnoses the problem and then deals with it once the client has been given the options and has been asked to make a decision about the most appropriate one for them. Problem solving is seen as an important part of the solicitor's role, but the solicitor is not trained in how to help the client make an informed decision about their instructions to the solicitor on the basis of the advice given by the professional (clear communication to the client is important, however). This is an interesting omission when the profession claims to take instructions from the client, rather than telling the client the action that will be taken.

The LPC also includes litigation and advocacy as a core skills set, but no longer includes negotiation.[282] Litigation theory is not included in contrast to mediation theory for family mediation training. It appears that advocacy skills are seen as tremendously important, interesting when one learns that there are many non-contentious solicitors who never engage in advocacy or litigation work, although non-contentious work appears to be dealt with within the context of conveyancing and probate, types of legal practice that many solicitors will never undertake after completion of the LPC.[283] In this regard, the

---

[282] This has been made an essential part of the training contract, as discussed in the next chapter.

[283] For a now rather old review of the decline of conveyancing in legal practice see Bowles, J. 'The Structure of the Legal Profession in England and Wales.' (1994) Vol. 10 No. 1 *Oxford Review of Economic Policy* 18.

contentious environment and values associated with it are privileged over the non-contentious, although admittedly students may choose to take non-contentious electives and undertake negotiation training on an optional basis. This is in marked contrast to the exhortations by the profession that divorce solicitors should seek to resolve issues in a non-adversarial manner. But, family law electives seek to instil this, even though they appear to run in a parallel consensual context to other aspects of LPC training.

Family mediation training, by contrast, revolves around skills development and in particular facilitation skills development. Courses are much briefer than training for legal practice, lasting approximately forty hours plus professional practice consultancy rather than the minimum of one academic year full-time for the GDL and another year full-time for the LPC. Family mediation training course content is strictly circumscribed – the skills that must be taught and learned are set out in great detail, both by the Law Society and the UK College of Family Mediators. The theory of mediation is also a core topic for both professional bodies' training requirements; this includes knowledge of communication theory and conflict theory. Negotiation theory, skills and negotiation facilitation are covered in the Law Society curriculum for family mediation training. Negotiation theory is covered in the UKCFM curriculum as its values are more to the fore in their documentation. The needs of the children joint decision-making, fairness, non-compulsion are all values that are highlighted as important during training. The Law Society curriculum also has those values embedded within them, but they are phrased in a very different way. The Law Society curriculum is outcome statement orientated – family mediators should have 'an understanding of' but may not necessarily believe the values espoused. The UKCFM curriculum very clearly states the principles and values that must be taught and learned during the training programme. The focus, once again, is on values although these remain somewhat vague within the curriculum.

Family mediation training explicitly addresses the process skills for mediation but covers little that is not directly relevant to the process. The theory behind the process is important to facilitate it, values associated with consensual decision-making are also considered to be important. However, a defined broader knowledge base is not taught or required prior to, or at the end of, family mediation training. Instead, the family mediator develops skills to help her assist those participating in the mediation to reach a decision, and the skills that the family mediator needs to give the best opportunity for the mediation session(s) to be successful (i.e. result in a consensual decision about the previously undecided issues). Facilitation skills are indeed the central skill set, knowledge base. For the UKCFM family mediator, the values of family mediator are also extremely important; the Law Society is more concerned with the competence than the belief of its members.

To conclude, solicitors are trained to be active, partisan problem-solvers for their clients. Law Society family mediators are trained to be actively informed as to the process of family mediation (and the legal system) with the intention of facilitating negotiations between the parties to reach a consensus based on sufficient knowledge for the agreement to be an informed one. The UK College family mediators is similarly an active, consensus focused solution facilitator, however, the family mediators is selected on the basis of believes and values rather than taught the process as a relatively value-neutral system. The family mediator is not taught detailed substantive law so as to inform the clients about legal norms and their potential application to the clients' situation.

Table 4.3: The Role of the Professional in Decision-Making:

Partisan, protector & problem-solver (solicitor); **actively impartial non-directive facilitator** (solicitor family mediator); **passively impartial & fair facilitator** (UK College family mediator).

Solicitors Law Society of England and Wales (GDL Route)

Context of the Professional Role

- *LPC:* The Ethical Context – Solicitor-client retainer; introduction to the principles of Professional Conduct and Client Care (Incl. Solicitors Accounts Rules and Financial Services Act); see chapter six for further information on the specifics of the ethical context.

The Professional & Decision-Making

- *LPC:* This is dealt with in the client care pervasive component of the course in the context of the client retainer. Little detail is given in the training material but reference is made to the code of conduct. This is discussed in detail in chapter 6. Family law is not a core component of the GDL or LPC, the nature of decision-making in the context of divorce is not discussed and thus the solicitor-client retainer is based on the traditional view of solicitor-client partisan relations rather than that set out in the Family Law Protocol.

Children in Decision-Making

- *LPC:* No mention of children within the training literature. This is a pertinent issue to family law practice, but as family law is not a core component of the GDL or the LPC this will only be taught if the student takes a family law elective on the LPC. Solicitors may not have been exposed to this when they enter practice.

Family Mediators Law Society of England and Wales

Context of the Professional Role

- *Initial Training:* Ethical understanding (mediation ethics and solicitor ethics, including codes of practice); knowledge of principles of confidentiality and evidential privilege; understanding of the ways in which the traditional solicitor's role differs from that of a mediator and an ability to cope with those different roles; understanding of the applicability of non-discrimination policy; awareness of counselling, therapy and other agencies for referral if necessary; understanding of cultural and gender issues; knowledge of how to draft appropriate records of agreement.

The Professional & Decision-Making

- *Initial Training:* Awareness of principles of impartiality and non-directiveness and their application; understanding of and ability to manage the mediator's own preconceived prejudices, assumptions and judgements; understanding of and ability to facilitate discussions, negotiations, option development and reality testing; managing and facilitating discussions and negotiations; ability to communicate and work with the parties' solicitors as necessary; knowledge of where it is inappropriate to mediate; employing impasse strategies; knowledge of the appropriateness of different methods of communicating; empathetic approach without forming alliances; an understanding of how to deal sensitively with the issues, concerns and aspirations of each party; knowledge of how to bring negotiations to a close; knowledge of settlement implementation including relevant court formalities, and post-termination requirements; awareness of couple and family dynamics and patterns of behaviour; an understanding of how to avoid the development of unwitting alliances with either party; knowledge of how to manage power-imbalances.

Children in Decision-Making

- *Initial Training:* Understanding of children's developmental stages and needs; understanding of how to deal with abuse concerning partner or chid, and child protection.

Family Mediators UK College of Family Mediators

Context of the Professional Role

- *Foundation Training:* Knowledge of College Standards & Code of Practice; cultural diversity within mediation and non-discrimination; needs of the children within the context of mediation; no compulsion; joint decision-making by the parties; impartiality of the mediator; fairness; freedom from pressure; confidentiality and privilege; co-mediation where appropriate; self-monitoring and the use of professional practice consultancy; organisational context within which the mediator works.

The Professional & Decision-Making

- *Foundation Training:* No compulsion; joint decision-making by the parties; clarity of the process; confidentiality and privilege; impartiality of the mediator; fairness; freedom from pressure; issues appropriate for mediation; procedural flexibility; sufficient time for parties to use the process; power and gender issues; dispute resolution; domestic abuse.

Children in Decision-Making

- *Foundation Training:* focus on needs of children; child protection procedures; indicators of possible child abuse; consulting with children; the needs of children.

Partisan, protector & problem-solver (solicitor); actively impartial non-directive facilitator (Law Society family mediator); passively impartial & fair facilitator (UK College family mediator).

The nature of the professional role is considered as part of training as are the ethical principles of the profession.[284] Solicitor training focuses on the solicitor-client relationship, legal provisions and their context, financial probity as well as the financial and property needs of the client – from conveyancing needs to estate planning and wills. This highlights the business context of legal practice training. Family mediation training highlights the need to assist clients to develop their own options. Facilitation is the key, as is the impartial role of the family mediator and also the role of teacher in some respects. The family mediator seeks to develop the parties' abilities to communicate with each other, to consider the needs of other members of their family rather than just their own, and to develop strategies to deal with each other after the mediation is concluded. This is particularly important, if continuing contact is necessary in respect of children or other family members. However, the UK College training requirements set out the values that the family mediator must possess to begin training, whereas the Law Society requirements set out the abilities that the family mediator must have developed as a result of the training, as well as the issues about which they must be aware. This is an interesting difference. The Law Society appears to be concerned with professional ability; the UKCFM appears to be concerned with professional approach.

The Law Society, in both the solicitor and family mediation contexts require knowledge of the principles of confidentiality, as does the UKCFM, as well as evidential privilege. The UKCFM also highlights privilege as an issue. At face value that may imply that solicitors, Law Society family mediators and UK College family mediators are all being sent similar messages. However, the language used by the Law Society, 'evidential privilege' is that of the litigation environment, as opposed to the language used by the UKCFM, which implies that privilege is an extension of confidentiality, rather than a product of the adversarial system and litigation based terms of disclosure. Instead, the UKCFM has a strong focus on the joint decision-making of the parties and power-balancing by the mediator, as well as the importance of children in the decision-making context. This is also there for solicitors and Law Society family mediators, however to a much lesser extent. The shadow of the law, and more directly the court, is evident in the documentation of one body, whereas the needs of the children and the role of the parties and their wider family circle, is more evident in the other. The latter comes through strongly in the next concept as well.

Appropriate decision-making, in terms of process and outcome, is an integral part of solicitor and family mediator training, although both have very different views on the nature of decision-making. This is particularly the case, if one of the parties is in a weaker position than the other. There is evidence to suggest that domestic violence occurs in fifty-eight per cent of cases which go to mediation in the USA and Britain.[285] Family mediation is often criticised for not providing a safe environment

---

[284] The content of the codes of conduct are discussed in detail in chapter six and consequently will not be mentioned in any detail in this chapter.

[285] Winner, M. 'Capacity To Mediate' Vol. 7 No. 2 *Family Mediation* 17.

for victims of domestic violence on the one hand, but if safety can be assured, for not providing an equal bargaining position for both parties. Unequal bargaining power may result in an unfair agreement at the end of the process. Solicitors, on the other hand, represent only one of the two parties and it is argued that the presence of the partisan redresses any imbalance between the couple. Alternatively, it has been argued that this is detrimental to decision-making as it promotes egocentric decision-making that fosters adversarialism rather than consensus.[286]

Family mediator commentators suggest that family mediators can counter balance power inequalities and assist the couple to reach settlements that are fair and appropriate for them. Richards concludes that victims of domestic violence should not be excluded from mediation, but instead that mediators should be aware of the potential problems associated with domestic violence and act to counterbalance their negative effects.[287] Research conducted by Davis and Roberts suggests that mediation does not in fact undermine the position of women as eighty-six per cent of the women they interviewed felt that the agreement reached had been fair.[288] This assumes that prima facie fairness necessarily equates with actual fairness or that actual fairness is either unquantifiable or less important. The clients' perception of fairness may be based on inadequate information as to the type of settlement to which they had legal entitlement. Davis and Roberts argue however that the more important point to take from mediation sessions is that the mediator respects procedural fairness, rather than that the outcome is necessarily objectively fair. Mediators can ensure this by allowing each party to express his or her views freely in a safe environment, through their intervention in the process where necessary. This is justified on the basis that agreements are rarely legally binding and the parties often chose to alter the detail during the course of its use.[289]

Family mediation training focuses on the need to redress power imbalances, and the professional training requirements do highlight this issue as they do as regards the need for procedural fairness. This is also placed alongside the need for the mediator to be impartial. This is a difficult juxtaposition because impartiality usually connotes even handedness whereas the ability to redress power imbalances suggests that the family mediator must reframe and steer discussions to allow the weaker party to assert his or her position with authority. This role is closer to the need for a family mediator to play an adversarial role with the stronger party, if he or she is not giving any ground to the weaker, although this is within the context of a process to reach consensus. The literature on this is discussed more fully in chapter three.

Appropriate decision-making in the context of a solicitor relates to the correct operation of the solicitor client retainer. The solicitor is charged with the responsibility of investigating the client's situation, making all necessary enquiries, in order to be able to provide an expert legal assessment of the most appropriate correct course of action for the client, or the options open to the client. The client is then

---

[286] Finlay, H.A. *op. cit.* note 129.

[287] *Id.*

[288] Davis, G. & Roberts, M. *op. cit.* note 195.

[289] Davis, G. & Roberts, M. 'Mediation and the Battle of the Sexes' (1989) *Family Law* 306.

asked to provide instructions upon which the solicitor should act, within legal and professionally recognised limits. Thus, the solicitor acts on the client's instructions. It is assumed that the solicitors for both clients, are relatively equally matched in terms of arms, and thus, appropriate decision-making is predicated on an adversarial system of partisan champions for the protection of each client's own interests. As shall be seen in chapter five, this is not the model adopted by the Family Law protocol for solicitors who have sought and achieved accreditation at family practitioner level through the Law Society. However, this is how the solicitor client relationship, and client decision-making, is represented within the non-family law client care pervasive component of the LPC, with reference to the Guide to Professional Conduct. It could be argued that this does not reflect the post Woolf reform world of litigation; however, there is no mention of this within the training literature examined for this research. Thus, the adversarial model is still firmly entrenched.

Role of the Profession in Respect of Children & Their Participation in Decision-Making

Studies in the UK have indicated that twenty per cent of marriages end in divorce within the first ten years and many of these marriages will include young children.[290] The Family Law Act 1996 was, in part, promulgated to safeguard the interests of children in the divorce process, since parents were not previously encouraged to reach agreements about their children in a non-legal environment (although the Children Act 1989 does encourage private ordering). The Act actively encourages parents to use family mediation to reach agreements about their continuing parenting role, in order to minimise bitterness and conflict between the parties and therefore the children and family mediators have often stressed their particular expertise in respect of children's issues.

Why is family mediation seen as important for children going through a divorce? Does it have benefits that cannot be met by the traditional legal process? Research by Cockett and Tripp suggests that children rarely understand why their parents are getting divorced or the change in their living arrangements as the result of a divorce, including why one parent may now be absent.[291] Kalter's research found that divorce and separation has a negative impact on children.[292] Children may be affected by the altered relationships between themselves and their parents, between their parents, with the introduction of a new person into their lives through a parent's new relationship. They may also be affected by the change in their standard of living at the point of divorce. Family mediators believe that they are in a good position to assist children at this time and to help their parents to agree terms that will put their children's needs to the fore. However, the involvement of children in family mediation raises ethical issues concerning the confidentiality of discussions with children and how far the mediator may actively counsel the child. Mediators have the potential to transform children's lives through their

---

[290] See Cockett, M. & Tripp, J. *The Exeter Family Study: Family Breakdown and Its Impact On Children.* (Exeter: Exeter University Press, 1994); and Simpson, B. *Being There: Fathers After Divorce.* (University of Newcastle: Relate Centre For Family Studies, 1995).

[291] See Cockett, M. & Tripp, J. *id.*

[292] Kalter N. Kloner, A., Scheier, S. *et al.* 'Predictors of Children's Post Divorce Adjustment' (1989) Vol. 59 *American Journal of Orthopsychiatry* 605.

involvement with the parents in the development of their parenting function; equally they have the potential to increase conflict. This gives rise to important training issues.

Family mediation training does highlight the needs of the children as distinct from the divorcing couple. In addition, the Law Society family mediator training standards include a provision that requires family mediation students to be given training in children's developmental stages to assist the mediator in focusing better on the needs of children. Children are not mentioned in the GDL training literature and are not overtly covered in the LPC either, other than perhaps in respect of minor children as clients as part of the pervasive client care component of the course. Children and their rights would be part of any family law module, but this is not a core part of training for solicitors. Consequently family mediators are taught to consider the couple's needs and to focus each party to consider their needs and their former spouse's needs, alongside the needs of any children, whereas solicitors are taught to focus on the needs of their clients and on their client's instructions to them, within the ethical and legal limitations placed upon them. The training for would-be solicitors does not directly focus on the wishes and needs of the children. Family law modules would consider the place of the child, the rights of children and the impact of divorce on children, this is not a core part of the training for a solicitor unless a solicitor wishes to become accredited as a family law specialist once qualified. Once again, the focus of solicitor training is on the solicitor-client relationship, in the partisan environment, whereas the focus on family mediation training is on the wider needs of the family unit that is the subject of the relationship breakdown.

In conclusion, the conceptual label that sums up the messages transmitted by the professional bodies to their members is: the solicitor as a partisan, client protector and problem-solver; the Law Society family mediator as an actively impartial (to stress the difference between the role of solicitor and the role of mediator), non-directive facilitator; the UK College family mediator as a passively impartial (as this in deemed to be inherent and requiring no special effort), fair, even-handed facilitator in the family mediation process.

Table 4.4: Legal Norms and Role of Law in Decision-Making:

The framework (solicitor); **the legal back-stop** (Law Society family mediator); **one possible framework** (UK College family mediator).

Solicitors Law Society of England and Wales (GDL route)

The Law Curriculum
- *GDL:* The seven foundations of legal knowledge must be taught and assessed: Contract law; Criminal law; Equity and Trusts; European Union law; Land law; Public law; Tort law.
- *LPC:* The law, procedure and practical skills associated with: Litigation and advocacy; Business law and practice; Conveyancing; Probate and Administration of Estates- basic principles of succession, practice and procedure of winding up estates; Plus three electives from a range of private client and corporate client work. EU law and revenue law are all pervasive topics.

Law & Practice
- Accounts, professional conduct and client care as well as the practical skills associated with the practice of law in relation to the LPC subjects and electives.
-

The Legal Process
- The legal process and procedure and evidential requirements are covered in litigation and advocacy.

Family Mediators Law Society of England and Wales

The Law Curriculum
- Knowledge of law and legal procedures relevant to marriage breakdown so as to appreciate the implications of the parties' circumstances and requirements, and available options.
- Detailed working knowledge of core areas family law including the Family Law Act 1996, the DPMCA 1978, the court's inherent jurisdiction; Private Children Act proceedings including CA 1989 Parts I & II; Financial provisions and property disputes, including pensions (married & cohabitants) including: Maintenance pending suit, financial provision and PAO, MWPA 1882, CSA 1991, FLA 1996, TOLAOTA 1996, welfare benefit and tax implications of financial arrangements, Child Support.

Law & Practice
- Knowledge of law and practice regarding financial disclosure, clarification and verification; knowledge of how to provide legal information covering contract law, housing, pensions, inheritance, trusts, tax and other aspects, without advising; understanding the place of rights in family mediation.

The Legal Process
- Knowledge of settlement implementation including relevant court formalities, and post-termination requirements.

Family Mediators UK College of Family Mediators

The Law Curriculum
- Appropriate knowledge of family law and legal processes, namely, current legislation concerning families.
- Family breakdown and financial support following separation and divorce; changes to divorce legislation or family law legislation; range of orders to children in CA 1989 & C(Scotland)A 1995; legislation relating to on pensions & divorce, Pensions Act 1995 and subsequent amendments and how this works in practice; Child

Support Act 1991 and recent changes, in particular how clean break settlements are dealt with and where the Act may not apply, domestic abuse and Part IV of FLA 1996.

- Law on maintenance and capital settlements court processes.

The Legal Process

- Rules of court (Scotland); Civil Evidence (Family Mediation) (Scotland) Act 1995; evidential rules (Scotland).

The framework **(solicitor)**; the legal back-stop **(Law Society family mediator)**; one possible framework **(UK College family mediator)**.

The framework or the legal back-stop (solicitor, and Law Society family mediator); **one possible framework** (UK College family mediator).

The role of law within the curriculum is understandably very different. Law is the backdrop to all professional training to be a solicitor, whereas it is only a tiny part of an already short course on family mediation. As discussed in chapter three, while few divorces will be defended in court, some issues ancillary to the divorce may result in a court order and even when this is not the case it is generally considered that solicitors will attempt to negotiate issues in the light of prevailing legal norms, however loosely. This appears to be particularly true in respect of finance and property issues in which solicitors may attempt to reframe their client's view about an appropriate settlement. Family mediation, however, is based on the principle that it is important for the parties to reach their own agreement, whether or not this resembles the type of order that would have been made through court adjudication or a solicitor bargained divorce. It is more important that the parties reach a mutually commodious arrangement, than that they achieve the best deal for themselves at the expense of the other party. The parties will, however, only discuss the issues that they consider to be pertinent, unless the mediator suggests that they should consider others. For example, the parties may not have considered pension rights or insurance policies, nor make any provision for these in their agreement. Indeed, one of the parties may be unaware that there is a pension that would have been of benefit to her. There is the potential to miss issues that will be of vital importance in the future, but which may not appear of relevance at the present. However, the key to judging the success of the mediation will be the extent to which consensus may be reached between the parties.

It is estimated that most foundation training courses focus on family and child law for approximately three hours during the course.[293] However, it is also true to say that a solicitor is entitled to practice family law without ever having studied it. A solicitor would have spent many hours learning the general principles of English law and would have covered property law in two modules during the GDL, but there is no requirement that he or she would have studied the law relating to children or to divorce prior to practice. Family mediation training under the UKCFM auspices treats law in the same category as one of a number of areas of knowledge that family mediators should know, along with mediation theory, negotiation theory, conflict theory and management, the needs of the children, cultural diversity and communication theory. The Law Society requires all solicitors to have a core of legal knowledge as well as an understanding of legal process, the role of the solicitor and the role of the courts and the litigation environment. It no longer requires solicitors to have knowledge of negotiation theory nor the skills to perform it (pre-training contract stage). Litigation is stressed over the role of negotiation, and by implication, the role of the court order over the parties reaching a consensus.

This raises an important point with regard to couples who do not have separate legal representation when entering into family mediation. They may try to rely on their

---

[293] See for example Webley, L.C. *op. cit.* note 16 at 86-90.

own knowledge and that of the family mediator to gauge whether or not they are mediating the relevant issues in respect of their divorce. In strict terms, a family mediator would say that the parties should discuss and try to reach consensus about the issues of importance to them, rather than ones that a solicitor would highlight as of importance. However, if the divorcing couple do not bring issues to the fore and a family mediator does not raise an issue, then some may be left unresolved as a result of the parties' ignorance rather than by design. Issues such as future pension provision may well be ones that the parties have not considered at the time of the divorce, because they are not pressing at that stage.

Should family mediators raise these issues with the parties? Some commentators consider this to be of vital importance, others see this as the role of a legal professional outside the legal process, but family law training has been included within the foundation training programme to raise awareness of potential issues with family mediators. This is where legal commentators claim that legal knowledge is imperative to aid the mediator in redressing imbalances of power and information, demystifying the parties of their erroneous assumptions and clearing the way for an equitable settlement. [294] They claim that this will result in better long term solutions for the parties, who may find otherwise that they are worse off in later life, as a result of a lack of long term financial planning at the time of the divorce. [295] Law Society family mediator training appears to adhere to this view. Knowledge of family law is assessed in a manner similar to that expected of a solicitor practising in an area of law – in other words to a standard that is expected of an advisor rather than an informer. However, for UKCFM training, family law teaching is brief. The training does raise awareness of the types of issues that could be the subject of discussion at mediation. It also highlights issues that are pertinent to couples in respect of finance and property issues. Critics claim that this may not be sufficient to ensure that couples reach well informed settlements. [296] Roberts has highlighted the distinction between legal information provision and legal advice. [297] She suggests that legal information may be a useful addition to a mediator's skills repertoire, but legal advice would jeopardise independence. Family mediator training does include the ability to provide

---

[294] Legal knowledge is considered to be invaluable by Foster and Kelly as the parties may lose important legal rights as a result of not having the information which is required to make an informed decision. Foster & Kelly op. cit. note 198 at 670. This is discussed in more detail in chapter three.

[295] Not all family mediation bodies share the same view of legal knowledge requirements and the role of law. The Academy for Family Mediators in the US states that family mediators should 'acquire substantive knowledge and procedural skill in the specialised areas of practice. This may include but is not limited to family and human development, family law, divorce procedures, family and human development, family finances, community resources, the mediation process, and professional ethics.' At The Academy of Family Mediators 1983, Standards of Practice, Part XI. Training and Education and VII. Professional Advice A. B. and C. It goes on to state that mediators should provide information to the parties only in so far as they are qualified by training or experience to do so. They should encourage the parties (as opposed to explain or suggest) to gain independent legal advice when the mediation may give rise to legal consequences for the parties and where an agreement is to be formalised.

[296] See Fiss, O.M. op. cit. at note 102 and Twining, W. op. cit. note 114.

[297] Roberts, M. Mediation in Family Disputes, Principles of Practice 2nd Ed. (Aldershot: Arena, 1997) 64.

legal information to clients where appropriate, although it is stressed within the literature that the parties should, however, be permitted to reach their own decisions on fairness through informed decision-making, which requires an understanding of the legal position.[298]

To this end, mediator and solicitor training distinguish between a family mediator's basic knowledge of law which they may use to provide basic information to the parties, in contrast to legal advice provided by solicitors who in providing advice give a view of an appropriate course of action for the client. However, Law Society and UKCFM messages appear to be distinctive. The Law Society requirements appear to suggest that law is the backstop – if the parties are about to reach a decision that is consensual and yet wholly at odds with current legal practice, the family mediator should terminate the mediation until the parties seek legal advice from solicitors. However, UKCFM appears to suggest that legal norms are one of a possible range of principles that may be considered when reaching a consensual settlement, but a settlement at odds with current legal practice is not in itself a cause for alarm, or for the suspension of the mediation process.

Family mediators are not in a dissimilar position to other professions, such as accountants and estate agents, who provide legal information. UKCFM appears to consider that family mediators' relationship with the law in a similar light. Information is viewed as a way of assisting couples in reaching an informed, consensual agreement, whereas legal advice is party specific. This may be a tool in assisting the party to reach an agreement with their former spouse, or it may be a tool to use to drive a hard bargain, and if necessary go to court to secure a good 'idea' where one cannot be reached through negotiation. Information is one piece in the jigsaw of consensual decision-making, advice is the key to securing a good deal for one party, which may include an assessment of what a court would order, against which an offer to settle can be assessed. The Law Society does not entirely distance mediators from the role of solicitors. While the Law Society does see the distinction between the role of a solicitor and a family mediator, it cannot sanction decisions that are totally at odds with legal practice unless the parties have reached an informed position on the basis of partisan legal advice. Thereafter, the family mediator is acting in a similar way to a family law solicitor – taking instructions about the terms of settlement albeit not necessarily the terms that they would advise to a client in a partisan solicitor-client relationship.

To conclude, both solicitors and Law Society family mediators view law as the framework within which agreements should generally be made, and if the parties seek to agree terms outside the legal norm they should do so in full knowledge of that. The family mediator is a backstop in this respect, and the mediator's intervention is an exception rather than a standard part of her role. The UK College family mediator considers law to be one possible framework for decision-making, as part of a wider range of decision-making norms that the clients may choose to adopt.

---

[298] Folberg, J. 'A Mediation Overview: History and Dimensions of Practice' (1983) *Mediation Quarterly* 3 at 11.

Table 4.5: Professional Attributes that Require Assessment at a Vocational Level:

A legally knowledgeable, informed, problem-solving, communicator with business & financial acumen (solicitor); a family law expert, competent, fair, legally acceptable consensual solution-facilitator (Law Society family mediator); a competent, fair, impartial, consensual solution-facilitator (UK College family mediator).

Solicitors Law Society of England and Wales (GDL Route)

PSC Assessment

- *Financial and business skills:* Written standards element 1 – no assessment; written standards elements 2-6 – open book exam of 1.5 hours.
- *Advocacy and communication skills:* skills assessment/appraisal.
- *Client care and professional standards:* no assessment.
- *Electives:* must be assessed, but no set requirements (other than for distance learning).

Training Contract Assessment

- Review and appraisal of the trainee's experience during the training contract against the criteria set out below. Trainee must keep a record of training. Trainee must have daily access to a supervising solicitor. His/her progress must be monitored regularly and at least three times during the two years. Must be prompt and adequate arrangements to deal with personnel concerns in respect of trainee. Trainees must have paid leave to attend required courses.
- Trainees are appraised on their overall ability to: (1)produce a schedule for a case/transaction, split into phases; (2) plan work in terms of time, cost and risk management; (3) diarise, follow-up and revisit matters at an appropriate time; (4) keep accurate records; (5) manage files effectively; (6) report back to clients regularly and fully; (7) co-ordinate teams to review progress and revise options; (8)brings matters to a timely conclusion satisfactory to the client; (9) wrap up the matter, closing the file and recovering costs and disbursements and must pay all fees and reasonable expenses.
  - *Client care and practice support:* Set and meet deadlines; review and report on progress; prioritise tasks; maintain files in good order; adopt a methodical approach to work; understand the process of setting fees and billing clients
  - *Communication:* Express ideas orally and in writing with precisions and logic in language appropriate to the recipient; use grammar syntax and punctuation correctly; listen actively, speak effectively; keep accurate notes; use email/word processing; identify client's goals and priorities
  - *Dispute resolution:* Take careful instruction from the client; identify the client's purposes in pursuing the dispute and advises on the possible outcomes and costs; thoroughly research the liabilities of the parties to the dispute; gather evidence from witnesses or elsewhere; consider fully the range of options for dispute resolution; meet necessary deadlines and keeps the client informed as the dispute progresses; draft or prepare papers to assist the resolution of the contentious matter; control information central to the client's interests through meetings, conference and hearings; ensure the settlement and judgments are secure and enforceable.
  - *Drafting:* Maintain a standard of care that protects the interests of the client; address all relevant factual and legal issues; identify relevant options; demonstrate a critical use of standard forms and precedents; draft document which are logical, coherent, clear and precise.

- o *Interviewing and Advising:* Prepare for interviews; use appropriate questioning techniques; identify possible courses of action and their consequences; help clients decide on the best course of action; agree action to be taken following the interview; accurately record the interview and establishes a professional relationship with the client dealing with any ethical problems which may arise.
- o *Legal Research:* Grasp of basic legal principles; knowledge and understanding of the law when researching; application of law in a practical and commercial way.
- o *Negotiation:* Identify the central issues and explains them to the client; assess the bargaining positions of each party; plan a negotiation; establish an agenda at the start of the negotiation; generate alternative solutions to resolve the issues; use appropriate negotiating style; identify the strategy and tactics used by the other side; document the agreement or settlement; explain the benefits and disadvantages of the agreement of settlement.

Family Mediators Law Society of England and Wales

FMC/ PPC Assessment
- Meet the requirements set out for Family Mediation Consultancy (FMC), including one-to-one consultancy.

Developmental & Direct Route to Practitioner Membership
- Demonstration of competence at the time of the research: submission of written answers to questions set by the Panel. The questions are scenarios which test the mediator's competencies, skills and knowledge against the Law Society standards.
    - o Question 1 – c. 40-100 word answer per section (of which there are 8); Question 2-16 should each be answered in 100-500 words.
    - o In addition, a mediator must complete summarises for 4 mediation cases which they have completed in the last two years and submit those for consideration.
- The family mediator is assessed against the family mediator competencies (summarised in the table above) and against the knowledge and skill standards (also summarised in the table above). This is a very detailed and extensive written form of assessment. The standards of competence against which they are judged relate to: (1)understanding of the Law Society's code of Practice for Family Mediators; (2)engaging the parties in the mediation forum; (3)obtaining commitment and agreeing mediation rules; (4) preliminary communications and preparation; (5) establishing the venue and meeting the parties; (6) establishing the issues and setting the agenda; (7) information gathering; (8) managing and facilitation discussions and negotiations; (9) employing impasse strategies; (10) concluding mediation and recording the outcome; (11) post termination skills. These and the knowledge and skills components are set out in the table above.
- If the mediator does not appear to have sufficient breadth of competencies, skills and knowledge then applications may be invited to attend an interview with two or more Family Mediation Panel assessors.
- Family mediators must also include two referees.
- A **general member** should have the knowledge of all aspects of mediation by having completed the foundation training.
- A **practitioner member** should the knowledge of all aspects of the mediation process and be able to demonstrate how this has been applied in practice.

Family Mediators UK College of Family Mediators

PPC Assessment
- Meet the consultancy requirements including one-to-one consultancy.

- Monitoring undertaken by sampling records kept by the mediation (permission of clients must first be sought and recorded)
- Consultant must make reasonable and appropriate enquiries about the mediator and his/her practice, and follow these up (if necessary). The consultant should review the mediator's documents with a careful and critical eye.
- Portfolio Assessment: The portfolio is examined by an assessor will then consider the portfolio, make a decision and forward the portfolio to the College's Internal Verifier who will ensure the assessment has been properly conducted.
- The consultant's formal assessment will include her assessment of the portfolio and an evaluation the candidate.

A legally knowledgeable, informed, problem-solving, communicator with business & financial acumen (solicitor); a family law expert, competent, fair, legally acceptable consensual solution-facilitator (Law Society family mediator); a competent, fair, impartial, consensual solution-facilitator (UK College family mediator).

The professional bodies require solicitors and family mediators to have some vocational experience prior to them becoming fully qualified as professionals. The Law Society requires solicitors to undertake a two-year training contract within a law firm or another organisation approved by the Law Society and successfully to complete the PSC. The Law Society does not require a trainee solicitor to undertake family law practice prior to becoming qualified as a solicitor, nor prior to carrying out family law work as a qualified solicitor. This suggests that the Law Society approaches divorce matters in the same way as other forms of legal practice, in other words that training in other forms of legal practice will fit trainees for family law practice. This is interesting as the role of the client's family and the needs and wishes of children are of little relevance to the solicitor's retainer in virtually all other forms of legal practice. Generic training will not fit a solicitor for this type of work and therefore one would anticipate a need to train solicitors in this mode or form of professional approach. This is indeed recognised by the Law Society, if solicitors wish to attain accredited family law status; however, this is not a prerequisite for family legal practice. The skill set developed by the PSC and the training contract is in addition to that taught during the GDL and LPC. It gives more weight to non-contentious skills than does the LPC and also includes negotiation skills and strategies which are more appropriate to legal practice, if adversarialism is truly a last resort.

PSC providers have to be accredited by the Law Society prior to being permitted to offer training. The role of the vocational stage of training is an interesting one, as both professions have a very different approach. Solicitors have an extended period of supervised vocational training, two years full-time in a training establishment – usually a law firm, compared with ten hours of supervised training for family mediators through professional practice consultancy. Both include appraisals of the professional's performance and both require a senior professional to consider the quality of the work carried out by the new professional. However, solicitor's vocational training is far more extensive and also far more controlled by the professional body. Solicitors appear to broaden out and deepen their knowledge, skills and experience as trainee solicitors through day to day supervised practice over a long period. Trainees work alongside more senior staff very closely and thus learn the principles, values and approaches of solicitors in an apprenticeship. Solicitors undertaking a family law 'seat' in their training contract may be exposed to a very different type of legal practice than the one they imagined through their GDL and LPC training, as this may be their first experience of family law. Their skills development is closely monitored and they are required to reflect on their practice. Adversarialism is present within training as there is further emphasis placed on advocacy skills, however, negotiation skills are also present as are the skills of identifying the client's goals and priorities, client care issues, and choice of appropriate dispute resolution mechanism, which may be inter partes negotiations, mediation, arbitration, or litigation. This does force the trainee to consider the solicitor's role in a wider context and to focus on the needs and wishes of the client.

This does not necessarily mean adversarial legal practice but does connote partisanship, as one would expect in a solicitor client-relationship.

The UKCFM requires all family mediators to undertake a minimum of ten hours of professional practice consultancy prior to completing their foundation training stage. After that they may practice as an associate member of the UK College as long as they have successfully completed their foundation training. Training then follows a professional practice consultancy route. This means that an approved professional practice consultant family mediator reviews the work of the associate family mediator, in person for at least one hour and either face-to-face with the family mediator as well as through checking family mediation files, discussing practice with the family mediator, reviewing practice via telephone etc. The family mediator then either presents him or herself for Panel assessment by a College approved body after a period of practice and professional practice consultancy, or alternatively goes through the portfolio based assessment route which seeks to establish the competence of the family mediator to the standards set by the UK College.

The Law Society has decided to adopt a similar regime for family mediators. The Law Society requires the solicitor-family mediator, in addition to their training requirements as a solicitor, to undertake a minimum of ten hours of family mediation experience and consultancy as part of their foundation training (it appears that this has now been increased to eleven hours). After that a family mediator may apply for general membership of the Panel, if the conditions are met, and practice on that basis. At the time of the research, practitioner status was gained, assuming the CPD and consultancy conditions were met, by competence assessment through an extended written assessment against the Law Society's family mediation competencies, skills and knowledge standards. In both instances, family mediation training at this stage appears to reinforce the principles and values set out in the initial training and also acts as a check on the quality of the work undertaken by family mediation – a gate-keeping and quality assurance function by the profession. It is, however, far less intensive than that of the solicitor' profession through the training contract as far as it is outlined in the professional literature. It relies very heavily on the family mediation/ professional practice consultants to provide feedback and development opportunities to family mediators at the early stages of their practice. There is now mandatory training for family mediators who wish to practice as professional practice consultants, which suggests that this role is given status and prominence within the profession as is the consultancy stage of training for family mediators. However, family mediation and professional practice consultancy is not a form of supervision in the sense of supervision during a training contract and unless the family mediator regularly co-mediates, most of the professional experience of the family mediator will be relatively isolated. This means that they are likely to reinforce the values and principles that they have learned at foundation stage, or they continue to hold in spite of foundation training, rather than take on those of other family mediators with whom they work. This is the opposite of the position of solicitors, as discussed below.

Family mediation practice based training is an extension of the foundation training, allowing mediators to practice the skills that they have learned or developed. It is also a way of providing enhanced feedback to associate mediators and to check that they are working appropriately. It does aim to reinforce the principles and values espoused by family mediators, however, there is little direct observation of face to face mediation work and consequently it is hard to say with any certainty that family mediators do indeed practice in the manner set out in their foundation training, other than in respect of observation of their work through PPC or co-mediation by other mediators. It is difficult to say with certainty that the principles and values are being put into practice, if the clients appear happy and the paperwork looks to be in order. Thus, this stage of training, whilst valuable, does not appear to provide greater insight into the approach adopted by family mediators to their work. The training contract for solicitors, coupled with the PSC, appears to embed, strengthen and widen the trainee's skills set in a supervised context and provide a less litigation based, more non-contentious approach to legal practice than is afforded by the earlier training stages. It also requires trainees to work alongside other more experienced solicitors, which will lead them to take on the values and approaches that their supervisors and colleagues demonstrate, rather than necessarily reinforce those raised at the LPC stage of training. This suggests that, if a solicitor works in a practice in which family law is practiced in an adversarial context, they may adopt a similar approach, and likewise, if their supervisor adopts a conciliatory approach they too may develop that.

The conceptual label adopted to describe this concept is: solicitors are legally knowledgeable, informed problem-solvers with strong communication skills, business and financial acumen. Law Society family mediators may be summed up as family law experts who are classes as competent, even-handed and fair, seeking to facilitate a legally acceptable yet consensual solution. UK College family mediators are described as competent, fair, impartial facilitators of consensual solutions for clients.

4.6 Conclusions

The training for would-be solicitors appears to broaden and deepen students' legal knowledge and to provide and develop the skills they need to be able to use substantive knowledge. Skills development also focuses on interpersonal skills to enhance the solicitor-client relationship, although there is no overt skills training in how to assist a client towards making decisions that lead to instructions to the solicitor. In other words, it is assumed that the client will be able to take the information and advice given to him or her by the solicitor and then formulate appropriate instructions for the solicitor to act on. This does not appear to represent the reality of family legal practice as discussed in chapter three, which has found that solicitors try to steer their clients towards appropriate settlements and to raise or lower their expectations, while taking into account the needs of any dependants such as children. However, this is not present within the core of legal training, whereas advocacy and litigation skills are present. Negotiation skills are also not core skills at LPC level. This provides some evidence for the proposition that solicitors are trained to practice in the shadow of litigation, even if they do not take cases on to court. Solicitors are taught to be analytical problem solvers, to use the totality of their skills and their knowledge to provide a solution that the client is able to accept. Teaching is within the context of the norm of partisanship. The solicitor is trained to be client's champion, who will protect the client from inappropriate demands from the other person or people involved in the matter.

Family mediator training appears to inculcate key values and principles into students, even though potential family mediators are selected on the basis of having appropriate values (in the context of selection using UKCFM criteria). Subsequent training is values and skills-based training rather than a knowledge-based one. Facilitation skills are the key to assist clients in reaching their own decisions; however, there is no normative structure within which clients should reach an appropriate agreement. The training literature reinforces the impartiality of the mediator and the need to redress power imbalances. It does provide some training in relevant legal norms and the Law Society family mediation training highlights the need for a family mediator to terminate mediation in certain situations. However, the training documentation does not grapple with the issue of when a mediator should intervene in the decision-making process to ensure that the needs of one of the couple are brought to the fore, or when the needs of the children should be taken into account by the couple, nor when an agreement is not an agreement that could in any way be described as fair. There is evidence within the literature to support the proposition that family mediators adopt a consensus based approach to practice, however, the literature stays silent about when a mediator must intervene to prevent a prima facie consensual settlement that is manifestly unfair for one of the parties or for the children. This goes to the heart of the distinction between information giving and advising, which appears to be the crux of the difference between family mediation and solicitor approaches to divorce.

The next chapter considers the accreditation requirements for family mediators and divorce solicitors including accreditation as a family law solicitor by the Family Law Panel. It also considers whether the accreditation and continuing professional development requirements give an indication of professional approach by solicitor or family mediators.

Chapter 5: Adversarialism & Consensus? Accreditation Requirements

The English Royal Commission on Legal Services described the five main features of a profession as being: the existence of a governing body of the profession with powers to discipline its members and to control their practice; mastery of a specialised field of knowledge with specific education and training as well as practical experience and continuing professional development; admission requirements based on training and assessment; some form of self-regulation to require members to adhere to high standards of practice; responsibility of the professional to his client, by exercising the care and attention to the case that the client would, if he had the knowledge and skill to do so himself.[299] Chapter four considered the Law Society and the UK College of Family Mediators' training course requirements for students wishing to become members of their professions, but they also set accreditation standards including continuing professional development requirements. These are the minimum standards that professionals must meet in order to become and remain members of the profession. This chapter considers those requirements to examine what the policy and regulatory documents indicate about appropriate professional approaches to divorce matters. Once again, the analysis has been conducted using a grounded theory method, as discussed in chapter two.

5.1 Professional Literature on Accreditation & Professional Standards: Relevance to Professional Approach?

Why refer to the literature on accreditation and continuing professional development, in order to consider what cues professional bodies give to their members about their professional role and approach? Professional bodies have an interest in setting the entry requirements into their professions, as discussed in chapter four, and accreditation and monitoring of professional standards are an extension of this. As Laster and Taylor comment,

> Professions distinguish themselves by claiming competence in certain skills not possessed by others. Guaranteeing professional competence is an important way of gaining legitimacy for a profession. Thus professionals ensure that incompetent members are penalised, so as not to undermine the standing of their professional peers. Competence is "created" through formal training and accreditation.[300]

In short, professional bodies have an interest in ensuring that their members reach a set of defined standards, or are viewed by their client group as meeting a set of defined standards, and to this end they set accreditation requirements for potential members.

---

[299] *The Royal Commission on Legal Services Final Report Volume One Cmnd 7648* (London: HMSO, 1979).

[300] Laster, K. & Taylor, V.L. *Interpreters and the Legal System* (Sydney: The Federation Press, 1994) at 208.

What do professional bodies hope to achieve by setting accreditation requirements for potential members? Abel argues that professional bodies construct the professional commodity. Consequently, they must require certain basic values, skills and knowledge from their members in order to maintain, and in a competitive situation, advance the profession. This is certainly an issue in respect of divorce services, as divorce solicitors are now vying with family mediators in relation to public funding of legally aided divorce dispute settlement. As Abel states, '[p]rofessions produce services rather than goods... Service providers confront two distinct problems in particularly acute form. First, the consumer must value the producer's services.... Second, consumers must be convinced they cannot produce the services themselves.'[301] Couples are permitted by law to reach their own divorce settlements and do not need to use the services of a solicitor or family mediator to do so. Therefore, professionals must point to their rigorous training and accreditation requirements including regular updating and monitoring or reaccreditation, to indicate that their professional project is an important one that takes years to learn, and which provides a service far superior to anything a lay person would be able to achieve themselves, or with the assistance of a non-expert.

Abel also suggests that professions must also market expertise – art and technical ability, and must continue to reinvent themselves in order to maintain their professional commodity.[302] Accreditation and reaccreditation requirements may play a role in this. Accreditation standards allow the professional body the opportunity to set the entry level qualifications for its new members, and provide a tiered competence level for more experienced staff. However, accreditation requirements alone will only assist bodies with new recruits to the profession, or members seeking to move between recognised tiered levels of expertise. These standards will not address continuing technical ability of existing members, nor provide a vehicle for professional bodies to refocus the skills and knowledge of their established professional members to develop or model the professional project. Reaccreditation and continuing professional development requirements provide this function. Professional bodies may also attempt to maintain the competence of their profession by setting continuing professional requirements and periodic renewal of membership to ensure that messages they have sent about professional approach are reinforced through-out professional practice. They may argue that continuing professional development promotes professional development and reflection, just as initial training provides substantive knowledge and skills development. This inculcates professionals with a sense of profession and identity, which may also result in a particular professional approach being adopted by members.

The professional accreditation requirements set by the solicitor and family mediation professions are greater than would be needed for the purposes of marketing a service, as set out below. Abel argues that the detailed content of education and training is far greater than is necessary for a professional to be competent. He states that, 'To the extent that mandatory education serves a purpose other than market control, it confers status through the association of the university with high culture, socialises entrants to their professional roles, and provides warrants of loyalty and

---

[301] Abel, R.L. *American Lawyers* (Oxford: Oxford University Press, 1989) at 18.

[302] *Id.*

discipline.'[303] Continuing professional development would appear to take this a stage further, socialising professionals but also highlighting the importance of the knowledge and skills that solicitors and family mediators need to refresh, in order to retain professional status. This in turn suggests that professional bodies also have some influence over their members as a result of professional requirements and standards, otherwise over a period of time the profession's marketing would be discredited and the professional commodity devalued.

Abbot argues that professionalisation is not a linear development and that in reality professions organise themselves and control and influence their members in order to retain a 'heartland jurisdiction', which they will defend in the face of competition from other areas of professional practice.[304] Laster further argues that lawyers defend themselves by persuading the public of their specialist knowledge and skills as well as their commitment to the public through altruistic ideals.[305] This is evidenced by the accreditation requirements they set including the technical and values based norms of the given profession. In the face of competition from family mediators, which have been viewed as less intimidating, more responsive and less expensive in the media and parliamentary debates at the time of the passage of the Family Law Bill, the Law Society has sought to distinguish between its generalist solicitors and its family law specialists, while family mediators have retained a distinctive identity, a step apart from other types of mediators.[306]

In response, or at least subsequent to this move by the Law Society, the UKCFM introduced an advanced family mediation qualification in 2004 (AQM), which seeks to recognise family mediators who have more extensive post-qualification experience (at least 80 hours of mediation experience making up at .least twenty mediation cases in the previous three years), who have been assessed against the College criteria via a taped practice mediation session, an assessed 3,000 word essay on an approved family mediation topic and an assessment of competence at this level by a professional practice consultant. However, further detail is not provided about the criteria against which the family mediator is to be judged and on this basis, even though it is billed as an advanced qualification akin to a specialist qualification although it does not appear to involved greater specialism but rather a more detailed assessment of competence. Solicitors too have sought to position themselves not only as solicitors but also as family mediators. This could be further evidence of professional realignment or, as Dingwall argues, of professional capture.[307] The

---

[303] *Id.*

[304] Abbot, A. *The System of Professions: An Essay on the Division of Expert Labour* (Chicago: University of Chicago Press, 1988).

[305] Laster, K. *Law as Culture* 2nd Ed. (Sydney: The Federation Press, 2001) at 19-20.

[306] See chapter one for a discussion. Non-family mediators are now organising themselves into a separate umbrella body, the Civil Mediation Council, which is seeking to establish itself as a professional body for mediators in the civil field in a similar way to the UKCFM did approximately ten years previously.

[307] Dingwall, R. 'Professions and Social Order in a Global Society' (1999) Vol. 9 International Review of Sociology 131; See further Dingwall, R. & Fenn, P. ' "A Respectable Profession'?

distinctions drawn between different groupings appear to have been accelerated by the Law Society and not as a result of individual members' decisions.

Weber argues that competitive advantage is one of the keys to a successful profession and that 'Market competition constructs categories of adversaries within classes.... Professions are distinguished by the strategies of social closure they use to enhance their market chance....'[308] In other words, professional bodies have an interest in extolling the virtues of their members in contrast to other occupations or professions that may be permitted to offer their services to a similar client group. There is some evidence as discussed by Dingwall that this strategy may be operating within the divorce services sector.[309] At a time when family mediation was marketing itself as a family focused rather than a generalist service for couples with specific needs, the Law Society introduced a specialist Family Law Panel with two tiers of membership, aimed predominantly at clients undergoing separation and divorce. Equally, it could be argued that the professional bodies for family mediators were marketing the benefits of mediation over legal assistance, for couples going through divorce and relationship breakdown. The rhetoric focused on consensual decision-making in place of adversarial partisanship,[310] from the mediator organisations, and expert legal help and protection of legal and financial interests over non-expert decision-making.[311] The messages were stark and oversimplified, but had the hallmarks of social closure for market advantage, as well as being genuinely held ideological differences between professions.

There are other explanations for professional bodies' creation of accreditation requirements. Durkheim, a structural functionalist, argues that professions operate as a means of constructing an apparent community in an otherwise fragmented capitalist society, which have a set of common values that mean that they do not use their 'privileged knowledge' for harm within society, but instead for altruistic rather than egotistical purposes.[312] Durkheim's view of professions suggests that accreditation standards are a means by which professional bodies may protect the public from harm, and promote the use of knowledge to further the professional

---

Sociological and Economic Perspectives on the Regulation of Professional Services' (1987) Vol. 7 *International Review of Law and Economics* 51.

[308] See Weber, M. *The Theory of Social and Economic Organisation* (New York: The Free Press, 1964). For a discussion see Abel, R.L. *op. cit.* note 301 at 34-39.

[309] Dingwall, R. *op. cit.* note 307.

[310] See for example National Family Mediation, *Looking to the Future: Mediation and the Ground for Divorce – A Response from National Family Mediation* (London: NFM, 2004).

[311] See further Law Society (1994) *Fairness for Families: The Law Society's Response to the Consultation Paper* (London: Law Society, 1994). For a discussion of the debates at that time Day Sclater, S. 'A Critical Approach to the White paper on Divorce Reform' (1995) Vol. 4 *Web Journal of Current Legal Issues*.

[312] See Durkheim E. *Professional Ethics and Civic Morals* Brookfield, C. *(trans.)* (London: Routledge & Keagan Paul, 1957). For a discussion of Durkheim and Weber see Abel, R.L. *op. cit.* note 301 at 34-39. For a critique of Durkheim see Habenstein, R.W. 'Critique of "Profession" as a Sociological Category' (1963) Vol. 4 No. 4 *The Sociological Quarterly* 291.

project and the needs of society. This is an idyllic picture of professionalism and of professional bodies. However, it could be argued that this aim is not inconsistent with a more market based perception of professional body activity. Returning to Abel's theory that professional bodies seek to maintain a dominant position in a given sector, market dominance may only be maintained, if the public are prepared to use a profession's services. Once the public believe that the profession is operating for the benefit of its members to the detriment of society, it is unlikely that market dominance will be maintained.

While it appears that academic opinion provides different explanations as to why the profession seeks to set professional training, accreditation and continuing professional development, none appear to suggest that the professional bodies believe that they do not have influence of their members. The accreditation and CPD requirements set by the professions have been analysed to consider what cues they send to professional members.

5.2 What Cues Do the Professions Send to Their Members through Accreditation & Reaccreditation Requirements?

The professional literature for family solicitors, Law Society family mediators UK College family mediators has been analysed line by line to consider what cues the professional bodies send to their members through their accreditation and reaccreditation requirements.[313] The UKCFM has established *Standards for Mediators* that set out the requirements a family mediator must meet, if he or she wishes to be enrolled on the UKCFM register of family mediators, or wishes to maintain that status. The *Standards for Mediators* document has been compared below with the *Law Society Family Mediation Panel Accreditation Requirements* for family mediators as well as

---

[313] The documents considered were as follows. For the Law Society of England and Wales: *Law Society Family Mediation Panel: Procedures and Conditions for Panel Membership* (version 1); *Law Society Family Mediation Panel: Application for Practitioner Membership–Passport Route Questionnaire* (version 1); *Family Mediation Panel: Application for Practitioner Membership- Development/ Direct Route Questionnaire* (version 1); *Law Society Family Mediation Panel: Application for General Membership* (version 1); *Law Society Family Mediation Panel: Criteria and Guidance Notes* (version 1); *Law Society Family Mediation Panel: Standards of Competence for Accreditation of Family Mediators* (version 1). For the UK College of Family Mediators: *Requirements for the Registration of Mediators* (October 2005); *Requirements for Providers of Professional Practice Consultancy – and Guidelines as to the Requirements of Professional Practice Consultancy* (April 2003); *Competence Assessment for Family Mediators: Portfolio Guidelines, Specification and Template* (November 2005); *Professional Practice Consultancy for Family Mediators: a Guide to Roles and Responsibilities* (June 2005); *Continuing Professional Development – Scheme Requirements*. For Law Society Family Law Panel: *Family Law Panel: The Law Society's Family Law Panel Assessment* (version 1); *Family Law Panel Criteria and Guidance Notes* (version 1); *Family Law Panel: Application for Membership* (version 1); *Family Law Panel Procedures*; (version 1); *Family Law Panel Advanced – Case Study Preparation and Submission Instructions* (version 1); *Family Law Panel Advanced- Case Report Preparation and Submission Instructions* (version 1); *Family Law Panel Advanced: Guidance Notes* (version 1).

Where there were more recent version of these documents prior to 31st December 2006, these were also considered to examine whether there were substantial chances that affected the theoretical and conceptual categories.

the Law Society requirements for entry on to the Roll as a solicitor in England and Wales. An additional level of professional accreditation has also been analysed for solicitors as the Law Society has established the *Family Law Panel Accreditation Requirements* and the *Family Law Advanced Panel Accreditation Requirements* for solicitors who wish to be accredited family law practitioners, with the right to use the Law Society Panel logo on their documentation. The Law Society Family Mediation Panel does not have a tiered level, unless one were to count family mediation consultant status, which is really a teaching status rather than a senior mediation status, and thus has not been considered here. Equally, the level of professional practice consultant for the UKCFM has not been considered as a separate level of expertise as the role is a supervisory and teaching role, rather than a status akin to an Advanced Panel role for family law solicitors. The Advanced Qualification in Mediation level was initially considered as a separate level until it became clear that this level appeared to be a more detailed assessment of the family mediator's competence (with greater levels of experience required) rather than assessment against a new or higher skill set. The qualification has, however, been noted in the tables where appropriate to do so.

The professional bodies set similar structural conditions for membership, which are the hallmarks of most professions. They require members to have met certain entry criteria, by undertaking accredited training. They require them to have had a certain amount of practical experience before conferring qualified status on them. They both require some level of supervision or monitoring of the quality of members' work before attaining full membership status; they also require references or signatures by more senior staff to vouch for the ability of the trainee. Finally, they both require reaccreditation or renewal of membership subject to continuing professional development conditions, as well as payment of a fee. These concepts in themselves do not shed much light on the professional approaches that members are required to adopt, other than that the bodies consider their members to be professionals who are subject to their direction and regulation. It does suggest that the bodies consider themselves to have influence over their members, which would indicate that professional approach may be influenced by the professional body.

5.3 The Data & Findings

The tables below set out the requirements that must be met to be a solicitor carrying out divorce matters (for which there is no specialist family law requirement), a solicitor Family Law Panel member and an Advanced Panel member, as well as a Law Society family mediator Panel member and a UKCFM family mediator member. Each table considers one of the theoretical concepts derived from analysing the professional literature using a grounded theory method of analysis. These may be described and explained as follows:

Professional bodies' membership levels and renewal requirements–meeting the standard and maintaining the standard: **pre-admission assessment after long term training & socialisation with no reaccreditation** (solicitor); **expert professional assessment with periodic reaccreditation with minimum practice requirements** (accredited family solicitor); **professional oversight & endorsement & a minimum number of mediations undertaken with periodic reaccreditation or renewal** (Law Society family mediator and UK College family mediator).

Secondly, the need for a minimum level of knowledge requirements, professional practice and/or experience, which defines the sphere of expertise: **Extensive pre-admittance experience** (solicitor); **extensive & continuing specialist experience** (Family Law Panel member); **some continuing experience** (Law Society family mediator); **minimal continuing experience** (UK College family mediator).

Thirdly, the demonstration of professional standards to senior professional members, to provide a professional recommendation of suitability to practice, which my be described as: **Continual assessment during training, not post-admittance monitoring** (solicitor); **benchmarked experience with detailed academic assessment of knowledge** (Family Law Panel solicitor); **recommendation by other professionals** (Law Society family mediator); **informed recommendation by family mediators** (UK College family mediator).

Fourthly, a set of minimum knowledge requirements, which defines the sphere of professional expertise. This may be reduced to the label: **transactional negotiation based practice within a business context** (solicitor); **in-depth family law knowledge, adherence to reflexive family focused practice with knowledge of mediation** (accredited family solicitor); **continued assessment against the initial training mediation value based criteria** (Law Society family mediator and UK College family mediator).

Finally, continuing professional development, which the professions use to keep control of the knowledge base. This may be described as: **annual updating & refreshing** (solicitor); **annual updating & refreshing in a specialism** (Family Law Panel solicitor); **additional family mediation updating & refreshing** (Law Society family mediator); **reflexive practice with refresher training** (UK College family mediator).

The nature and extent of the conceptual categories are out in tables later in this chapter, in some detail. Many of these concepts are susceptible to further subdivision. The tables contain summaries of the information contained within the professional documentation, providing a brief account (for illustrative purposes) of some of the material that led to the adoption of the concepts. As discussed earlier, it is sometimes difficult to display the evidence in support of the conceptual categories without providing all memos drawn up during the initial data cycles. The compromise was to set out in summary form some of the material that led to the conceptual categories. It is admitted that this is not ideal, but it appeared to be the most reliable compromise in the context of a PhD thesis. Secondly, there is some overlap between the conceptual categories, indicating that the analysis has reached a point of saturation, in-keeping with grounded theory. This is developed further in the final chapter.

Table 5.1: Professional Bodies' Membership Levels & Renewal Requirements – Meeting the Standard & Maintaining the Standard:

Pre-admission assessment after long term training & socialisation with no reaccreditation (solicitor); **expert professional assessment with periodic reaccreditation with minimum practice requirements** (accredited family solicitor); **professional oversight & endorsement and minimum mediations undertaken with periodic reaccreditation or renewal** (Law Society & UK College family mediator).

Law Society Solicitor Requirements

- *Two levels of membership:* Student Member of the Law Society; & Solicitor of the Supreme Court of England & Wales.
- *Duration:*
  - *Student members:* must apply prior to undertaking their LPC. LPC qualification only valid for seven years, student membership renewable annually.
  - *Solicitor:* Must renew practising certificate annually, but no reaccreditation is required if the solicitor continues to practice.

Law Society Family Law Panel/ Advanced Panel Requirements

- *Two levels of membership:* Family Law Panel Member & Advanced Member.
- *Duration:*
  - *Family Law Panel membership:* Must apply for reaccreditation every five years.
  - *Family Law Panel Advanced membership (FLP Adv.):* Must apply for reaccreditation every five years.

Family Mediators Law Society Family Mediation Panel Requirements

- *Two levels of membership:* General Member & Practitioner Member.
- *Duration:*
  - *General membership:* is valid for three years and cannot be renewed. If a general member has not gained practitioner member status at the end of the three years, (s)he will be removed from the Panel. A fee is payable for general membership.
  - *Practitioner membership:* is valid for three years initially, after which members will have to apply for reselection. Successful reselection will be for a further five-year period.

Family Mediators UK College of Family Mediators Requirements

- *Two levels of membership:* Associate Member & Member.
- *Duration:*
  - *Associates:* must apply to renew status on the Register annually, including payment of a fee.
  - *Members:* must apply to renew their status on the Register annually, including payment of a fee.

Pre-admission assessment after long term training and socialisation with no reaccreditation (solicitor); expert professional assessment with periodic reaccreditation with minimum practice requirements (accredited family solicitor); professional oversight and endorsement & minimum mediations undertaken with periodic reaccreditation or renewal (Law Society family mediator and UK College family mediator).

Both professional bodies have initial or training levels of membership as well as full membership levels. The training levels of membership are interim or temporary membership levels and ensure professional regulation as regards those who have the potential to become full members of the profession. The Law Society has a student (which includes trainees) membership level and then a generalist category of 'solicitor' for solicitors regardless of their area of specialism, unless solicitors apply for specialist accreditation through the Family Law Panel at either level. This is interesting as it suggests that the specialist knowledge requirements for a competent family law solicitor do not include substantive knowledge of family law, as family law is not a core element of pre-entry training and is not specified as a requirement for accreditation as a full member of the Law Society. This is fascinating as it could be argued that the knowledge that solicitors have of the legal system coupled with their litigation expertise is considered to be sufficient to be a competent family law solicitor. This runs contrary to Abel's view of professional commodity, unless it is to be argued that the professional commodity relates to the legal system and litigation rather than to consensual decision-making between the parties. If so, this would indicate that the professional cue is that family law practice is a subset of other areas of law, rather than an area of professional practice in itself. It is perhaps with this in mind, that the Law Society relatively recently set up the voluntary but specialist Family Law Panel. All specialist panels are currently under review by the Solicitors Regulatory Authority.

The Law Society stance on reaccreditation for the Family Law Panel for both levels of membership is in contrast to their lack of reaccreditation for the status of solicitor. Solicitors are required to review their practising certificate annually as well as fulfil their CPD requirements (as discussed later) but there is no reassessment of knowledge or skill post-qualification unless a solicitor wishes to become specialist reaccredited. Family Law Panel Members and Advanced Members are required to submit to reaccreditation every five years. This provides the professional body with a mechanism to monitor and refocus the skills and knowledge of their members periodically, in a way that is not open to them for the standard solicitor level of membership. Members of this Panel are distinguished from their generalist counterparts in terms of knowledge and expertise, but are also more susceptible to control by their professional body. The knowledge requirements associated with accreditation and reaccreditation to the Panel are discussed in more detail below.

The Law Society family mediation Panel and the UK College both also include two levels of membership. General (Law Society) or Associate (UK College) membership is the initial level, and in turn Practitioner or Member level is the higher. Both initial forms of membership are time limited. In the case of Law Society family mediators, General membership is valid for only three years and on expiration is non-renewable, whereas Associate status is time limited to one year, but is renewable. Both professional bodies maintain control of their early stage professionals, but in different ways. The Law Society requires early stage mediators to meet full professional standard within a time period, or else be removed from the Register. The UK College also requires full members to meet a defined set of criteria before moving on to full membership; however the College allows members as much time as they need to attain those standards, as long as the Associate member resubmits to accreditation for each year (s)he wishes to remain on the Register. This suggests that competence may be achieved over time, whereas the Law Society standards suggest that, if General members cannot meet the criteria within three years, then they will not be able to meet the standard required of a Law Society family mediator.

In conclusion, the conceptual label applied for this theoretical concept is: solicitors have pre-admission assessment after long term training and socialisation with no reaccreditation; whereas accredited family law solicitors are subject to expert professional assessment along with periodic reaccreditation assuming relatively high minimum practice requirements. Law Society family mediators and UK College family mediators are subject to professional oversight and endorsement, having undertaken at least a (relatively low) minimum number of mediations, along with periodic reaccreditation or renewal requirements.

Table 5.2: The Need for a Minimum Level of Professional Practice and/or Experience:

Extensive pre-admittance experience (solicitor); **extensive & continuing specialist experience** (Family Law Panel member); **some continuing experience** (Law Society family mediator); **minimal continuing experience** (UK College family mediator).

Law Society Solicitor Requirements

- *Student Member Requirements:* Successful completion of GDL & LPC, plus met the honesty and integrity character requirements, but no practice experience required.
- *Solicitor Requirements:* 720 full days of work, usually discussed as two years full-time work, during training contract. No further hours or day practice requirements after completion of training contract.

Law Society Family Law Panel/ Advanced Panel Requirements

- *Panel Member Practice Requirements:* Practised as a solicitor for at least three years (with practising certificate) hold an unconditional practising certificate & meet the requirements for either the assessment or the interview route.
    - *Assessment Route.* At least 350 chargeable hours of E&W family law work in each of previous three years.
    - *Interview Route.* Minimum general litigation experience of 1,000 chargeable hours in E&W law within previous three years & minimum family law post qualification experience of 350 chargeable hours in E&W law within previous five years.
- *Advanced Panel Member Requirements:* Admitted to the roll for at least five years, hold current practising certificate and be a FL Panel Member. Demonstrate that carried out at least 550 chargeable hours family work in E&W jurisdiction in each of three years before date of application.

Law Society Family Mediation Panel Requirements

- *General Membership Requirements:* No requirement to become a general member, but must meet the practitioner membership threshold requirements within the maximum period of three years as a general member.
- *Practitioner Member Requirements:* At least 160 hours of mediation practice during the period of General Membership (may be over a maximum of three years) which includes: foundation training of at least 40 contact hours; at least five mediations together which total at least 25 hours during General membership period; at least eleven hours CPD for each year of General Membership; consultancy of at least eleven hours of which at least five hours must be face-to-face during period of General Membership; remaining hours up to the 160 - further training, practice, CPD and consultancy, drafting summaries or outcomes and writing articles or appropriate reading.

UK College of Family Mediators Requirements

- *Associate Member Requirements:* At least ten hours mediation practice per year within a three year period.
- *Member Requirements:* At least fifteen hours of mediation practice per year.
- *Advanced Qualification:* UK College membership over at least the three previous years. Eighty hours of mediation made up of at least 20 cases.

Extensive pre-admittance experience (solicitor); extensive & continuing specialist experience (Family Law Panel member); some continuing experience (Law Society family mediator); Minimal continuing experience (UK College family mediator).

The similarities and differences between the professions become more apparent at the level of content. Of the four professional groupings examined in the research, three set a minimum number of practice hours for their members, and the fourth sets a minimum number of 720 days of experience in a law firm. Trainee solicitors are required to carry out a two year training contract. Family law practitioners applying to be accredited members of the Family Law Panel have to provide evidence that they have undertaken at least 350 chargeable hours of family law work in the previous three years, or a minimum of 1,000 chargeable hours of general litigation within the previous three years and a minimum of 350 chargeable hours in family law post qualification and within the previous five years to be eligible for the Family Law Panel memberships. Family Law Panel Advanced membership requires at least 550 chargeable hours family work in each of three years before date of application. Practitioner membership of the Law Society Family Mediation Panel requires at least 160 hours of mediation practice during the period of General Membership, although this is made up of a wider category of work than mediation practice with clients, and as regards family mediation experience it may be as little as twenty-five hours over a three year period. Associate Members of the UKCFM must have carried out at least ten hours mediation practice each year within a three year period to maintain their status, followed by fifteen hours of mediation practice each year to retain their status, expect in exceptional circumstances, for example illness, pregnancy, geographical isolation or lack of practice opportunities beyond the control of the mediators including closure of the mediation service. The professional bodies clearly require their members to keep up their professional experience, although without supervision or monitoring, professional experience reinforces the values and approach already adopted rather than adding an extra level of training or reflection or appropriate practice.

These requirements highlight differences in approach and the different messages that are sent to members. The Law Society does not require a continued level of work from its members once a solicitor has become qualified, however, there are relatively high threshold levels of family law work, if a practitioner wishes to apply for Family Law Panel Membership or Advanced membership. These are far higher than family mediation requirements by either of the two mediation accreditation routes. For those solicitors who apply for Panel membership under the interview route of the Family Law Panel, general litigation experience is taken into account as well as family law experience. This sends an interesting message to the profession, as general non-litigation experience is not considered towards Panel membership. This adds an adversarial element to family law practice rather than a non-contentious slant to it. Litigation experience is only important, if a solicitor does not complete the competence assessment, which suggests that knowledge of litigation is an alternative to detailed knowledge of family law tested via assessment. This sends interesting signals about the importance of litigation within the work of a family law solicitor. Neither the assessment route nor the Advanced Panel route required minimum levels of litigation experience but instead relied on family law practice experience. Both couple this with a detailed assessment of family law knowledge, abilities, ethics and approach.

Family mediation experience requirements are similar to those in other aspects of the accreditation process. The Law Society sets standards for General members, which must be met before full Practitioner membership may be awarded to the mediator. The UK College, on the other hand, has a continuing practice requirement of ten hours per year at both Associate and General membership levels, for the duration of membership of the College. The Advanced Qualification requires at least eighty hours of practice made up of at least twenty mediation cases, although this too is relatively low over three years – on average only twenty-seven hours of practice per year rather than the hundreds of hours of family law practice per year that is needed for Advanced level status in the Family Law Panel. The professional bodies adopt different approaches to accreditation, one – the Law Society, has initial standards that must be met before full membership is conferred but thereafter does not require continued evidence of practice experience, as compared with the UK College which requires an ongoing minimum standard of practice. This difference, and theories as to why this may be the case, will be considered below in more detail in respect of the need to demonstrate professional competence.

The conceptual category that has developed from the data as follows: the Law Society requires solicitors to have extensive pre-admittance experience prior to a solicitor being granted fully qualified status, thereafter the solicitor is subject to little professional body modelling. The Law Society Family Law Panel Members (or Advanced members) is required to have extensive and continuing specialist experience in family law cases. The Law Society family mediator is required to have some continuing experience of family mediation in order to retain Practitioner membership as compared with the UK College family mediator, who is required to retain a minimal level of continuing family mediation experience. The next section will consider how the professional bodies require their members to demonstrate their professional standards.

Table 5.3: Demonstration of Professional Standards to Senior Professional Members – Professional Recommendation of Suitability to Practice:

Continual assessment during training, no post-admittance monitoring (solicitor); **benchmarked experience with detailed academic assessment of knowledge** (Family Law Panel solicitor); **recommendation by other professionals** (Law Society family mediator); **informed recommendation by family mediators** (UK College family mediator).

Law Society Solicitor Requirements

- *Student Member:* No requirements specified.
- *Trainee to Fully Qualified:* Suitability to practice assessed by the firm (as regards continued employment post training contract completion). Once a member becomes a Solicitor of the Supreme Court of England and Wales there is no further monitoring, although the solicitor may be reviewed in Legal Services Commission requirements, if (s)he is to receive legal aid funding for legal work.
- *References/ recommendations:* One reference of suitability is required to become a student member of Law Society. None subsequent to the completion of the training contract.

Law Society Family Law Panel/ Advanced Panel Requirements

- *Panel Member:* one of two routes.
  - *Assessment Route.* Must complete a detailed assessment form examining the range and extent of application of family law practice, including 300 word written answers to eighteen questions posed on family law, marked by a Law Society assessor.
  - *Interview Route.* Complete the detailed form (but not written answers to eighteen questions); & successfully completed a mandatory interview with two Family Law Panel assessors.
- *Advanced Panel Member:* Take home exam: completed cases reports, one 3,000 word case report for each of two specialist subjects within the area of family law that is applied for (discussed in the text below); & answered questions posed in set case studies for each of the selected areas in no more than 3,000 words per case study. If an applicant passes (s)he becomes a FLP Adv. member, if borderline invited for an interview.
- *References/ recommendations:* References from two people who are competent to comment on family law practice e.g. another solicitor, a barrister, district judge, magistrate or court clerk, but not someone employed within their firm applicant/ employers.

Law Society Family Mediation Panel Requirements

- *General Member:* No requirements specified.
- *Practitioner Member:* If a Practitioner member has not passed the LSC competence assessment they will not be permitted to undertake publicly funded work.
- *References/ recommendations:* For General Membership & Practitioner Membership: Details of 2 referees from family mediation mentor, supervisor, professional practice consultant, other family mediators, solicitors, barristers, district judge, magistrate or court clerks who have knowledge of and can comment on the applicant's family mediation practice, but are not a member of the applicant's firm.

UK College of Family Mediators Requirements

- *Associate Member:* Demonstration of standards through four hours of peer observation by an approved consultant (individual consultancy) p.a or 10% face to face mediation hours, whichever is greater. At least one hour must be on an individual basis, the rest may be group consultation or pair grouping
- *Member:* The greater of at least two hours peer observation (individual consultancy) or 5% face to face mediation hours. At least one hour must be on an individual basis, the rest may be group/pair consultation. Member is to be recommended for continued membership by a PPCt.
- *Advanced Qualification in Family Mediation.* Assessment via a taped mediation session, 2,000 word commentary on it, assessment by a PPCt & a 3,000 word paper on an approved topic. Assessment is made by a panel.
- *References/ recommendations:* PPCt witness testimony as part of assessment of competence prior to membership being granted.

Continual assessment during training, no post-admittance monitoring (solicitor); benchmarked experience with detailed academic assessment of knowledge (Family Law Panel solicitor); recommendation by other professionals (Law Society family mediator); informed recommendation by family mediators (UK College family mediator).

The professional bodies require their professionals to have demonstrated professional competence by meeting a set of professional standards to senior members of the profession. They also require that the professional has received a positive reference or a form of professional endorsement from another member of the profession or a member of an allied profession. Solicitors are required to demonstrate their professional standards to their tutors at the academic and professional stages of training and to more senior colleagues as part of the training contract phase, but not subsequently unless the solicitor applies for specialist accreditation. The accreditation requirements for membership of the Family Law Panel (at Member of Advanced Member level) are stringent, either through written answers to questions testing family law expertise or an in-depth interview with the Family Law Panel assessors.[314]

Advanced Panel accreditation requirements are even more stringent, focusing on specialist in-depth case reports. Up until full solicitor status, students and trainees are assessed on a range of skills and knowledge based criterion. Specialist accreditation focuses on knowledge of substantive law coupled with practical application of that knowledge to a fact based scenario. Solicitors are therefore considered to have demonstrated sufficient levels of professional competence during their GDL phase of study, their legal practice course training, professional skills course and training contract period, and are not required further to prove themselves, unless they are applying for specialist status. As this specialist status is being sought outside of an educational and training environment, specialist status is dependent on demonstration of professional standards to senior members of the profession.

Family mediators have shorter periods of professional training than do solicitors. Family mediators are consequently required to demonstrate their professional standards in different ways. The Law Society does not set post-qualification standards to be met, in a similar way to their solicitor membership requirements, perhaps due to the fact that Law Society family mediators have also had to qualify as solicitors and demonstrate competence as solicitor. The UK College, without pre-entry undergraduate and postgraduate standards to be met, sets demonstration standards at Associate and Member levels. Associate members must demonstrate their ability through peer observation by an approved consultant. This requirement is not restricted to early stage professionals. Members have a slightly reduced peer observation requirement, but this is a continuing obligation and must give rise to a recommendation for continuing membership, if the member is to be permitted to continue as a member. Family mediators who have applied for the Advanced Qualification in Family Mediation are subject to further assessment against the foundation training skills, knowledge requirements, principles and values. Assessment is via observation of a taped mediation session as well as a 3,000 word

---

[314] The application procedure is contained in Law Society: *Family Law Panel Procedures.*

paper on family mediation. UK College members are required to continually demonstrate their professional competence, whereas Law Society family mediators are not.

All professional bodies require their applicants or members to obtain references at some stage: potential solicitors from their tutors for student membership, Family Law Panel applicants from other solicitors or barristers or from court based professionals in related professions, but not from employers. Law Society family mediators require references at both General and Practitioner membership levels, similar to UK College requirements, although the UK College requires members to obtain a professional practice consultant 'witness testimony', a recommendation, as part of competence assessment, and this is a continuing requirement. The UK College continues to vet its members, whereas the Law Society does not once a solicitor or family mediator has been granted full membership.

It could be suggested that the solicitors profession sets detailed and multiple forms of assessment of competence for applicants to the profession, before accrediting them as full solicitors, but once accredited it is presumed that they are competent professionals. This early stage assessment is coupled with in-depth training, which the professional body oversees, particularly at the LPC stage of training. It could be argued that the Law Society is relatively confident that solicitors who are admitted to the profession have demonstrated adequate professional standards, or alternatively, that as solicitors cannot practice as sole-practitioners until they have three years post-qualification experience, that potential employers will act as a check on professional competence. It may suggest that the profession believes that the extended period of training and assessment, the need to meet entry requirements for the GDL, the LPC, the securing of a training contract with a law firm, and then to succeed in the training contract and secure a long-term position as a solicitor weeds out potentially weak members of the profession as well as the socialisation of the remaining professionals. The Law Society adopts a similar approach to its Law Society family mediators, all of whom will have undergone assessment of competence as solicitors. However, the period of family mediation training is brief, and unlike the UK College, the Law Society does not continue to demand demonstration of professional competence from its Law Society family mediators once they have been granted Practitioner status.

The UK College, without its extended period of training and testing for its professionals adopts a post-qualification assessment of competence and on an ongoing basis. This may reflect the different pattern of employment of family mediators, many are self employed and there is not a well developed family mediation market with a sophisticated repeat player client base as yet. It may also reflect the differing mode of training of family mediators. The professional bodies' approach is further evidenced by the requirement for recommendations and references. The Law Society vets its applicants prior to membership but then, in the absence of complaints to the professional body, leaves the process of vetting solicitors to their employers. It could be argued that this is more apt in a largely employed rather than self-employed profession, whereas, as many family mediators work as self-employed professionals, the professional body, the UK College, may need to undertake this function itself. The Law Society regards its qualified members as having demonstrated adequate professional standards, so as to leave further scrutiny to other professionals but without the need to report to the Law Society. The UK College regards its obligation to scrutinise professional competence as an ongoing one, regardless of the level of professional, having had less input (as regards the time taken for training as well as the depth of that training) into the development of its members.

To conclude, the Law Society requires continual assessment of would-be solicitors during training, but there is virtually no post-admittance monitoring of solicitors once they are qualified. Family Law Panel members (and Advanced Members) are subject to the requirement of extensive pre-accreditation experience in family law coupled with a detailed academic assessment of knowledge by other family law specialists; Law Society family mediators need recommendations from other professionals as evidence of their professional standards, whereas UK College family mediators need recommendations from other more senior family mediators who have assessed the family mediator's competence through a number of different mechanisms prior to membership or advanced status being granted. The next section will address minimum knowledge requirements and the defined sphere of expertise.

Table 5.4: Minimum Knowledge Requirements - A Defined Sphere of Professional Expertise:

Transactional, negotiation based practice within a business context (solicitor); **in-depth family law knowledge, adherence to reflexive family focused practice with knowledge of mediation** (accredited family solicitor); **continued assessment against the initial training mediation value-based criteria** (Law Society & UK College family mediator).

Law Society Solicitor Requirements

- *Student Member:* As required to meet QLD/ GDL and LPC requirements.
- *Trainee Solicitor:* As required to meet PSC & training contract requirements above.
- *Solicitor:* No further requirements once the solicitor has met threshold requirements to become a solicitor.

Law Society Family Law Panel/ Advanced Panel Requirements

- *Panel Member:* **Substantive knowledge & practice**: divorce, judicial separation and nullity; financial provision disputes; private law Children Act proceedings; injunctions; CSA jurisdiction and enforcement; welfare benefits; taxation, role an scope of mediation; adoption; child abduction; public law matters; Children Act proceedings as well as client care; access to information issues; plus the qualifications of the applicant, experience and CPD.

- *Advanced Panel Member:* **Substantive knowledge & practice**: As above plus two specialist areas: children law private; child abduction and wardship; cohabitation; violence in the home; limited means cases; advice in and conduct of ancillary relief proceedings and complex asset cases. **Skills:** legal analysis, communication, drafting including court pleadings and consent orders; advocacy (where appropriate); negotiation; case management and numeracy; ability to analyse and reflect upon their work, including what other appropriate courses of action; demonstrated commitment to personal development.

  o *Client skills & abilities:* (1) ability to understand the client's issues, needs and objectives & to advise appropriately; (2) demonstrate an awareness of issues of race, gender, or other diversity & ability to communicate appropriately with the client when those issues are identified; (3) detailed client skills & an understanding the client's emotional state; Obtaining relevant information for the client, as well as details & understanding of the client's objectives & needs (immediate & long term) & advising accordingly; (4) managing the client's expectations & giving early advice on likely outcomes; (5) undertaking & explaining to the client any risks involved in pursuing a particular course of action; (6) agreeing & implementing with the client a strategy for dealing with the issues & keeping it under review & amending as appropriate; (7) keeping the client properly informed, including regular information about costs through-out the case.

  o *Analytical skills and abilities::* (1) awareness of & ability to apply alternatively methods of resolving disputes (including mediation, early neutral evaluation and negotiations between solicitors); (2) identifying underlying as well as presenting issues; (3) analysing material presented by the client & other parties.

  o *Legal skills and abilities:* (1) a detailed knowledge of & ability to apply legal knowledge and rules of evidence; (2) applying the relevant law to the issues presented & advising the client appropriately; (3) detailed knowledge & ability to apply the ethical principles particularly relevant to the issues arising from family breakdown including codes of conduct, Practice Directions, the Family Law Protocol & Law Society best practice guidance.

- o *Professional skills:* (1) clear understanding & ability to comply with professional & statutory obligations & duties & detailed knowledge and ability to apply all confidentiality obligations (particularly children cases); (2) identifying & meeting key dates.

Law Society Family Mediation Panel Requirements

- *General Member:* As required to meet training requirements to proceed to practitioner member status.
- *Practitioner Member:* None once attained practitioner member status.

UK College of Family Mediators Requirements

- *Associate Member:* As required to meet training requirements to proceed to member status.
- *Member:* The Member is to be recommended for continued membership by an approved consultant. The mediator and the consultant must produce written material that demonstrates: (1) that the member mediator has a body of work of at least 75 hours face-to-face mediation (transitional arrangements in place following implementation of FLA 1996 Part III); (2) evidence of at last eight recorded case outcomes, at last 50% must show evidence of some arrangement, or other outcome approved body has agreed with the College, proof of consultancy as set out above; (3) The knowledge, skills and abilities set out below.
    - o **Skills:** Core mediation skills as taught and assessed in foundation training (see table 4.2).
    - o **Substantive knowledge & practice:** Core mediation principles & values; core mediation knowledge as taught in foundation training (see table 4.2).
    - o **Abilities:** (1) Take responsibility for professional development; (2) positive use of consultancy; (3) ability to mediate a range of cases (4) ability to produce agreements (as part of mediation outcomes requirement above).

- *Advanced Qualification in Family Mediation:* **Knowledge requirements:** No specific requirements but the candidate should conduct an extended piece of research and writing (3,000 words) on an approved family mediation topic, to demonstrate knowledge. **Abilities:** Reflection on what has been learnt in foundation training and employed to date via the commentary on her videoed mediation session. This should include a reflection on (1) her response to the problems posed; (2) the measures taken to engage the parties & address the issues; (3) the reasons for their use; (4) the impact of the measures employed; (5) alternative strategies; (6) the wider implications of this to mediation models and theory.

Transactional negotiation based practice within a business context (solicitor); in-depth family law knowledge, adherence to reflexive family focused practice with knowledge of mediation (accredited family solicitor); continued assessment against the initial training mediation value based criteria (Law Society family mediator and UK College family mediator).

All four professional groupings set knowledge and skills requirements that they assess. However, there are substantial differences between them. As discussed in chapter four, solicitor training focuses on legal knowledge of cases and statutory material, alongside legal skills which are angled towards an adversarial paradigm until a trainee solicitor takes up a training contract, and then become more transactional and less adversarial. Further core legal knowledge and legal skills development is not set by the professional body unless a solicitor wishes to gain accreditation through one of the Law Society subject specialist panels. The Family Law Panel, with its two levels of membership, requires family law solicitors have to demonstrate family law and practice based knowledge as well as adherence to the Family Law Protocol,[315] with a modified set of ethics. This will be discussed further below. Family mediators of either the Law Society Panel or who are members of the UKCFM do not have to learn new or to demonstrate further understanding, skill development and knowledge of family mediation and related areas once they are qualified, unless they apply for a training role in the College as professional practice consultants. However, this is a teaching, training and supervising role rather than a further level of specialism. Instead they are monitored to ensure that they maintain their skills and keep knowledge current. Professional approach is set at the training stage and then developed through experience of practice.

Family Law Panel knowledge and practice requirements are assessed for both routes of entry via completion of a very detailed questionnaire on family law experience, as well as client care, access to information issues, qualifications of the applicant, experience and CPD. Those aspirant members who undertake the assessment route rather than the interview route also have to complete in eighteen brief (300 words) answers for assessment by a Law Society assessor. Family mediation is highlighted as one of the areas within which a Panel member must demonstrate knowledge. The emphasis on client care is an interesting one as Panel members must show evidence that they adhere to the Family Law Protocol, which requires solicitors to adopt a conciliatory rather than an adversarial approach to family law practice. Although the solicitor remains a partisan for the client, he or she must consider the wider implications of any decision-making, as well as the long term effects any decisions may have. This reflective and longer range approach to advising the client fits in with some of the findings set out in the literature in chapter three in which solicitors have been observed taking a more conciliatory approach to the divorce than has been reflected in the media and public discussions.

Family Law Panel Advanced knowledge of family law and practice and ethical standards are assessed via a take-home exam. The Family Law Panel Advanced Chief Examiners Report for the first round of assessment in 2001 noted that there had been 351 applications for Advanced membership. Sixty-one per cent of those who took the exam passed, although the specialist papers had varying pass rates from fifty-seven

---

[315] This is discussed in more detail in chapter six in connection with professional ethics.

per cent to eighty-eight per cent. An Advanced member must claim expertise in two family law areas, as set out in the table. They must also be able to demonstrate detailed knowledge and ability to apply the ethical principles particularly relevant to the issues arising from family breakdown including codes of conduct, Practice Directions, the Family Law Protocol and Law Society best practice guidance for their specialist areas. They should have an awareness of and ability to apply alternatively methods of resolving disputes including in particular mediation, early neutral evaluation and negotiations between solicitors. They must also demonstrate their ability to understand the client's issues, needs and objectives and to advise appropriately; and demonstrate an awareness of issues of race, gender, or other diversity and an ability to communicate appropriately with the client when those issues are identified. The list of how this may be evidenced is very long indeed as set out in the table. Areas of particular interest in relation to theory development are:[316]

- Understanding the client's emotional state;

- Identifying underlying as well as presenting issues;

- Obtaining details of the client's objectives and advising accordingly;

- Understanding the client's needs, both immediate and longer-term and advising accordingly;

- Managing the client's expectations and giving early advice on likely outcomes;

- Agreeing and implementing with the client a strategy for dealing with the issues;

- In consultation with the client; keeping the strategy under review and amending as appropriate.

These abilities are very similar in nature to those set out in family mediation training in chapter four, except for the focus on the client rather than the focus on both parties. In addition, the solicitor is providing advice rather than information about the range of options open to the client. The first ability, the ability to understand the client's emotional state, is not set as an ability in earlier training to become a solicitor and appears to be very much family law orientated. Managing the client's expectations may be of relevance in other areas of law, but was highlighted in the literature in chapter three as one of the key abilities of a divorce solicitor as female clients tended to try to settle lower than a court would order and male clients tend to try to settle higher. These attributes do not rule out an adversarial approach to practice but tend to militate against it. They are focused squarely on the emotional as well as financial needs of the client and require a solicitor to assist the client in generating options and considering their implications in the short and long term, rather than fighting hard to achieve the best financial result for the client, as an adversarial approach would tend to suggest.

---

[316] Element 2 (i) of Law Society of England and Wales, *Family Law Panel Advanced Knowledge and Skills Criteria* version 1 at 6.

The abilities also focus on the importance of working with the client in order to assist the client in providing instructions, whereas earlier training has implied the need to obtain full instructions without setting out how this is to be done. Emphasis has not been placed on litigation practices in this set of abilities, even though litigation may be one of the options open to a client. Indeed, knowledge of non-court based forms of dispute settlement is required instead, and thus highlighted as desirable, in the form of alternative methods of resolving disputes including in particular mediation, early neutral evaluation and negotiations between solicitors. Solicitors must also demonstrate their ability to understand the client's issues, needs and objectives and to advise appropriately; and demonstrate an awareness of issues of race, gender, or other diversity and an ability to communicate appropriately with the client when those issues are identified. These are similar requirements to those in family mediation training except that solicitors are required to have negotiation skills rather than an understanding of how negotiation works so as to facilitate others' negotiations. Once again, while these do not expressly provide for a consensus based approach to family law practice they certainly do not imply adversarialism.

Legal skills development is also taken further at this level. An applicant to the Family Law Panel Advanced Members must demonstrate skills appropriate to those undertaking family cases including: legal analysis, communication, drafting (including pleadings and consent order – contentious and non-contentious drafting); advocacy (where appropriate); negotiation; case management and numeracy; as well as an ability to analyse and reflect upon their work, including what other courses of action may have been appropriate. These are tested through the case reports that candidates submit, one for each area, as well as the exam section of the paper which covers their two areas of specialism. Within the case reports candidates must demonstrate skill and competence in legal and practice issues including case management and client care to a high standard, critical reflection on the outcome of their cases and how matters could have been dealt with different with the benefit of hindsight. Candidates are also marked on the basis of ethics, strategies, protocols and guides to best practice as well as costs benefits and the risks involved in the transaction. Reflection should assist a solicitor in personal development but also require the solicitor to consider other ways of approaching cases in the light of experience and against a set of criteria that are considered desirable to the profession. This is a distinctive non-adversarial approach to family law work, although the option of litigation is still present in the skills set, alongside settlement based skills.

Practitioner members of the Law Society Panel and UKCFM members continue to be assessed against the criteria to which they would have been introduced during introductory/ foundation training and General (Law Society) and Associate (UKCFM) member status. However, they rely far more heavily on family mediation consultancy or professional practice consultancy rather than assessment in the form of written case reports or answers to given scenarios. The UKCFM's professional practice consultancy (PPC) has the stated aims of providing support and professional guidance to qualified family mediators and to supervise and teach family mediators who are working towards qualification; to oversee the maintenance of standards to ensure that family mediators undertake the required amount of PPC, CPD and professional practice in order to be eligible for continued membership of the College. The third stated aim is for consultants to assess the quality of family mediation being practised by members of the College and to assess the quality of mediation being undertaken by mediators who are working towards full qualification. It also aims to provide on-going monitoring of the work being practised by mediators to ensure that it does not fall below an acceptable standard.[317] The Law Society has a similar requirement entitled family mediation consultancy. Both are really supervision and detailed peer observation requirements to monitor the quality of the work being carried out by professionals and also a time for mediators to be forced to reflect on their practice.

For UK College family mediators, reassessment runs alongside consultancy and peer observation. Members must periodically be reassessed by a professional practice consultant to consider whether the consultant may recommend the family mediator for continued membership. Assessments is made against the College's core mediation principles & values; core mediation knowledge; core skills; capacity to deal with a range of cases; the extent to which the professional has demonstrated a responsibility for professional development; positive use of consultancy; a body of work of at least seventy-five hours (transitional arrangements were in place following implementation of FLA 1996 Part III), evidence of at least eight recorded case outcomes, at least fifty per cent must show evidence of some arrangement or other outcome that an approved body has agreed with the College; and the family mediator must be able to provide proof that (s)he has undertaken the required number of consultancy (supervised) hours. This is an extensive form of monitoring conducted by senior members of the profession, which instils the core values into family mediators on a regular basis and keeps professionals in line with a defined professional approach. By contrast, full members of the Law Society Mediation Panel – Practitioner members, do not have any continued assessment of their competence. This is consistent with the Law Society's approach to fully qualified solicitors.

The UK College has introduced its own form of specialist status – the Advanced Family Mediation Qualification, which assesses family mediators on their ability to employ the principles, values, skills and knowledge that they have been taught previously in foundation training as well as their ability to critique and reflect upon their own performance. There is a more detailed assessment of knowledge via a 3,000 word essay on an approved family mediation topic, although the criteria against which this is judged are not evident from the documentation. The Advanced Qualification provides a mechanism through which more experienced family mediators may be delineated from the less experience, but does not set a distinctive knowledge or skills set for more experienced mediators. As such it does not follow the specialist assessment methods employed by the Law Society, although this is not unsurprising for a profession that is early in its development, with a relatively small market.

On the face of it, the Law Society's assessment of professional competence for admission to the Family Law Panel (at Member and Advanced Member levels) appears to be out of step with its approach to assessing the competence of non-specialist solicitors, as the former is largely tested in academic and training establishments and the latter is largely tested in service and without a period of prior academic training. However, this reflects the fact that Panel membership is a

---

[317] UK College of Family Mediators, *Professional Practice Consultancy for Family Mediators: A Guide to Roles and Responsibilities*, Version January 2003.

specialist status resulting from a prolonged period of professional practice in the area. The detailed assessment of skills, abilities and knowledge of solicitors who wish to attain Family Law Panel specialist or advanced specialist status is actually in-keeping with the Law Society's approach to assessment of professional competence at the undergraduate and postgraduate stages of training. The assessment criteria are delimited as they are in academic and training institutions and the assessment mode used to test competence is also very similar to academic modes of assessment. The Law Society has set extremely detailed requirements, which are specified as outcomes that must be demonstrated by the applicant. The UK College also has a set of criteria against which it continues to assess its professionals, including those that have awarded full membership status. The criteria also cover skills, abilities and knowledge, although are more skills focused than knowledge focus, perhaps a reflection of family mediation more as a process than as a series of more or less appropriate outcomes for the client. As UK College members have not undergone the minimum of two year full-time study with assessment of competence coupled with two years full-time supervised practice, they continue to be assessed by senior members of the profession which are required to report back to the professional body on the competence of that member. The Law Society does not extensively test family mediators pre or post-qualification, which suggest that qualification as a solicitors is the primary means of competence assessment. The professional body retains a watching brief over professional competence, whereas the Law Society appears to leave this to its professional members.

In sum, the label for this conceptual category is: Transactional negotiation based practice within a business context (solicitor); or in-depth family law knowledge, adherence to reflexive family focused practice with knowledge of mediation (accredited family solicitor); or continued assessment against the initial training mediation value based criteria (Law Society family mediator and UK College family mediator). The next section will consider continuing professional development and the messages that this sends to professionals.

Table 5.5: Continuing Professional Development – Continued Professional Control of Knowledge Base:

Annual updating & refreshing (solicitor); **annual updating and refreshing in specialism** (Family Law Panel solicitor); **additional family mediation updating & refreshing** (Law Society family mediator); **reflexive practice with refresher training** (UK College family mediator).

Law Society Solicitor Requirements

CPD Hours
- Solicitor (first three years of admission): Any CPD courses Law Society direct & at least one hour of CPD for each whole month in legal practice/ employment between admission and the next 1st November.
- Solicitors (from year four of admission): sixteen hours of CPD during each complete year in legal practice.

Other Requirements
- Solicitors must keep a written record of CPD attendance for six years and produce this record to the Law Society).
- The Law Society provides a detailed pack to assist solicitors to identify their training and developmental needs in order to set up a training development plan to get the most out of their training.
- At least 25% of CPD hours must be met by participation in accredited courses. Up to 75% may be met by attendance at unaccredited courses, and other non-attendance activities.

CPD Includes
- Undertaking scholarship: writing law books & articles; research into legal topics of relevance to practice; writing a dissertation; research into legal topics of relevance to practice.
- Undertaking further education/ training- certain NVQs in business & management; distance learning modules (if interactive); watching videos/ listening to cassettes by authorised providers; study towards certain professional qualifications. Undertaking training – preparation and delivery of certain training courses; undertaking coaching & mentoring sessions of less than one hour.
- CPD cannot merely be to advance a particular fee earning matter.

Law Society Family Law/Advanced Panel Requirements

CPD Hours
- *Panel.* Minimum of six hours solicitor CPD p.a. must be family law.
- *Advanced Panel.* Minimum of six hours solicitor CPD p.a. must be in family law.

Other Requirements
- As for solicitors.

CPD Includes
- As for solicitors

Law Society Family Mediation Panel Requirements

CPD Hours

- *General Member::* Undertake to gain eleven hours CPD.
- *Practitioner Member.* eleven hours CPD per year.

Other Requirements
- None mentioned, although it is presumed that the context is similar to solicitor CPD.

CPD Includes
- No reference, although it is presumed that the context is similar to solicitor CPD.

UK College of Family Mediators Requirements

CPD Hours
- *Associate Member:* ten hours CPD approved by the College.
- *Member:* Minimum ten hours CPD approved by the College.

Other Requirements
- CPD must be relevant to the needs and professional standards of the College.
- It should show evidence of a range or learning, including active participation in mediation practice.
- Training must be authorised, which includes that course content and training materials must be reviewed by two members of the training sub-committee. Training must be evaluated.
- Professional Practice Consultancy (PPC) must include a range of activities. Satisfactory completion of peer observation of at least 10% of a mediator's face to face mediation hours, by a College approved consultant (If the family mediator is already a member of the College this is reduced to 5% of face to face mediation hours).Consultancy must be done even if the mediator is not practising.

CPD Includes
- Participation in training courses, seminars, conferences, workshops & lectures. Other programmes & methods of approved individual study.
- Providing family mediation training to others.
- It is intended to raise professional standards.

PPC Includes
- Professional accountability & quality assurance issues
- Professional development including training & CPD.

Annual updating & refreshing (solicitor); annual updating & refreshing in specialism (Family Law Panel solicitor); additional family mediation updating & refreshing (Law Society family mediator); reflexive practice with refresher training (UK College family mediator).

The professional bodies both require their professionals to undertake annual continuing professional development (CPD). The Law Society has differential CPD requirements for newly qualified solicitors and for more experienced solicitors, the standard requirements being sixteen hours of CPD per year. A quarter of that time must have been spent attending Law Society accredited courses, and the remainder may be spent on that or on other CPD recognised activities. These encompass a wide range of options including: attendance at unaccredited courses, writing law books and articles, undertaking certain NVQs in business and management, and preparation and delivery of certain training courses, undertaking coaching and mentoring sessions of less than one hour, undertaking distance learning modules (if interactive), research into legal topics of relevance to practice, writing a dissertation, watching video/listening to audio cassettes by authorised providers, participating in development of specialist areas of law and practice, study towards certain professional qualifications. None of the activities can be merely to advance a particular fee-earning matter. Solicitors on the Family Law Panel (Members and Advanced Members) must undertake at least six hours of their CPD in respect of family law matters. The majority of CPD is not controlled by the Law Society, solicitors are only required to undertake twenty-five per cent of CPD by attending Law Society accredited courses, and consequently CPD cannot be used as a way of instilling particular values into the profession, except perhaps the importance of professional and personal development as a professional.

The need regularly to practice the skills acquired during the initial training programme has been recognized by some family mediators within the UK, who have also highlighted the importance of supervision and continuing professional development.[318] Supervision is also seen as the key to ensuring that family mediators practice their skills and learn to develop in competence. National Family Mediation (NFM) suggests that it is: 'wasteful and incomplete to train mediators who have no work and/or no supervision...'[319] NFM believes that it is important for them to keep a tight reign on entry into the profession, in order to ensure that sufficient mediation practice is available to trainees, coupled with effective supervision by a more experienced family mediator. Family mediation training is thus now being viewed as a first step in a longer term learning process, rather than a licence to mediate. This is in line with moves towards comprehensive continuing professional development in other professions in England and Wales – medicine, law, veterinary practice, *etc.*

Family mediators have a lesser level of CPD hours by comparison with solicitors. Practitioner members of the Law Society Family Mediation Panel must undertake at least eleven hours of CPD per annum, although they will also be required to undertake solicitor CPD as well. Members of the UKCFM were required to undertake seven hours per annum although this increased to ten hours as of the

---

[318] Martin, P. 'The Hitch-Hiker's Guide to Mediation' (1995) *Family Law* 589.

[319] Fisher, T. 'Training For Family Mediation' (1995) *Family Law* 571.

beginning of 2005. They do, however, also have to undertake professional practice consultancy in addition to their CPD requirements. The range of activities that are treated as CPD for these purposes are also wide, including anything that falls within the definition of raising professional standards including training course, seminars, conferences, workshops, lectures and other programmes or methods or approved individual study or providing mediation training to others. However, it must be relevant to the needs and professional standards of the College and training must be authorised by the College who consider the content of the course and the training material by at least two members of the training subcommittee and training must also be evaluated. This permits the College to keep a watching brief over CPD and also gives it the opportunity to control the content of courses to a certain extent. Many of the currently advertised CPD courses appear to be mediation refresher skills training or legal and financial training rather than courses on the theoretical underpinnings of family mediation, which are covered in detail in foundation training, or new skills development.[320] Family mediation CPD training appears to focus on substantive material to aid family mediators in providing information to clients.

Interestingly, only the UKCFM mentions return to professional practice after a period of absence in its training and accreditation literature. This may be because family mediators may well be self employed and could begin mediating as soon as they returned from a long break, whereas most solicitors would be employed and would have to satisfy other solicitors within the firm that they were ready to take on an individual case load before being given that level of responsibility. Mistakes can be costly in a legal context and, although solicitors are insured, a firm may also find that it has to write off the cost of work done, if a complaint is upheld through its complaints procedure or through the Law Society's regulatory function (now performed by the Solicitors Regulatory Authority).

The UKCFM requires some staff retraining, usually a five hour re-entry course plus consultant approval to practice before the family mediator may resume work. In addition, there is a more onerous CPD requirement for the year of return to practice, tiered according to the length of time for which the family mediator has been absent from practice. After more than four years' break the family mediators has to retrain by following the foundation training programme at associate level and reapply to the College. This may suggest that the UKCFM is keen to make sure that family mediators keep up their professional practice and maintain their standards and keep in touch with up-to-date professional approach, or it may signal a concern that as yet there is insufficient mediation work to maintain the level of family mediators currently trained and eligible to practice and the only way to control numbers and to keep the profession current is to set a requirement to retrain after four years absence from practice.

The Family Law Panel goes a step further than that in its requirement that family law solicitors maintain their standards, skills and keep up-to-date with current

---

[320] UKCFM CPD approved training includes courses on updating mediation skills and new developments in family mediation, particular issues in relation to family mediation and also a number of courses on legal and financial issues such as the Child Support Act and Tax traps and complex finances. See the UK College of Family Mediators *Approved Training for CPD Points*.

professional approach. Family Law Panel membership and Advanced membership is time bound – members and advanced members must apply for reaccreditation every five years and the literature suggests that reaccreditation includes reassessment. Assessment for both levels of membership is stringent and complex and thus the requirement that professionals seek reaccreditation every five years maintains the elite nature of the group and provides the public with confidence in the ability of these professional members and allows the professional body to dictate the terms upon which Panel members continue to practice with their endorsement. Professional approach is tightly controlled by adopting this approach. Practitioner membership of the Law Society Family Mediation Panel will be for three years initially after which members will have to apply for reselection, and then for a further five years. Once again, this requires members to remain current, although the accreditation procedure does not appear to be as stringent for this group as it does not require reassessment.

The documentation reveals that the messages that the professions send in respect of CPD are that CPD is required for updating and refresher purposes for solicitors and that solicitors may choose the areas they wish to address, for family law accredited solicitors, they must updated and refresh themselves on areas of family law practice. For Law Society family mediators CPD is viewed in a very similar way as for solicitors, however, family mediators do need to focus on some family mediation within their solicitor CPD. For UK College family mediators CP is more associated with reflexive practice, along with refresher training, rather than with updating. This may reflect that balance of knowledge and skills between the two professional groupings.

5.4 Conclusions

The rules that have been laid down by the professional bodies for entry on to the professional Roll or Register provide some clues about the nature of professional practice in respect of professional approach. They provide an insight into the issues that the professional bodies wish to place firmly on the agenda for their professionals, for clients and potential clients and for the wider public and regulatory frameworks. All bodies stipulate that those wishing to become professionals must have completed a period of approved training, thus requiring all who wish to attain membership through this status to have undertaken a prescribed curriculum. All potential members must have had their competence assessed and have been graded as at least competent at each of the components described in more detail in chapter four. All must have completed a minimum period of vocational experience and have been supervised or observed during that period. It is important for both professional bodies to control membership to their organisations and to exercise continued control. It is also important to them that their professionals are seen as current in their professional expertise and that they have been assessed by another professional or they have been overseen by another professional who has vouched for their abilities.

Solicitors are required to continue in their practice as they were taught in their classroom based courses and socialised by their supervisors in their training contract. There is a requirement that they refresh their knowledge and skills through CPD, but it is up to the solicitor to select the courses they wish to attend from a wide array of those on offer in the legal sector. Family mediators who are members of the Law Society Panel will undertake their CPD to be a solicitor but also undertake family mediation CPD as well. They also have to reapply for selection to the Panel periodically. This challenges them to reflect on their professional practice and it is likely that their approach to being both a solicitor and a family mediator will be influenced, at least to some extent, but their membership of two different professions. Accreditation does not require them to learn new skills or to demonstrate vast tracts of substantive knowledge, unlike the status of Family Law Panel membership and Advanced membership. Family Law Panel members are required to have the characteristics of solicitors but also to adopt a conciliatory approach to family law matters, including alternative modes of resolving disputes if appropriate, which brings their professional approach closer to the approach that has been identified as consensus based rather than adversarial. Family Law Panel members *do* maintain their partisan stance, but attempt to use that role, along with the solicitor for the other member of the couple, to broker a settlement that they and their clients consider to be appropriate.

The accreditation requirements set by the Law Society and the UK College reflect their view of their role. The Law Society appears to regard its role as a gate-keeper, a body to ensure that those who wish to receive the status of full membership of the Society, regardless of whether this is solicitor or Law Society family mediator status, meet a minimum standard of competence to be assessed in detail against specific outcome based criteria. Once a professional is admitted to full membership, scrutiny of competence is left to the profession itself – the Law Society does not require further evidence of competence. The exception to this is specialist accreditation to the Family Law Panel and Family Law for members and advanced members. Those solicitors who wish to attain specialist status must resubmit to assessment every five years. As much of the assessment is knowledge based, and the law changes at a rapid rate, it could be argued that resubmission to assessment is a necessary condition of continued specialist status, and the continued endorsement of the Law Society, although it is not within usual Law Society practice for non-specialist solicitors.

The UK College appears to regard its role as a continuing one, more as the supervisor of its members than a gate-keeper. This may reflect the fact that the UK College is of relatively recent inception and it oversees a relatively new profession without a large, established and competitive market. Accreditation requirements for family mediators are set at a relatively low level in some respects – professional experience is measured in hours rather than in days, but again this may reflect the lack of a developed market, rather than an unwillingness to set stringent standards. Instead, the UK College compensates for this low experience requirement with an ongoing surveillance of members. It will be interesting to examine whether, in time, the UK College adopts a role more akin to that of gate-keeper than supervisor, as the market develops and the profession matures.

The next chapter will examine the codes of conduct that regulate the professions to consider what these indicate about professional approach to divorce matters, which is the final piece in the professional jigsaw through which the profession regulates and controls its members.

Chapter 6: Adversarialism & Consensus? Good Practice & Ethical Conduct for Divorce Solicitors & Family Mediators

This chapter examines what the codes of practice for divorce solicitors and family mediators indicate about the professions' approach to divorce dispute settlement. It begins with a brief examination of previous research findings; the focus will then turn to consideration of the codes of practice for solicitors and for family mediators. The Law Society of England and Wales has a mandatory code of conduct for all solicitors who practice law, the *Guide to the Professional Conduct of Solicitors*.[321] In addition, the *Family Law Protocol*[322] provides a guide to good practice for family law solicitors, against which family law solicitors' conduct may be examined in the event of disciplinary action being taken. Adherence to the Protocol is a requirement for Members and Advanced Member of the Family Law Panel. This research considered the first version of the Protocol, although the second version has been considered (coming into force as I did in early 2006) to examine whether the later version has an impact on professional approach. In addition it also has the voluntary code of conduct for solicitors carrying out family mediation the Law Society's *Code of Practice for Family Mediators*. The UK College of Family Mediators has a mandatory code of practice, the *Code of Practice for Family Mediators*[323] for its members. The research has focused on these codes.

6.1 Are Codes of Conduct Really an Indication of Professional Approach?

Is it possible to isolate ethics for professions, what role do codes of ethics play in the profession and how are these expressed to members? What cues do the codes give to

---

[321] The new *Solicitors Code of Conduct* came into force on 1st July 2007 and is not reflected in this study.

[322] The Protocol was first published by the Law Society's Family Law Committee, the Solicitors Family Law Association (now Resolution) the Lord Chancellors' Department (now Ministry of Justice) and the Legal Services Commission in March 2002. The second version, which has been amended to reflect legislative changes such as the Civil Partnerships Act 2005, was published in January 2006. Part 1 – The Main Protocol; Part 2 – Proceedings for Dissolution of Marriage: Divorce, Judicial Separation or Nullity; Part 3 – Children: Private Law; Part 4 – Protocols for Ancillary Relief; Part 6 – Domestic Abuse; and Part 7 – Alternative Dispute Resolution were considered. The changes did not appear to make any amendments to the developing conceptual categories and thus the detail from version 1 has been retained in the tables.

[323] UK College of Family Mediators Code for Family Mediators April 2000 – still in force. These have been read in conjunction with the College's policy as follows: *Children, Young People and Family Mediation–Policy and Practice Guidelines* September 2002 – still in force; *Policy on Conflicts of Interest and Similar Conflicts and Good Practice Guidelines* 2000 – still in force; *Domestic Abuse Screening Policy* – still in force; *Notes for Guidance in Respect of Court Proceedings* February 2004 – still in force; *Form E* (financial settlement terms) – still in force.

solicitors and to family mediators and do they influence professional behaviour and if so how? In *Codes of Ethics and the Professions* edited by Coady and Bloch,[324] codes are examined in detail, across a number of professions including the legal profession, to consider their essential characteristics and purpose. Solicitors certainly do take notice of their code, whether or not this is a result of a fear of being disciplined for breaching it, or a respect for professional ethics. In the first 'Ethics in Practice' in *Legal Ethics* the editors offered an overview of ethical issues raised by legal practitioners and others. They noted that solicitors were concerned with ethical issues, it was a misnomer to call solicitors unethical, as in 1997 the Law Society received a total of 56,417 telephone calls for guidance on ethics and a further 4,996 requests for guidance in writing. The majority of calls related to practical issues, many concerning the interpretation of the rules of professional conduct. This indicates that the rules of professional conduct, the code of ethics, is known and is taken seriously by practitioners even if the code does suffer from the problems associated with such codes, their practical rather than aspirational guidelines.

Typical ethical issues raised in a small scale survey of legal practitioners were: issues around billing and fees, taking on too much work in order to maintain profits and conflicts of interest between firm and client were.[325] Some may view these as ethical issues whereas others may view them as simply the meat and drink of business life rather than legalcentric ethical concerns, however, it is of interest that so many calls are received on the ethics hotline from practitioners who are eager to check that they are doing the right thing. Legal practitioners in the study felt that while the profile of legal ethics had been raised in the public's mind, this was due to the increased awareness of the public to media coverage, which tended to denigrate the legal profession, rather than due to a decline in ethical standards amongst lawyers world wide.[326] On the other hand they did acknowledge that lawyers had not helped themselves in recent times, particularly in cases such as the O.J. Simpson case and that in some instances lawyers' standards had been lowered as a result of financial pressure upon them to increase their workload for competitive advantage.[327] Thus, there is evidence that codes of conduct indeed reveal insight into professional characteristics and professional approach to their work, but do they reveal the ethics of a given profession and could codes be used to provide an insight into solicitors and family mediators' approaches to cases of divorce?

Some suggest that professional ethical rules are ways to instil ethical behaviour into lawyers. Previous studies have concluded that codes of conduct are little more than attempts to promote professional cohesion and a method of enhancing a profession's standing with the public by appearing to behave honourably according to a defined

---

[324] Coady, M. & Bloch, S. (eds.) *Codes of Ethics and the Professions* (Melbourne: Melbourne University Press, 1996).

[325] Economides, K., Nicholson, D. & Webb, J. 'Ethics in Practice: Welcome!' (1998) Vol. 1 No. 1 *Legal Ethics*. 19.

[326] *Ibid.* at 20.

[327] *Id.*

standard.[328] Abel has suggested that the rules are merely there out of professional self interest.[329] As Laster and Taylor comment,

> Professions frequently seek to create their autonomy and legitimacy by defining and promulgating their own professional standards... Like training, licensing, accreditation and referral networks, ethics are devices for promoting consistency in conduct and good business practice among members...[330]

Hutchinson has suggested instead that codes of conduct further distance professional practice from the public, according professions a monopoly over the practice of certain areas in return for a 'quality' service. Some argue that codes of conduct simply placate the public and provide a method of distinguishing professions from other commercial pursuits. Codes have been used to keep market dominance in their areas of technical expertise, rather than to promote competent, ethical practice [331]

Hutchinson states that the legal profession is the embodiment of George Bernard Shaw's view that 'every profession is a conspiracy against the laity.'[332] Is the legal profession simply a group of legally trained individuals who hold a monopolistic position and who obfuscate divorce, in this instance, to maintain their grip on the process and therefore on the market? Do family mediators, as an emerging professional grouping wish to adopt a market position, offering a different service by pointing out the negatives of the traditional order, while replicating the monopolistic ideal? Do either or both professions have an ethical stance that recognises the role they can play in assisting couples at a difficult time, while shoring up their practice with ethical considerations and exhortations to good practice? Shaw's view was probably more appropriate to a time when professions tended to replicate themselves, to draw upon a limited cultural and educational base, with a limited set of ideals and a similar background. The present legal profession is increasingly diverse, as is professional practice.[333] It may be more difficult to construct an appropriate ethical code that can be accepted and applied by solicitors or by family mediators with such differing backgrounds. Hutchinson suggests that, 'a fragmented society deserves a fragmented legal profession which, in turn, warrants a more fragmented idea and implementation of legal ethics.'[334] However, codes generally operate within practice in the round, to promote professional cohesion, rather than to serve the needs of particular groups within a profession.

---

[328] See for example Abbot, A. *op. cit.* note 304 at 83 for a discussion.

[329] Abel, R.L. 'Why Does the ABA promulgate Ethical Rules?' (1981) Vol. 59 *Texas Law Review* 639. See too Laster, K. and Taylor, V.L. *op. cit.* note 300 at 204.

[330] See Laster, K. and Taylor, V.L. *op. cit.* note 300 at 204; Abbot, A. *op. cit.* note 304 at 83.

[331] Abel, R.L. *op. cit.* note 329.

[332] Hutchinson, A.C. 'Legal Ethics for a Fragmented Society: Between Professional and Personal' (1998) Vol. 5, Nos. 2/3 *International Journal of the Legal Profession* at 175.

[333] For details see *Trends in the Solicitors' Profession Annual Statistical Report 2006* (London: Law Society of England and Wales, 2007) at 33-34, 54-55.

[334] *Id.*

What does the code of conduct reveal about the role and approach of solicitors? Hutchinson argues that traditional ethics are premised on lawyers as 'super-technocrats', as morally neutral on the stance that the law takes, considering that they job is to apply the law rather than to reform it or use it in furtherance of their ethical principles.[335] He argues that the traditional understanding is based on a number of underlying principles: law is objective and certain and the role of the lawyer is to elicit and then apply the law; all clients are to be treated the same in order for the Rule of Law to be upheld; no client has a morally superior claim on the law than another; the criminal trial is the paradigm of legal responsibility, an adversarial contest between lawyers, and this is the benchmark against which all law is measured even in the civil context; finally lawyering is apolitical, lawyers are neutral as to the law and its application.[336] It is further argued that this 'formalistic theory' has been discredited in the main, however, rule based morality still pervades the codes of conduct that regulates the profession. However, the fragmented profession makes formalism difficult, but a move towards heterogeneity would require a rethinking of the professional norm and role, a certain reflexivity on what it is to be a lawyer. And as we have seen in the chapter on training, this is not something we train our lawyers to do very readily.[337] If the traditional understanding is taken, then the role of solicitor is defined by the adversarial context, and the code furthers this role.

Codes of conduct have a number of aims, some stated some not. The Chartered Institute of Arbitrators Code of Professional and Ethical Conduct spells out the aims of the code:

> The purpose of adopting a Code of Ethics for arbitrators and others involved in alterative dispute resolution is not only to serve as a guide to arbitrators and those conducting the resolution process but also to serve as a point of reference for users of the process and to promote public confidence in arbitration and other dispute resolution techniques. The Code itself is not a rigid set of rules but is a reflection of internationally acceptable guidelines.[338]

Hutchinson suggests that the reasons for having codes of conduct are to educate solicitors about what is expected of them by the professional body and other solicitors; to affect professional behaviour and to be used for disciplinary purposes.'[339]

---

[335] *Ibid.* at 176.

[336] *Ibid.* at 177.

[337] For a discussion of concerns that law students are taught to use ethical rules as they do legal rules. See Menkel-Meadow, C. *op. cit.* note 256. For a discussion of how to increase reflexivity and develop ethical professional practices see Moliterno, J.E. 'On the Future of Integration between Skills and Ethics Teaching: Clinical Legal Education in the Year 2010' Vol. 46 No. 1 *Journal of Legal Education* 67 at. 68; See further Powles, G. 'Taking the Plunge: Integrating Legal Ethics in Australia' (1999) Vol. 33 No. 3 *Law Teacher* 315 and Webb, J. 'Developing Ethical Lawyers: Can Legal Education Enhance Access to Justice?' (1999) Vol. 3 *Law Teacher* 284.

[338] *The Chartered Institute of Arbitrators' Code of Professional and Ethical Conduct Final Draft April 2001* (2001) Vol. 17 No. 3.*Arbitration* 273.

[339] Hutchinson, A.C. *op. cit.* note 332 at 182.

Critics, in particular those of Abel and Rhode,[340] consider that codes of conduct make it appear that the profession is tackling ethical issues and give the impression of ethical respectability, retaining professional status and a market place monopoly. Hutchison argues that professional bodies adopt their rules to deal with past problems, in others words they are reactive. He argues that the rules are designed to develop conformity as much as solicitors' conscience, as solicitors approach ethical rules in the same way as legal ones.[341] In other words, codes foster professional cohesion, an accepted set of norms and a certain degree of self-interest, but surely that is true of any body of rules, whether professional or societal? Others would suggest that some standards are better than no standards at all and, at least with a push to conformity, there is also a push to meet a minimum standard of service and behaviour at least. Solicitors are disciplined for breaches of the code, although family mediators with their newly drafted codes of conduct may fear their own disciplinary bodies less. This will be discussed later below.

There are obvious limitations to codes of conduct as well as some strengths.[342] Codes rarely offer definite solutions to ethical dilemmas, but Hutchinson notes that where the rules fall short there must be ethical debate. In other words, the limitation of the code in itself promotes a degree of reflexivity, albeit at an individual level and in a sporadic fashion with little systematisation. Personal responsibility cannot be relinquished to a code, as codes do not provide definite answers to many ethical dilemmas; there are too many permutations of professional life for a code to become mechanistic and entirely formalistic. Codes may develop conformity through defensive practice, but may not increase ethical awareness and behaviour. Without a movement towards ethical exploration through training, it is unlikely that members of a profession will not move from formal compliance with a code of conduct, through passivity and neutralism to an active engagement with ethics and the fundamental role of the profession. Moving legal practitioners from rules to theories without training is tantamount to asking them to hang up their professional cloaks at the door and engage with legal problems as they would have done before their training.[343] Whereas this may be more rational for family mediators who are not solicitors, who have not been trained to use rules as tools to justify a particular position.

Even if codes of conduct are there to promote professional cohesion or to maintain a monopolistic position, it is suggested that professional rules will also have an impact on the way in which professionals' ethics are constituted and how they then behave. However, it would be unwise to suggest that codes of conduct determine the behaviour of members of the profession. Indeed, research carried out on divorce lawyers in America by Maiman, McEwen and Mather concludes that,

---

[340] Abel, R.L. *op. cit.* note 329. See too Rhode, D.L. 'Why the ABA Bothers: a Functional Perspective on Professional Codes' (1981) Vol. 59 *Texas Law Review* 689.

[341] *Id.*

[342] Hutchinson, A.C. *op. cit.* note 332 at 183.

[343] Menkel-Meadow, C. *op. cit.* note 256 at 9.

...lawyers' work decisions are not produced solely or primarily by either abstract professional ideals or narrow economic interests. Rather, they result from complex interactions involving personal values, preferences and identities; formal and informal norms of groups of professional colleagues; local legal rules and institutions; the demands of work itself; and specific workplace and clients characteristics ...[344]

They do highlight 'collegial influence' as a key characteristic and codes of conduct are an important collegial influence. Maiman *et al.* consider that these collegial standards and norms convert the independent reasoned decisions into professional decisions when the collegial standards are introduced, it turns the service from a consumer service to a professional service as the collegial standards and norms set the benchmark by which the profession can evaluate its decision-making and set levels of expertise.[345] Codes of conduct play an important role in the setting of standards and norms and provide a public expression of the way in which the profession would like to view itself and would like to be viewed by others. They are an important source of information about the professional approach. It has been argued that codes are less important in large commercial firms that employ vast numbers of solicitors, as the firm culture may become dominant,[346] however much family law practice in England and Wales is carried out within small law firms and therefore this would be less of an issue. But, work colleagues do have an important influence on the way in which solicitors practice and therefore the role of codes should not be viewed as determinative by any means.[347] The professional ideology theory, favouring professional rules, is too narrow in and of itself; however the work-place theory also falls short of providing the answer. Maiman *et al.*'s research into divorce lawyers in the US found that divorce lawyers took their cues from both sources, thus leading them to conclude that 'collegial influence' would be a better term for influencing behaviour. Maiman *et al.* found in interviews with divorce lawyers that formal rules, codes, were not frequently mentioned, however as divorce cases were the ones that provoked the most complaints and with formal grievance procedures being embarrassing for lawyers (at least), many lawyers felt they practiced defensively to try to avoid complaints.[348]

While accepting that codes are probably not determinative of solicitors' and mediators' behaviour, it is none the less asserted by many that codes do have an impact on members of the profession, either in noble terms, in encouraging members to act ethically, or in cynical terms, in encouraging members to act in a way that

---

[344] Maiman, R.J., McEwen, C.A. & Mather, L. 'The Future of Legal Professionalism in Practice' (1998) Vol. 2 No. 1 *Legal Ethics* 71.

[345] *Ibid.* at 72.

[346] See for example Galanter, M. & Palay, T. *Tournament of Lawyers: The Growth and Transformation of the Big Law Firm* (Chicago, Ill: University of Chicago Press, 1991). See further Nelson, R.L. 'Ideology, Practice and Professional Autonomy: Social Values and Client Relationships in the Large Law Firm' (1985) Vol. 37 *Stanford Law Review* 503.

[347] Maiman, R.J. *et al. op. cit.* note 344 at p. 75.

[348] *Ibid.* at 75-76.

permits them to retain their professional status and thus their livelihood. They will shape professionals' approach and their identity. In other words, they either influence behaviour positively through exhortations of good practice or negatively through constraining unacceptable behaviour, but they do influence the way in which professionals practice regardless. Both solicitors and family mediators have the luxury of self-regulation at present. The Law Society (now the Solicitors Regulatory Authority) regulates solicitors; the UK College of Family Mediators regulates its own members. Family mediators are not required by law to be members of nor regulated by the UK College, whereas the Law Society statutorily regulates solicitors even if they choose to be one of the few who is not a member of the Society. Solicitors who also act as family mediators will still be subject to Law Society regulation, if they are practising as solicitors or if mediation is part of their solicitors' practice. Solicitors who are also members of the UK College as mediators will be subject to UK College regulation while they act as family mediators as well as being subject to the Law Society code as a solicitor. Thus in some situations solicitors will be subject to dual regulation. This is discussed further in the next section.

6.2 The Role of the Professional Bodies

The Law Society of England and Wales is the professional body charged with the function of governing the professional practice of solicitors in England and Wales. It has statutory recognition,[349] it was established under Royal Charter[350] and it has statutory functions in respect of the regulation of solicitors. Since January 2007 it has handed this function to the Solicitors Regulatory Authority – an independent body of the Law Society. In order for an individual to be permitted to practice as a solicitor in England and Wales he or she must have been entered on the Roll of Solicitors and have an up-to-date practising certificate.[351] This permits the Law Society to regulate the entrance qualifications of those who are admitted as solicitors and to require solicitors to comply with the rules of professional conduct set from time to time. The rules of professional conduct contain some mandatory provisions and some that are considered to be best practice statements. Solicitors are advised to telephone the Law Society ethics hotline for advice, as discussed above, if they are concerned about what constitutes appropriate professional or ethical conduct in a given situation.

---

[349] The Solicitors Act 1974; the Administration of Justice Act 1985 and the Courts and Legal Services Act 1990 are the principal statutes that relate to the Law Society's role.

[350] Granted in 1831 as the Society of Attorneys, Solicitors, Proctors and others, not being Barristers, practising in the Courts of Law and Equity in the United Kingdom, although other Royal Charters have been granted subsequently as stated in the *Guide to the Professional Conduct of Solicitors* 8th Ed. at 6.

[351] The Solicitors Act 1974 sets out the law relating to suspension of solicitors from the Roll of Solicitors and situations in which a solicitor may be struck from the Roll and unable to practice as a solicitor. Practice Rule 15 sets out client care information and the requirement that a firm has a complaints' handling procedure. Part VII of the Guide to Professional Conduct deals with complaints and discipline including the role for the Legal Complaints Service (LCS). A client may complain directly to the LCS (formerly the Office for the Supervision of Solicitors – OSS) although clients are to be encouraged to voice their concerns to the firm in the first instance and to use the firm's complaints handling procedure first.

Complaints made of solicitors may be reported to the Legal Complaints Service[352] and solicitors. They may also be reported to and investigated by the Legal Services Ombudsman[353] and they may also be the subject of legal proceedings, being sued in tort for negligence by a client.

A solicitor acting as a solicitor is bound by the mandatory sections of the Law Society's code for solicitors as well as being legally bound by the provisions set out in the Solicitors Act 1974. Rule 1 of the code states that a solicitor should not do anything in the course of practising as a solicitor, or allow another to do for them, anything that would or would be likely to compromise or impair the good reputation of the profession or 'the solicitor's proper standard of work'.[354] Rule 15 sets out how solicitors are required to deal with their client in terms of client care, including the way in which they must handle any complaints made against them. Part VII deals with how complaints and disciplinary matters are conducted including the role of the Legal Complaints Service (LCS), including the right of a client to complain directly to the LCS, if the complaint is not satisfactorily resolved by the firm. The complaints' handling procedure is formalised, has an independent investigation element associated with the process and may lead to sever penalties for a solicitor including the loss of professional status and livelihood, if the solicitor is struck from the Roll.

The UK College of Family Mediators is an umbrella organisation which was set up by three existing mediation bodies, National Family Mediation, the Family Mediation Association and Family Mediation Scotland, but which sought to widen its membership during 1998 to anyone who is able to meet its standards.[355] The UK College seeks to provide initial training and continuing professional development for mediators and to protect the public from poor service. Its objectives, as set out at the time of launch, were,

> To advance the education of the public in the skills and practice of family mediation; to set, promote, improve and maintain the highest standards of professional conduct and training for those practising in the fields of family mediation; and to make available the details of registered mediators qualified to provide family mediation.[356]

---

[352] See for example Moorhead, R., Sherr, A. & Rogers, S. *Willing Blindness? OSS Complaints Handling Procedures, A Report to the Office for the Supervision of Solicitors* (London: Law Society, 1999).

[353] See for example James, R. & Seneviratne, M. 'The Legal Services Ombudsman: Form versus Function?' (1995) Vol. 58 No. 2 *Modern Law Review* 187-207; and Seneviratne, M. *The Legal Profession: Regulation and the Consumer* (London: Sweet and Maxwell, 1999) Chapter 6.

[354] The new code of conduct came into force on 1st July 2007. It has not been considered as part of this research.

[355] The UK College of Family Mediators came into being on the 1st January 1996 and was formally launched on 17th September 1997. See Booth, M. 'The UK College of Family Mediator – An Update' (1997) Vol. 6 No. 2 *Family Mediation* 6.

[356] The UK College of Family Mediators *The Policies and Standards of the UK College of Family Mediators - Objects and Functions of the College* at 3.

The College's powers relate to: setting up and maintaining a register of mediators who have met the College's selection, training and supervision standards; establishing and maintaining a code of professional practice for family mediators; and establishing and maintaining quality assurance systems that are considered necessary to ensure the quality of service delivered by family mediators. There were approximately 800 Associates and General Members registered as family mediators with the College in 1997-1998 at its inception and around 640 members currently.[357] The UK College considers itself to be in the process of developing into a professional organisation and as such is in a period of evolution. It has established committees with responsibility for professional standards, membership, discipline and complaints as the College also has a disciplinary function in respect of its members, in addition to its regulation of the register and training and accreditation standards. This will be discussed later.

The College has yet to reach the status of a mandatory professional body, comparable to the status enjoyed by the Law Society of England and Wales and the General Council of the Bar. Family mediators are not required to be members of the body in order to be able to call themselves mediators, nor to be able to practise. Other bodies with an interest in regulation and professional standards are consequently also developing regulatory functions that will apply to their own members. The UK College of Family Mediators has a number of national family mediation bodies affiliated to it and to its Code. This makes for an interesting regulatory framework. [358] If a client wishes to make a complaint about a mediator, there is a complex complaints' procedure. In the first instance they should approach the mediator in order to try to resolve the problem. The next stage, if unsuccessful, is to complain to the mediator's professional or service organisation through his or her own complaints' procedure. The UK College provides further elaboration to explain this tier. The mediator's local service provider may be one of the professional bodies such as National Family Mediation. The mediator's provider could instead be a senior mediator or senior partner in the solicitor-mediator's law firm, or the manager of the mediation group practice. If this stage also does not resolve the complaint the next tier of complaints' handling would be the mediator's approved body, which may be the body that provided initial training for the mediator or the one with which the mediator initially registered prior to seeking UK College registration. The final tier would be to take an unresolved complaint to the UK College itself, which will ask that the complaint be mediated in the first instance and, if unresolved then to a ruling by the College. This document makes it clear that this is not an appeal against an earlier decision, but a full hearing of the complaint, with evidence provided as to earlier decisions. The UK College will use the UK College Code along with good practice guidance as the basis for consideration of complaints, if the complaint cannot be mediated.[359] This complaints' procedure is a somewhat convoluted one,

---

[357] It is not clear whether this includes Associates, although it is presumed from the wording that it does not. See Head, A., Head, M. & England, H. *Privately Funded Work in Family Mediation: Calculating the Volume of Privately Funded Family Mediation Cases:* A report prepared for the UK College of Family Mediators (London: UKCFM, December 2006) at 8.

[358] This is set out in the UK College of Family Mediators *Complaints' Procedure and Disciplinary Code* (January 2006).

[359] The table below sets out the Code of Conduct. The UK College has also drawn up a

but does illustrate the range of professional organisations that have an interest in regulating the work of family mediators. It also provides an insight into the early of development of a professional body. The UK College has not, at the time of the research, yet taken over the role of mandatory professional body for all family mediators; other longer established bodies consider that their role as regulator should be preserved for their members.

The Law Society of England and Wales also has a code of practice for family mediators who are also solicitors. The code applies to solicitors who practice as family mediators, in addition to the code of conduct that regulates their members' conduct as solicitors. The code of conduct for solicitors in England and Wales contains sections that have mandatory force, sections that are voluntary although express best practice recommendations as to conduct, and sections that are aspirational. The code for family mediators is expressed as best practice recommendations, and is therefore not mandatory. It is similar in status to the Law Society and Lexel *Practice Management Standard* which remains voluntary (PMS). The PMS are being redrafted so as to incorporate models of good administrative and management practice to cover solicitors acting as Law Society family mediators. Mediators who are also solicitors may be disciplined for conduct unbecoming a solicitor, whether or not they are practicing law, although other aspects of the solicitors' code relate solely to their legal practice. The mediation code of practice is voluntary at present; its breach will need to be explained as there is a rebuttable presumption that the code should be followed by all solicitor family mediators. The Law Society also reminds its family mediators them that they remain subject to the rules and principles which govern solicitors' conduct generally.[360] Solicitors offering mediation outside their practices remain officers of the Court by virtue of being members of the solicitors' profession and may be subject to disciplinary sanction, if their behaviour tends to bring the profession into disrepute.

Self-regulation of family mediators in England and Wales therefore currently operates at a dual level. Individual professional organisations operate their own system of regulation and discipline through their own codes of practice and their own complaints procedures. The UK College operates at a similar level as these organisations for those members who only belong to the College. It operates as a regulator of regulators for professional organisations who are on their approved list and whose members also apply for membership of the College. This is in addition to mediators' existing organisational affiliation. This suggests that the UK College is seeking to establish overall responsibility for discipline, although devolving the exercise of its power to approved bodies as its agents, for the purposes of both training mediators and regulating their own members. It remains to be seen whether this complex system of regulation and accountability will result in tighter regulation or whether it will allow breaches of codes to go unchecked as professional organisations assume that their counterparts, rather than they, will exercise this function.

---

number of policies and good practice guidelines for different aspects of family mediation practice including conflicts of interest and similar conflicts and good practice guidelines, domestic abuse screening policy, children, young people and family mediation policy and preliminary guidelines.

[360] See section 22 of the Law Society Code for Family Mediators.

There are real differences between the complaints and discipline provisions within the Codes. The UK College states that family mediators must abide by the complaints and disciplinary procedure of the College and the ethical and other quality requirements of the College. The Law Society Code for family mediators recommends that solicitors who act as family mediators should comply with the Law Society's Code of Practice for Family Mediators. It is consequently not mandatory, although the Law Society strongly recommends that a solicitor follows the code. Breach of the Code will not in itself give rise to disciplinary sanctions but evidence that they have not followed the code may be relevant in any disciplinary proceedings against the solicitor for breach of duties as a solicitor. The Legal Complaints Service is likely to consider the Code as evidence of good practice and compare the solicitor mediator's behaviour against this in respect of the complaint. Solicitors are, however, still bound by the Law Society's code for solicitors, if they act as a family mediator as part of their practice and they may be disciplined for breach of the Code. Solicitors who offer mediation services out of their practice are still solicitors and bound by their duty as officers to the Court and members of the profession. As a result they can still be disciplined if they act inconsistently with these duties.

6.3 The Data & Findings

This section compares the conduct rules for solicitors acting in family law matters, if they were to comply with best practice guidance for family solicitors, with solicitors acting as family mediators and with the code of conduct that regulates family mediators who are members of the UK College of Family Mediators. The tables below set out the requirements that must be met to be a solicitor carrying out divorce matters (for which there is no specialist family law requirements), a solicitor Family Law Panel Member (and Advanced Member) as well as a Law Society Family Mediator Panel Member and a UKCFM Family Mediator Member. Each table considers one of the theoretical concepts derived from analysing the professional literature using a grounded theory method of analysis. The first concept may be explained as the relationship between the client(s) and the professional in relation to voluntary participation of clients in the process and impartiality and independence of the professional. This may be described as:

Firstly, **partisan protector to the willing and free** (solicitor); **impartial guide to the willing and (some) safeguard to the vulnerable** (Law Society family mediator & UK College family mediator).

Secondly, the duty of the professional to the client(s) as regards power imbalances and threats to the client: **solid wall of protection** (solicitor); **protective buffer & legal crash barrier** (Law Society family mediator); **protective buffer** (UK College family mediator).

Thirdly, the nature of the decision-making process, the role of information and advice and the relevance of legal norms in decision-making, which may be described as: **legal adviser, guide & touchstone** (solicitor); **legal informer and backstop** (Law Society family mediator); **and legal awareness raiser & sign poster** (UK College family mediator).

Fourthly, the importance of other family members (including children) within the decision-making process. This may be reduced to the label: **third party issue** awareness raiser & (possibly) guide (solicitor); **third party guide and facilitator** (Law Society family mediator); **third party guide and expert facilitator** (UK College family mediator).

Finally, the responsibility of the professional as regards confidentiality and privilege. This may be described as: **trusted adviser & secret keeper** (solicitor); or **trusted, private facilitator** (Law Society family mediator and UK College family mediator).

The nature and extent of the conceptual categories are out in tables later in this chapter, in some detail. Many of these concepts are susceptible to further subdivision as indicated in the tables, which contain summaries of the information contained within the professional documentation, indicating what led to the adoption of the concepts.

Table 6.1: Relationship between the Client(s) and the Professional – Voluntary Participation of Clients in the Process & Impartiality & Independence of the Professional:

Partisan protector to the willing & free (solicitor); **impartial guide to the willing & (some) safeguard to the vulnerable** (Law Society family mediator & UK College family mediator).

Solicitors as Family Solicitors
Law Society Guide to the Professional Conduct of Solicitors & Law Society Family Law Protocol

Voluntary Participation of the Client
- A solicitor must not do anything in the course of practising as a solicitor, or permit another to do anything on his or her behalf, which will or is likely to compromise or impair a person's freedom to instruct a solicitor of his or her choice (Rule 1, 1(b)).

Impartiality and Independence of the Professional
- A solicitor must not do anything in the course of practising as a solicitor, or permit anyone else to do anything on his or her behalf, which will or is likely to compromise or impair the solicitor's independence or integrity (1(a)) or the solicitor's duty to the court (1(f)). This may override the solicitor's duty to the client. Chapter 21 deals with the role of the solicitor in litigation and advocacy including 21.01 which addresses the duty of the solicitor not to mislead the court. The Law Society has a Code for Advocacy.
- The Law Society's Solicitors Anti-Discrimination Rule and Solicitors' Anti-Discrimination Code contain a non-discrimination rule prohibiting discrimination on the grounds of race, sex or sexual orientation and unfair or unreasonable discrimination on grounds of disability as regards professional dealings with clients, staff, other solicitors, barristers and others.
- A solicitor is generally free to decide whether to accept instructions from a particular client, but must not act or must stop acting, where the instructions would involve the solicitor in a breach of the law or a breach of the principles of professional conduct, or where another solicitor is acting for the client in this matter (rule 12).
- A solicitor must not act or continue to act, where the client cannot be represented with competence or diligence, or accept instructions which (s)he suspects have been given by the client under duress or undue influence.
- A solicitor must obtain written instructions for the client, if instructions have been received via a third party.
- A solicitor must carry out a client's instructions diligently and promptly; must not abuse the solicitor/client fiduciary relationship by taking advantage of the client; must deal promptly with communications relating to the matter of a client or former client; must not terminate his or her retainer with the client except for good reasons and upon reasonable notice.
- Communications should focus on identification of issues and how they are to be resolved rather than contain protracted, unnecessary, hostile and inflammatory exchanges and trial by correspondence'. Solicitors should be aware of the effect of correspondence on all parties and should not further inflame or antagonise the parties.
- In addition, the Family Law Protocol states that solicitors should not give personal opinions or comments within letters.

Solicitors as Family Mediators
Law Society Code of Practice for Family Mediation

Voluntary Participation of Clients
- Parties participate only if willing and not influenced by fear of violence or other harm (section 1).

Impartiality and Independence of the Professional
- Mediators must not have a personal interest, must conduct the process in an even-handed and fair way, and may not act if there is actual/potential conflict of interest (section 3).
- Mediators may express a comment/view that may be more acceptable to one party than the other, but should not comment on the merits of the issue.
- Mediators must ensure the parties agree to the terms and conditions, ordinarily in writing, in line with the code and including likely costs.
- Mediators are free to make management decisions on the conduct of mediation and may suggest possible solutions.
- Mediators have no obligation to verify information. Mediation does not provide for disclosure and discovery in the same way or to the same extent as court rules.
- Mediators should inform parties, if resolutions appear likely to be outside those likely to be approved by court. This may include writing a summary to be given to the parties' legal advisers. The mediator may terminate the mediation process or refer the parties to legal advisers.
- The mediation may advise the parties to seek other professional advice. Other parties may be present, if the mediator and the parties agree
- See sections 1, 3 & 4 of the Code for further details.

Family Mediators
UK College of Family Mediation Code of Conduct

Voluntary Participation of Clients
- Participation is always voluntary. Parties are free to withdraw. Mediators may terminate if concerned about fear of violence.

Impartiality and Independence of the Professional
- Mediators must remain impartial and conduct the process even-handedly and in a fair way. They must not act if they have acquired or may acquire relevant information in any capacity. Mediation must be an independent professional activity (section 4.3 & 4.4).
- Mediators must remain neutral as to the outcome and not seek a preferred outcome (section 4.2).
- Participants must be told how mediation differs from other services, including the extent of disclosure. Mediators must provide written information on mediation.
- It may not be possible to guarantee secrecy between the participants, except the confidentiality of their addresses.
- The terms of mediation are to be agreed in advance in writing where finance and property are involved.
- Mediators must ensure that participants have the opportunity to ask questions about information disclosed in the mediation and to seek further information. It must be made clear that mediators do not verify accuracy of information.
- They must not guarantee the accuracy of Child Support Act calculations either.
- See section 6 of the code for further details.

Partisan protector to the willing and free (solicitor); impartial guide to the willing and (some) safeguard to the vulnerable (Law Society family mediator & UK College family mediator).

Voluntary participation in the process by clients is a key feature of family mediation and is enshrined in the UK College code of conduct. Mediators may terminate the mediation, if they are concerned that one party may be acting under fear of violence or other form of coercion. The Law Society code for family mediators states that the mediation should only take place, if neither is in fear of violence or other harm. Consequently there are similar provisions for solicitor and non-family mediators in this respect. Could this be a key difference between family mediators and family solicitors; family mediators require a consensus to mediate whereas family solicitors are willing to take a case regardless of circumstance? Rule one of the solicitors code states that a solicitor must not do anything that could impair a client's right to instruct a solicitor of his or her choice. This could be interpreted as the requirement that solicitors make sure that clients instruct a solicitor voluntarily. This is not quite the same a voluntary participation in the legal process, but it does suggest freedom of action and choice of a legal adviser and advocate.

The second issue examined from the codes was the impartiality and independence of the professional. According to the UK College code, family mediators must remain impartial and conduct the process even-handedly and fairly. They must not act for the clients, if they have partial knowledge via another route. The family mediator must remain neutral as to the outcome for the clients. Law Society family mediators adhering to the Law Society code are required to act in a similar way; however, they may comment or give a view that may be more acceptable to one of the clients. The comment must stop short of being a comment on the merits on a particular issue. Again, the view is that the clients should reach their own consensual outcome without being steered by the family mediator towards a particular outcome. The duty to cease to act for Law Society family mediators is more similar to that of solicitors than it is to the duty imposed on family mediators by the UK College code. The issue for Law Society family mediators relates to conflicts of interest rather than knowledge received about one party. While both family mediator codes aim to ensure even handedness by the family mediator, the potential conflict of interest is drawn more widely for Law Society family mediators than for family mediators regulated by the UK College. This is in part related, it appears, to the view that there are some agreements that are considered as objectively undesirable or unfair, to which the family mediator should not be a party even in a facilitative role.

The stark difference in professional role becomes most apparent between family solicitors and family mediators when considering even-handedness between the clients. Solicitors are required to act in a way that is independent and has integrity, as are family mediators, and they must not do anything or allow another to do anything that may compromise their duty to the Court, which is much wider than for family mediators. Aside from these limitations, a solicitor is expected to provide the best advice to their client, which is necessarily partisan.

There are some limits to partisanship, however, as imposed by law and as set out in the latter stages of the code and by best practice guidance. Solicitors are expected to investigate a client's financial and personal situation to the extent that the factual basis is required to make a legal assessment of entitlement, provide advice to the client and to set out a bargaining position with the other party to the divorce. The investigation may require use of the court process, if the solicitor does not believe that the other party is providing the appropriate level of disclosure to permit the solicitor to provide full legal advice to his or her client. A Law Society family mediator may seek to verify financial and property information provided at mediation, but is under no obligation to do so. This renders the Law Society family mediator's view on whether the clients are about to reach an agreement outside the norm for their circumstances rather less reliable, although it is open to a mediator to terminate mediation, if he or she believes that one client is being obfuscatory, and that this damages the integrity of the consensual decision-making process. Mediators operating under the UK College code must state that they do not verify the information being provided by the parties. The parties must be reminded that they may have to provide the information that they have given to a court, at a later stage, Law Society family mediators must remind the clients of this in similar terms, after that, the UK College mediator does not attempt to check whether the information given is correct. On this basis the solicitor does not only provide partisan advice but also acts as a fail safe to check that the client's interests are being properly safeguarded through appropriate and accurate information exchange, as compared with a Law Society family mediator who may not act as a partisan but may act as safeguard both as regards the terms of an arrangement and the accuracy of information upon which the arrangement is to be based. This can be juxtaposed against the approach of the UK College mediator, which is to assume (unless evidence is presented to the contrary) that the parties are acting in a fair manner towards each other, and to assist the parties towards an agreement upon which they both agree. The mediators takes no part in providing a safeguard to the clients except to the extent that is required to ensure equal power in negotiations, to remind the clients that they may seek safeguards from other professionals (such as solicitors), unless the welfare of a child is in issue. Consensual decision-making is the key feature, rather than safeguarding the client's financial position.

It appears that the solicitor acts as the partisan protector for her client who has chosen her willingly and free from undue influence. The Law Society family mediator acts as a guide to the parties who participate in the process voluntarily, but may step in to safeguard the interests of a vulnerable client and provide a view that the agreement under discussion is outside the norm for the clients' situation. The UK College family mediator acts likewise, although the extent to which the family mediator may intervene to safeguard the vulnerable is less evidence from the code. The next section considers the professional's duty to the client(s).

Table 6.2: The Duty of the Professional to the Client(s):
Power Imbalances & Threats to the Client

Solid wall of protection (solicitor); **protective buffer and legal crash barrier** (Law Society family mediator); **protective buffer** (UK College family mediator).

Solicitors as Family Solicitors
Law Society Guide to the Professional Conduct of Solicitors & Law Society Family Law Protocol

Power Imbalances & the Role of the Professional

- If the other party is legally represented, the solicitor must deal directly with the legal representative rather than the other party. If the other party is not legally represented, there is guidance on how the solicitor should deal with that party. This is contained within 17.01 on 'fairness' and 19, which sets out professional relation with other solicitors.
- No specific mention of domestic violence in the Code, although Rule 12 deals with duress and undue influence, stating that solicitors must not accept instructions, if they suspect that the client has given them under duress or as a result of undue influence. The guidance note under that rule notes that particular care may need to be taken where a client is elderly or otherwise vulnerable to pressure from others.
- The Family Law Protocol contains a whole section on domestic abuse in section 6. Solicitors must treat the safety of clients and children as a priority, screen for domestic abuse, keep it under review if it is not apparent at the first meeting, and where it is revealed undertake a needs assessment and safety planning with clients. There may be a need for urgent action to protect the client and any children.

Solicitors as Family Mediators
Law Society Code of Practice for Family Mediation

Power Imbalances & the Role of the Professional

- Section 6 is devoted to dealing with power imbalances and what steps may be taken to redress the imbalance including termination of mediation, where necessary.
- References to domestic violence are made in the commentary on power imbalances. See also voluntary participation above.

Family Mediators
UK College of Family Mediation Code of Conduct

Power Imbalances & the Role of the Professional

- Mediators should seek to prevent manipulative/ threatening/ intimidating behaviour, redress power imbalances, and, if necessary, terminate the mediation. Section 4.3.2 and 4.8.
- Mediators must discover where there is fear of violence or other harm. If violence is an issue then the family mediator must discuss whether the participants wish to take part in mediation. Mediators must ensure the safety of all participants where mediation does take place.

Solid wall of protection (solicitor); **protective buffer & legal crash barrier** (Law Society family mediator); **protective buffer** (UK College family mediator).

Power imbalances are raised as an important issue in the context of family mediation. The UK College exhorts family mediators to seek to prevent behaviour by a client that may be manipulative, threatening or intimidating towards the other client. They should seek to redress any power imbalances in the mediation and, if necessary, terminate the mediation if this is not possible. The Law Society takes a similar stance for Law Society family mediators. The Law Society is also concerned about power imbalances between the parties in a legal context to the extent that it requires solicitors to deal with the other party's solicitors rather than with the other party directly. Some would see this as the maintenance of the professional monopoly, whereas others would argue that professional dealings prevent abuse by a professional with a dominant position in the legal process. The Code makes provision for non-legally represented parties as well. If the other party is non-legally represented then guidance is provided in 17.01 to ensure fairness as far as possible between the legally represented and non-represented party. All professionals are required to terminate the professional relationship, if it is not possible to adequately counterbalance power balances between the divorcing couple of others who may have influence of the parties' decision-making (the solicitor's client, or the parties to the mediation). This is left to a matter of professional judgement for solicitors, Law Society family mediators and family mediators from the UK College.

There is a duty to clients in all three situations – solicitors in divorce matters, Law Society family mediators and family mediators. A solicitor's general duty relates to ensuring that there is no undue influence being placed on his or her client in reaching a decision on instructions to the solicitor, but the duty may also extend to the other party in the matter. Solicitors should deal with the other party's legal representative and not directly with the individual, to ensure that the equality of arms is maintained in the adversarial process. The party who has not consulted a solicitor may agree to an offer being made by the other party's solicitor, in ignorance of the law or in ignorance of the facts of the matter. With the benefit of legal advice he or she may have reached a different, hopefully more appropriate decision. However, the duty to redress a power imbalance extends to the other party when that party is not legally represented. In this instance there is a due to act fairly towards the other party so as to provide some counter-balance to the power disparity between the solicitor's client and the client's soon to be former spouse. This does not override the partisan nature of the solicitor-client retainer, however, and consequently the redressing of a power disparity is more a question of fair play than a duty to put both parties in a similar position as regards legal knowledge and advice on their situations. Family mediators deal with both clients and therefore this issue does not arise in the same way, but both codes require steps to be taken to redress power imbalances, and mediation should be terminated if this proves impossible. Domestic violence is specifically mentioned in the Family Law Protocol (although not the Guide to Professional Conduct), and the two mediation Codes. All three documents set out a safety-orientated approach to domestic violence and consequently there is little difference in this regard. Differences relate more to information imbalance and undue influence where solicitors are concerned and negotiating skill strength in family mediation. The former appears to aim at allowing the solicitor correctly to assess and advise the client so that they may reach the best possible outcome for their situation with the other party receiving the benefit of similar advice from another professional, the latter, to establish and maintain a level playing field to allow the clients to reach a mutual, consensual decision.

This explains the wall of protection and the protective buffer in the conceptual label, but what of the 'solid' wall of protection and the 'legal crash barrier'? These refer back to the legal normative stance that the solicitor, and to an extent the Law Society family mediator take, as discussed in the next section. The solicitor is required to protect her client's interest by reference to the law, and the courts if required. The Law Society family mediation is required to consider whether the agreement under discussion is outside the range of those usually reached by a court in a similar situation, to advise the parties to seek legal advice and, if necessary, to terminate the mediation if it appears that a real unfairness may be the result of the negotiations. These are discussed further, below.

Table 6.3: The Nature of the Decision-making Process, Information, Advice & the Relevance of Legal Norms:

Legal adviser, guide & touchstone (solicitor); **legal informer & backstop** (Law Society family mediator); **legal awareness raiser and sign poster** (UK College family mediator).

Solicitors as Family Solicitors
Law Society Guide to the Professional Conduct of Solicitors & Law Society Family Law Protocol

- A solicitor shall not do anything in the course of practising as a solicitor, or permit anyone else to do anything on his/her behalf, which will or is likely to compromise or impair the solicitor's duty to act in the best interests of the client (I(c)).
- Rule III makes it clear that it is fundamental to the solicitor-client relationship that a solicitor must be able to give impartial and frank advice to the client. This includes freedom from outside pressures or interests, which could destroy or weaken the solicitor's independence or professional relationship with the client (explained as a fiduciary relationship), or may impact on the client's freedom of choice.
- Rule 15 requires that a solicitor or firm should not accept instructions to act for two or more clients where there is a conflict or a significant risk of one between the interests of those clients and the solicitor or firm must cease to act, if a conflict arises between existing clients. In addition, a solicitor or firm in receipt of confidential information about an existing or former client during the course of acting for that client, the solicitor or the firm must not accept instructions to act against the client.
- The Family Law Protocol states that it is bad practice to issue proceedings to pre-empt the other party. The other party should be given notice of the intention to commence proceedings at least seven days before doing so.
- The use of family mediation should be kept under review and should be discussed with the client, as should other forms of dispute settlement. Section 7 of the Protocol sets out the appropriate role of the solicitor during mediation.

Solicitors as Family Mediators
Law Society Code of Practice for Family Mediation

- Mediators may not provide legal advice to the parties but may provide legal information on relevant principles of law and how these may be applied.
- Parties should be given the opportunity to consult their own solicitors before reaching a binding agreement.
- Mediators should inform the parties, if resolutions are likely to be outside those generally approved by a court.

Family Mediators
UK College of Family Mediation Code of Conduct

- Mediators may inform the parties of possible solutions and of the legal implications. They must not give legal or other advice, but may inform the parties of broad principles of law that are applicable to disputed matters.
- Parties must be advised to notify any legal adviser that they are undertaking mediation. Mediators must not communicate with solicitors without parties' express consent. Information would be given to both solicitors whenever appropriate or required by the parties.
- Mediators must prepare a written summary of the factual outcome and inform the parties of the advantage of seeking legal advice whenever desirable and before a final agreement.

Legal adviser, guide & touchstone (solicitor); legal informer & backstop (Law Society family mediator); legal awareness raiser & sign poster (UK College family mediator).

The decision-making process shows the differences between solicitor and family mediator roles very clearly. The UK College of Family Mediators states that a family mediator may inform the parties of possible solutions and the legal implications of these solutions. However, family mediators are not permitted to give legal advice, or other advice for that matter, as their role is seen as facilitative rather than directive. They are expected to provide legal information in broad terms and to advise clients to take legal advice, if they require further information or advice. In addition, mediators must not communicate with the parties' solicitors without the parties' express consent and, if they do so they must provide the same information to both parties' solicitors. The parties must be informed that they should tell their own legal advisers that they are undertaking family mediation. The UK College also requires family mediators to provide a written factual statement stating the outcome of the mediation, and they must inform the parties of the benefit of seeking legal advice whenever it is desirable to do so and in any event before reaching a final agreement. Consequently, the UK College does not advocate mediation outside of a legal framework *per se*, but seeks to encourage the parties to seek legal advice, if they so wish. The UK College makes a complete distinction between the professional project of legal advice giving and providing legal information. Family mediators must provide information on broad principles of law but go no further. This is an interesting point to note in the context of the training given to family mediators on legal issues as discussed in chapter four, as little legal training is provided to facilitate this process.

The Law Society in its code for Law Society family mediators makes similar provision i.e. it states that family mediators must not provide legal advice to the parties, but they may provide legal information on relevant law and how the law may be applied. This could be considered to be a step further than the UK College, which maintains that legal information on the broad principles of law should be provided but does not state that the law may be given in the context of how it may be applied to the parties' situation. This is similar to the UK College provision – the Law Society requires family mediators to encourage the parties to seek legal advice being sought by the parties prior to reaching a final agreement, however, the Code makes it explicit that the parties should be given the opportunity to consult a solicitor prior to reaching a binding agreement rather than that the parties should be advised to seek legal advice. The Law Society's provision could be seen as an active engagement with the need to consult a solicitor rather than the UK College's more passive stance, although this is perhaps to be expected in view of the professional affiliations of the two organisations. The final provision on the decision-making process is rather different for the two family mediator codes. The Law Society provides that family mediators should inform the parties, if resolutions are likely to be outside those likely to be approved by the court. This is an interesting point. Law Society family mediators are in one sense expected to act like a solicitor, to evaluate the parties' potential solutions and to provide a non-adversarial but nonetheless 'legal' opinion on the potential outcome. Their view may be seen as neutral but within the legal norms of the time, which, as discussed earlier in the thesis, may be considered to be forged within the context of an adversarial paradigm. Obviously this would not prevent the two clients from reaching an agreement outside of the legal framework, but, a note of caution would be introduced by the family mediator as a result of the knowledge gained by the mediator in his or her professional experience as a solicitor. The family mediator is also empowered to terminate the mediation session, if she is concerned about the inequality of the agreement under negotiation.

The decision-making provisions in the Law Society code for solicitors prescribe that a solicitor should give legal advice if representing a client and must act in the best interests of his or her client. The solicitor must provide frank, impartial advice to the client within the context of the client's freedom to exercise choice. Solicitors may not accept instructions or to seek to act for two or more clients where there may be a conflict of interest between clients, which would certainly arise if a solicitor were to accept instructions from or act for both parties in a divorce case. A solicitor would also have to cease to act if a conflict of interest later arose between clients being represented by the firm. This is an interesting point as commentators often view this as the major distinction between solicitors and mediators, at least between solicitor family mediators and family solicitors as regulated by the Law Society Codes and to an extent this is of course true. A solicitor may not advise both clients, nor may he or she provide advice to a client that is not in that client's best interests. This highlights the partisan role of the solicitor, as the client's champion acting against the interests of the client's spouse. Having said that, the best interests of the client are now being interpreted rather more widely than they have previously in the context of family cases, as discussed shortly in the context of the section on other family members and the decision-making process.

The process that solicitors and family mediators must follow in their professional practice are also included in the Codes of conduct and these give an indication of the nature of the professional project. The UK College of Family Mediators sets out the process terms of family mediation. Family mediators are instructed to tell the participants how it differs from other forms of dispute resolution and the extent to which disclosure operates in family mediation. Family mediators must, as part of this process, give written information on family mediation. The parties are required to agree the terms of mediation in writing in advance where finance and property are to be involved in the context of the mediation. Participants must have an opportunity to make further enquiries about information disclosed as part of the mediation and to seek further information. However, family mediation does not in itself seek to verify the accuracy of the information given by participants. Family mediators must not guarantee that the Child Support Act calculations made in the mediation are accurate.

This is a different position taken from that of family mediators adhering to the Law Society code. Although family mediators are required to ensure that the parties agree the terms and conditions under which the mediation is to be conducted and usually in writing and including the likely costs of mediation, Law society family mediators have slightly different provisions in respect of disclosure. While the Code states that mediation does not provide for disclosure and discovery in the same way as the legal process and mediators have no obligation to verify information, it does not state that family mediators may not attempt to verify the information given by the parties. In addition, Law Society family mediators are required to tell the parties, if they believe that the solutions that are being proposed are likely to be outside the range that a court would approve. The mediator may terminate the process or refer the parties to seek legal advice from their legal advisers or advice from other professional advisers. The Law

Society family mediator may also include a summary of the solution to the parties' legal advisers. In fact, family mediators may make management decisions about the conduct of the mediation and may also suggest possible solutions. This approach suggests that the shadow of the court is ever present, that some solutions are more legally appropriate than others and that the law has an important role to play in the context of divorce settlement.

Solicitors are generally free to decide whether or not to accept the prospective client's instructions. However, a solicitor must stop acting for a client if by doing so it would involve the solicitor in a breach of the law or of professional conduct rules, unless the client is prepared to change his or her instructions. This indicates the difference between the nature of solicitors and family mediators, as solicitors assist the client and therefore to an extent they 'aid' and transact their legal business. Family mediators are there to facilitate the clients in reaching a resolution but they do not transact the settlement in any way. A solicitor must cease to act if he or she is unable to represent their client with competence or diligence. They have to consider whether they are able to provide a certain level of professional service to their client. Solicitors may not accept instructions, if another solicitor is acting in the matter until the retainer has been determined. There have been discussions about whether this relates to the protection of professional interests or whether this protects clients from conflicting or partial advice. Protection of the client does seem to be an important value established in the Code. Solicitors must not take advantage of their client, they must deal promptly with communications, they must not terminate the retainer unless the solicitor has good reasons and upon reasonable notice. A solicitor must also carry out their client's instructions diligently and promptly. This is an extremely important point; a solicitor must act on the client's instructions, not on their own initiative. The solicitor must provide advice to the client, may suggest solutions and ways of dealing with the matter, however, the client is fundamentally in charge. The conflict of interest issue reinforces the partisan role of the solicitor, who is required to act in the best interests of his or her client. Partisanship pervades the solicitor client retainer, the assessment of the client's best outcome and the advice that flows from that, this may extend to adversarialism on the face of the wording of the code. This is the traditional role of a solicitor, across all areas of law, however, as indicated in the next table, the *Family Law Protocol* indicates a more consensus based approach to family law practice that could be argued to modify or even contradict the role of the solicitor in providing partisan advice to the client as discussed in this section, and certainly appears to contradict an emphasis on adversarialism.

To conclude, the conceptual labels that have been applied to solicitors. Law Society family mediators and UK College family mediators relate to the role that they are required to adopt in relation to legal norms. The solicitor is a legal adviser, guiding the client on appropriate settlement terms and courses of action and is a legal expert – a touchstone on the law. A Law Society family mediator is legally knowledgeable and may inform the client on legal principles, may suggest a range of possible solutions and is fundamentally a backstop if the terms under discussion appear to be at odds with what a court would normally decide in this situation. As such the impartial facilitator may become a partisan backstop. The UK College family mediator may raise the clients' awareness of relevant legal principles and may signpost clients to further legal information and advice. However, the family mediator is not required to consider possible court discussion and the application of legal norms to the clients' scenario. The next section will consider the importance of other family members, including children, in the decision-making process.

Table 6.4: The Importance of other Family Members within the Decision-making Process:

Third party issue awareness raiser & (possibly) guide (solicitor); **third party guide & facilitator** (Law Society family mediator); **third party guide & expert facilitator** (UK College family mediator).

Solicitors as Family Solicitors
Law Society Guide to the Professional Conduct of Solicitors & Law Society Family Law Protocol

Consideration of Other Family Members (Including Children)
- The Family Law Protocol encourages a constructive and conciliatory approach to family disputes, to narrow the issues, to reach effective and timely solutions; to consider the interests of children and continuing family relationships; to minimise the costs.
- Solicitors should adhere to section 3 of the protocol as regards children, even if there is no apparent dispute between the parties in respect of the children. They should emphasise the continuing nature of the parenting relationship and the benefits to children or parental co-operation (includes encouraging them to talk together to the children about separation). Solicitors are expected to be aware of the benefits of parenting plans. Solicitors should remind parents that the interests of children will be treated as paramount by the court and that they should operate on the same basis. They should emphasise the potentially damaging effects of involved in children in disputes concerning the parents.

Involvement of Children
- No mention of direct involvement.
- Solicitors should also keep negotiations about children separate from all other negotiations and to discourage use of negotiations pertaining to children as a way of putting pressure on the other party about other issues.

Children at Risk
- *Protocol: 'To endeavour to minimise any risks to the parties and/or the children and to alert the client to treat safety as a primary concern'.* Solicitors should be sensitive to suggestions from clients that any children involved are showing serious signs of emotional disturbance. If so, solicitors should refer where appropriate to other agencies. This has to be juxtaposed against the solicitor's general duty to the client (see table 6.1 above).

Solicitors as Family Mediators
Law Society Code of Practice for Family Mediation

Consideration of Other Family Members (Including Children)
- The Mediator must have regard to the needs and interests of children. Mediators shall have regard to the provisions of Part I of the Family Law Act 1996.

Involvement of Children
- Children might be directly involved in mediation, although it is anticipated that this will be the exception rather than the norm. Mediators should, generally, be specifically trained to involve children in mediation, if they intend to do so. They must be aware of the dynamics of involving children and also of confidentiality issues in this respect.

Children at Risk

- Where a child is suffering or likely to suffer significant harm. Mediators should consider with the participants (if appropriate) what steps should be taken to remedy the situation. The mediator should contact an appropriate agency or take other appropriate steps.

Family Mediators
UK College of Family Mediation Code of Conduct

Consideration of Other Family Members (Including Children)

- Mediators have a special concern for the welfare of children. They must encourage participants to consider their children's welfare and where appropriate discuss their involvement in the mediation (section 4.7 and 4.8).

Involvement of Children

- The mediator must be trained to involve children, if he or she intends to do so and must obtain the child's consent and provide appropriate facilities.

Children at Risk

- The mediator must withdraw and outline her reasons to parties' legal advisers where there are issues of child welfare. The mediator must also consider the involvement of court welfare officer.

Third party issue awareness raiser & (possibly) guide (solicitor); **third party guide & facilitator** (Law Society family mediator); **third party guide and expert facilitator** (UK College family mediator).

There are many differences in the provisions of the codes for family mediators and for solicitors, however, many of them are cosmetic as regards standards of professional behaviour. The fundamental difference remains the fact the family mediator's objective is 'to help the parties to arrive at their own decisions regarding their issues, on an informed basis with and understanding, so far as reasonably practicable, of the implications and consequences of such decisions for themselves and any children concerned.'[361] Whereas the solicitor's duty is to the provide advice to the client and act on the client's own instructions without the need to consult the other party as to their preferred settlement options. But, the Law Society Family Law Protocol version one for solicitors[362] (the Protocol) stated in its aims that the solicitor is:

1. To encourage a constructive and conciliatory approach to resolution of family disputes.

2. To encourage the narrowing of the issues in dispute and the effective and timely resolution of disputes.

3. To endeavour to minimise any risks to the parties and/or the children and the alert the client to treat safety as a primary concern.

4. To have regard to the interests of children and long term family relationships.

5. To endeavour to ensure that costs are not unreasonably incurred.

This suggests that the solicitor should not be adopting a position that is focused entirely on the needs of his or her client, but instead to consider the wider implications of the divorce for other family members including not only the children but also to long term family interests, which may include the client's spouse in a continuing parenting role, for example. Naturally this could be considered to be a shift in emphasis rather than a radical change of the solicitor's focus, as in a divorce where children are involved it could be said that it is never in the client's interests for the agreement between the parties to be drafted so as to favour the client over the interests of the other spouse, if that spouse is to be the child carer.[363] The Protocol could have stopped short at requiring the solicitor to consider only the interests of the children rather than including long term family relationships. These points have been developed further in version two of the (much extended) Protocol. It is interesting to note that this definition has narrowed slightly from the draft that

---

[361] Section 5.1 *Law Society Code of Practice For Family Mediators* version 1 – still in force.

[362] *The Law Society's Family Law Protocol*, 26th November 2001. Available at www.lawsocietyinternetp.aspective.com/documents/downloads/Familylawprotocol.pdf . The Second version came into force in January 2006 *Law Society Family Law Protocol* (version 2) (London: the Law Society, 2006).

[363] See Webley, L. *op. cit.* note 28.

preceded version one, which include 'wider family members' within it as well,[364] but it is clear that the solicitor's role is no longer, if it were ever, to ignore the interests of others in order to secure the best deal for his or her client. In addition, the second version of the Protocol has shifted the emphasis yet again - it provides far more detail on the needs and welfare of children, and mentions other parties in specific terms (in relation to religious issues, and in relation to abuse, and in the general dealings between solicitors and clients) but not in relation to financial matters. Indeed the phrase 'long term family relationships' has been removed from this section. The content of the Protocol suggests that the adversarial charge levelled at solicitors may not be as accurate as it once was in the family law context, although partisanship is still evident and is clearer in the second version of the Protocol than in the first, even though the tenor of all communications should be conciliatory and constructive. It may be that solicitors' and family mediators' professional ethics have more in common than one would expect at first glance, particularly in terms of professionalism towards clients and other members of the profession. However, the core difference of identification of who one is to serve, one's client or the wider family unit in the context of divorce, brings the two professions closer together through their common purpose, while maintaining the wider professional distinctions in a generic solicitor, mediator context.

By contrast Law Society family mediators are required by the Law Society Code to have regard to the needs and interests of children and they must consider with the participants what steps should be taken to resolve the situation, if a child is suffering or is likely to suffer harm. If necessary, the Law Society family mediator should contact appropriate agencies. The Law Society code also specifies how a family mediator should act, if a child is involved in the mediation process. Law Society family mediators' attention is particularly drawn to Part I of the Family Law Act 1996, a reminder of the legal responsibilities of family mediators. There are no such provisions concerning children in the Solicitors' Code of Conduct although there are best practice guidelines where a solicitor's client is a minor. The UK College makes provision for the special concern that family mediators must have for the welfare of the children. They must encourage participants to consider their children's welfare and where appropriate they should discus their involvement in the mediation. There are provisions relating to the need for family mediators to be trained, if they are to involve children in family mediation sessions and the need to gain the child's specific consent prior to the child being involved in family mediation. Where the family mediator is concerned about the welfare of a child, the family mediator must, according to the UK College, withdraw from the family mediation, explain the issue to the parties and where necessary consider the involvement of the court welfare officer. This duty appears designed to endeavour to get clients to engage with the welfare of the child and, if this is not possible to hand the matter over to the clients' solicitors or a court welfare officer, all acting as agents of the court. There are major similarities between provisions relating to family mediators set out in the two mediator codes. The voluntary code for solicitors does encourage the solicitor to encourage conciliatory approaches to divorce and brings in the importance of the interests of children and other family members. There is less explicit mention of the interests of the chid in relation to solicitors, and also of their direct involvement in

---

[364] As at draft date 4th April 2001.

the process. The solicitor still has legal responsibilities towards any child that she considers may be in danger. This is, however, a less onerous responsibility than the requirement to consider the welfare of the child in the broader sense of term.

Solicitors and Law Society family mediators are reminded of their own legal responsibilities and the principles upon which the court would reach a decision on the welfare of the child. There is a focus on children in the Family Law Protocol and the duty on solicitors is explained in the context of the legislation that makes the interests of the child as paramount in court, a reminder of the legal arena in which settlements are being made. Solicitors are given detailed guidance on the way in which negotiations concerning the children are to be conducted, including their own duty towards the child. At the point at which the child's welfare is an issue, the solicitor's role appears to switch from partisan for the client to partisan for the child. Where a child is involved in a divorce matter, the solicitor's role could not be deemed to be adversarial in the commonly used sense, but consensual, with regard to assisting his or her client to work with the other party and his or her legal representative to reach an appropriate set of arrangements taking into account the child's welfare and where this is not possible to work with other agencies with this aim. The family mediator operating under the UK College code also engages in a consensual decision-making process with regard to arrangements for the child, however, this is done by encouraging the clients to operate in this way rather than making suggestions of appropriate arrangements for the children. Where this proves impossible the mediator must terminate mediation and the decision-making process is handed over to others, rather than managed by the mediator. This requires the family mediator to make an assessment concerning the welfare of the child, which goes beyond a facilitative role and moves towards a directive one, but does not involve the family mediator in any way in representing the child as the solicitor is effectively required to do in negotiations between the parties and, if necessary, with his or her own client.

In conclusion, the solicitor is required to consider children's welfare, to raise any issues about their welfare with her client and in some instances possibly also guide her client in a direction that emphasises and ensures the children's safety and well-being. The Law Society family mediators guides clients in respect of child welfare issues and concerns and may facilitate a child welfare focused approach by involving outside agencies in the family's situation. The UK College family mediator similarly acts as a guide with respect to child welfare, but with her greater training in child psychology and child welfare and with an explicit duty to raise and facilitate child welfare issues with the clients, as well as involve third party agencies, the UK College family mediator is also an expert facilitator in focusing negotiations on the welfare of children. The UK College family mediator is required to respect child welfare to the extent that she is not permitted to involve children in mediation sessions unless she has received specialist training.

Table 6.5: The Responsibility of the Professional as regards Confidentiality & Privilege:

Trusted adviser & secret keeper (solicitor); trusted private facilitator (Law Society family mediator and UK College family mediator).

Solicitors as Family Solicitors
Law Society Guide to the Professional Conduct of Solicitors & Law Society Family Law Protocol

Confidentiality of Client's Situation
- A solicitor is under a duty to keep confidential to the firm the client's affairs, but this duty can be overridden by certain exceptional circumstances (rule 16).
- A solicitor cannot act against a client if (s)he or the firm acquired relevant confidential information about that client during the course of acting for him/her (rule 15).

Requirement to Use Information for the Benefit of the Client
- A solicitor is also usually under a duty to pass on to the client and use all information which is material to the client's situation regardless of its source, except in exceptional circumstances (rule 16).

Solicitors as Family Mediators
Law Society Code of Practice for Family Mediation

Confidentiality of Clients' Situation
- Mediators must maintain confidentiality except where the parties and the mediator agree on disclosure, the law imposes an overriding obligation, or where a child may be suffering or likely to suffer significant harm. Mediators must discuss arrangements about confidentiality with each party separately (section 7).
- However, all financial information must be provided on an open basis, so that it can be referred to in court.
- Discussions about terms of settlement should be conducted on a 'without prejudice' basis and claim mediation privilege to allow options to be explored freely. Mediation privilege should not apply in communications concerning significant harm to a child, where other public policy considerations prevail, or where the rules of evidence render it inapplicable.

Family Mediators
UK College of Family Mediation Code of Conduct

Confidentiality of Clients' Situation
- Mediators must not disclose information about or obtained during mediation to anyone including a court welfare officer or a court, without the express consent of the participants or order of court, except where a child is in danger of or may have suffered significant harm.
- However, participants must agree disclosure in legal proceedings of facts related to property or finances (sections 4.5 and 4.6).
- Discussions and negotiations must be conducted on a legally privileged basis, which should only be waived if all the parties agree or if the law imposes an overriding obligation on the mediator.

Trusted adviser & secret keeper (**solicitor**); trusted private facilitator (**Law Society family mediator and UK College family mediator**).

There are confidentiality provisions within all three Codes. The UK College code provides that family mediators must not disclose information about or obtained during mediation to anyone unless the family mediator has the express consent of the participants or unless there is a court order, unless a child is in danger or may have suffered significant harm. This prohibition extends to disclosing information to the court welfare officer or the court without the participants' consent or a court order. Participants are required to agree to disclosure of facts related to property or finances in any legal proceedings. The participants' discussions and negotiations must be conducted on a legally privileged basis. This privilege should only be waived by a party, if both clients agree or if the family mediator is required to breach privilege as a result of an overriding legal obligation to disclose. The Law Society Code sets out similar obligations for Law Society family mediators in respect of maintenance of confidentiality. They must establish that financial information be provided openly, so that it may be referred on to a court, if necessary. Family mediators must discuss arrangements about confidentiality with each party separately. Settlement discussions are to be conducted on a 'without prejudice' basis, and mediation privilege should be claimed to allow options to be explored freely by the parties. Interestingly, both family mediator codes consider confidentiality in legal terms.

The Law Society Code for solicitors states at rule 16 that solicitors are under a duty of confidentiality, which may only be overridden in a limited number of exceptional situations, as discussed above in relation to family mediator's duties to disclose, but also as provided by law relating to money laundering. Solicitors are under a duty to pass on information that is pertinent to the client's business regardless of the source of that information. The solicitor is also under a duty to use that information, in his or her client's best interests. Again, there are statutory limits on this duty. The solicitor is also under a duty to cease from acting for someone else against an existing or former client, if the solicitor has gained relevant confidential information about that existing or former client. The duty of confidentiality extends beyond the client's case and pervades all of her dealing, past and present, with clients.

Solicitors are under more stringent duties in respect of clients, in the adversarial tradition, to maintain the balance of arms against both sides. Family mediators are under fewer obligations, other than the duty of confidentiality, as they facilitate negotiations of the parties, otherwise there are few differences between the professional approaches of solicitors and family mediators. Consequently, the conceptual label developed from the codes is that of a solicitor as trusted adviser acting under legal privilege who is required to maintain confidential the information provided with the solicitors-client relationship. This duty also extends into the future in relation to conflicts of interest with potential news clients, and thus the solicitor has been described as a 'secret-keeper' through time. Family mediators are trusted professionals who are under a duty of confidentiality within the context of private ordering, however, their duty is not legal privileged in quite the same way as solicitor-client relations. Thus, there is not quite the same level of confidentiality protection as is afforded via solicitors.

6.4 Conclusions

The theoretical concepts have been considered further to consider what they reveal as regards professional practice in divorce matters. They indicate the relative importance placed on the role of legal norms within divorce matters by solicitors and family mediators, not necessarily that legal norms should provide a definitive statement of the arrangements that ought to be reached between the clients, but as a guide to a range of appropriate settlement arrangements. This in turn has an impact on the way in which a solicitor advises his or her client on appropriate settlement alternatives, as the solicitor will provide information then advice. The UK College stresses the importance of facilitative approaches to mediation in which it is for the clients to seek value-ladened views, advice, on the legal implications of different settlement alternatives from a solicitor. The family mediator provides only legal information to the parties, if it is appropriate to provide it. The Law Society code for family mediation adopts a half way approach. It requires Law Society family mediators to put clients on notice, if they are reaching an agreement that is not one that a court would normally reach in their situation, but leaves the clients free to go ahead with the arrangement after being reminded that they should seek legal advice before finalising the agreement other than in wholly exceptional circumstances. This provides a degree of protection to the clients, as it may mitigate the effects of reaching an agreement on the basis of inadequate knowledge of one's legal entitlement, assuming that the Law Society family mediator has a full enough knowledge of the clients' situation to permit her to provide an assessment of divergence of any agreement from the legal norm.

The basis for decision-making is viewed differently between the solicitors and family mediators – the former views decision-making in the context of the law (even for Law Society family mediators), the latter views decision-making in the context of consensus whether or not it conforms to legal entitlement. The former attempts to guide decision-making on the basis of individually tailored legal advice about what a client could expect to get, were the case were to go to court, the bargaining power of the other party and the strength of his or he legal representative in the matter, but taking due regard of the welfare of any children. Where the welfare of the children is in issue, the solicitor must switch allegiance, as a court would, to operate in the best interests of the child. The latter, the family mediator, will seek to facilitate consensual decision-making, redressing any imbalance in negotiating power by one party, and turning the clients' attention to the welfare of the child. Where it is not possible to create an arena of consensual negotiations, then the mediator must step away from the process and, if necessary, let partisan advisers assist the parties. All three recognise the shadow of the law behind negotiations, but to different extents.

Solicitors have the stated intention of being partisan whereas family mediators do not, yet both are there to assist and to protect clients while attempting to settle issues relating to divorce. Solicitors have a final role of championing the client's case through the formal legal process if necessary, but the Family Law Protocol makes it clear that their role is not the role of an adversary, using whatever tactics they may legally employ in order to obtain the best deal for their client. The Family Law Protocol instead places the responsibility for a conciliatory process on to solicitor for each party. They are required to consider the emotional effects of their correspondence, to remind their client of their duties towards their children and the long-term family interests. They are asked to narrow down the issues to be debated and not to use the children as a way of gaining leverage on ancillary relief and property issues. In fact, their role is to encourage, cajole and if necessary intervene to get clients to behave as responsibly as possible towards their families. This takes the solicitor away from the model of 'hired gun' for the client, towards a conciliator with knowledge of the law and of many previous divorces, as well as an understanding of how to navigate the client through a difficult time. This is an interesting development in the role of the solicitor, influenced, some would say by the emergence of family mediation and the ethics of mediation. The next chapter considers how the training, accreditation and ethics of the professions, when taken together, may influence the professional identity of divorce solicitors and family mediators.

Chapter 7: Conclusions

This study has sought to examine the extent to which assertions made at the time of the passage of the Family Law Bill in the mid 1990s as regards the approach adopted by family law solicitors (assertion of adversarialism) and family mediators (assertion of more constructive consensus-based approaches) discussed in chapter one and to an extent in chapter three, are evident within the messages transmitted by the professional bodies to their members.   As discussed in chapter three, previous research relating to solicitors in England and Wales by Davis, Cretney and Collins, Ingelby and Eekelaar, Maclean and Beinart suggested that there was little evidence of overt and systematic adversarialism by solicitors undertaking divorce work. Little observational research has been undertaken in England and Wales in relation to family mediation sessions, although research by Roberts, Davis *et al.* and Dingwall has been instructive as regards the complex relationship between family mediator and clients, indicating that the publicly discussed tag of 'consensus-based approach' may mask the range of facilitative and evaluative approaches to family mediation. This in turn has an impact on whether family mediation is genuinely consensus-based and facilitative or rather more interventionist and directive. It is clear that the assertions made in the press and, in some instances in the parliamentary debates, were at best oversimplified and possibly also misleading.

This research has not examined the individual work of family law solicitors and family mediators to examine whether their professional approach tends towards an adversarial or consensus model. Instead, it has been a macro rather than a micro study of the influences that the professional bodies may have on their members via their training, accreditation, codes of conduct and best practice requirements. Chapters four, five and six chapters have considered the messages sent by both professional bodies in detail. The tables in these previous three chapters provide summaries of the detailed material that has led to the construction of the categories, whereas this chapter considers the final theory that has developed through the links between those categories.[365]   This final chapter seeks to discover whether the categories developed in this study may be synthesised into a theory that explains the messages that the professional bodies transmit to their members about approach and identity.[366] This is referred to as the 'core theory' when a grounded theory method is employed, as explained in chapter two. The findings from the review of training, accreditation, codes of conduct and best practice statements will be briefly set out in this introduction, followed by a table that displays all the categories together by professional grouping. The main body of the chapter integrates these categories and explains the unified core theory before providing some final conclusions.

---

[365] See chapter two and in particular 2.1 for a discussion of grounded theory method.

[366] For a discussion of identity in a professional capacity see Skeggs, B. *Formations of Class and Gender; Becoming Respectable* (London, Thousand Oaks. New Delhi: Sage Publications, 1997) and Sommerlad, H. 'Researching and Theorising the Processes of Professional Identity Formation' (2007) Vol. 34 No. 2 *Journal of Law and Society* 190.

7.1 Summary of Categories

As explained in chapter four, the training for would-be solicitors appears to broaden and deepen students' legal knowledge and to provide and develop the skills they need in order to be able to use substantive knowledge.[367] Skills development also focuses on interpersonal skills to enhance the solicitor-client relationship, although there is no overt skills training in how to assist a client towards making decisions that lead to giving appropriately advised instructions to the solicitor.[368] This does not appear to represent the reality of family legal practice as discussed in chapter three, which has found that solicitors try to steer their clients towards appropriate settlements and to raise or lower their expectations, while taking into account the needs of any dependants such as children.[369] The lack of negotiation skills training (in formal training courses), and the inclusion of advocacy and litigation skills provides some evidence for the proposition that solicitors are trained to practice in the shadow of litigation, even if they do not regularly take cases on to court.

Family mediator training, on the other hand, appears to reinforce, and if necessary inculcate, key values and principles within students. It is values and skills-based training rather than a knowledge-based one. [370] Facilitation skills are the key to assist clients in reaching their own decisions; however, there is no normative structure within which clients should reach an appropriate agreement for UK College family mediators. Impartiality is emphasised. There is evidence within the professional documentation to support the proposition that family mediators adopt a consensus-based approach to practice, however, the documentation is vague, particularly for UK College family mediators, about when a mediator must intervene to prevent a *prima facie* consensual settlement that is manifestly unfair for one of the parties or for the children. This goes to the heart of the distinction between information giving and advising, which is one of the major distinctions between family mediation and solicitor approaches to divorce.

The theoretical categories from chapter four may be reduced to the following labels. Some of the categories overlap, which reinforces the point of saturation in the grounded theory process.

- **Potential ability followed by benchmarked level of competence in law and skills** (solicitor); **solicitor qualification & inclination to mediate** (Law Society family mediator); **appropriate family mediator beliefs & values** (UK College family mediator).

- **Active partisan problem-solver** (solicitor); **actively informed consensus solution-facilitator** (Law Society family mediator); **active consensus solution-facilitator** (UK College family mediator).

---

[367] See chapter four and in particular sections 4.5 and 4.6.

[368] This is set out in table 4.2 and following.

[369] See in particular section 3.5.

[370] See chapter 4 and in particular sections 4.5 & 4.6.

- Partisan, protector & problem-solver (solicitor); actively impartial non-directive facilitator (Law Society family mediator); passively impartial & fair facilitator (UK College family mediator).

- *The* framework or the legal back-stop (solicitor and Law Society family mediator); or one possible framework (UK College family mediator).

- A legally knowledgeable, informed, problem-solving, communicator with business & financial acumen (solicitor); a family law expert, competent, fair, legally acceptable consensual solution-facilitator (solicitor family mediator); a competent, fair, impartial, consensual solution-facilitator (UK College family mediator).

As set out in chapter five, the professional bodies exercise continued control of their membership. The accreditation requirements set by the Law Society and the UK College reflect their view of their role. The Law Society appears to regard its role as a gate-keeper, a body to ensure that those who wish to receive the status of full member, regardless of whether they wish to be a solicitor or a Law Society mediator, meet a minimum standard of competence to be assessed in detail against specific outcome-based criteria. Once a professional is admitted to full membership, scrutiny of competence is left to the profession itself – the Law Society does not require further evidence of competence.[371] The exception to this is specialist accreditation to the Family Law Panel (at Member and Advanced Member levels).[372] Those solicitors who wish to attain specialist status must resubmit to assessment every five years, which involves an element of reflective practice. As much of the assessment is knowledge-based, and the law changes at a rapid rate, it could be argued that resubmission to assessment is a necessary condition of continued specialist status and the continued endorsement of the Law Society; although resubmission to assessment is not within usual Law Society practice for non-specialist solicitors. Family Law Panel members are required to have the characteristics of solicitors but also to adopt a conciliatory approach to family law matters, including alternative modes of resolving disputes (if appropriate), which brings their professional approach closer to the approach that has been identified as consensus-based rather than adversarial. Having said that, Family Law Panel members do maintain their partisan stance, but attempt to broker a settlement that they and their clients consider to be appropriate.

The UK College appears to regard its role as a continuing one, more as the supervisor of its members than a gate-keeper. This may reflect the fact that the UK College is of relatively recent inception and it oversees a relatively new profession without a large, established and competitive market.[373] Accreditation requirements for family mediators are set at a relatively low level in some respects – professional experience is measured in hours rather than in days, but again this may reflect the lack of an established market, rather than an unwillingness to set stringent standards. Instead,

---

[371] See chapter 5 and in particular sections 5.3 and 5.4.

[372] See in particular table 5.1 and following 5.1.

[373] For a discussion refer back to Wilensky, H.L. *op. cit.* note 253 in section 4.1; Larson, M. *op. cit.* note 258; Abel, R.L. *op. cit.* note 258.

the UK College compensates for this low experience requirement with ongoing surveillance of members, including peer observation of the family mediator and the need for professional endorsement by a professional practice consultant.[374]

The theoretical categories that have been developed from the accreditation documentation are as follows. Once again, there is some overlap between these categories.

- Pre-admission assessment after long term training & socialisation with no reaccreditation (solicitor); expert professional assessment with periodic reaccreditation with minimum practice requirements (accredited family solicitor); professional oversight & endorsement & minimum mediations undertaken with periodic reaccreditation or renewal (Law Society family mediator and UK College family mediator).

- Extensive pre-admittance experience (solicitor); extensive & continuing specialist experience (Family Law Panel member); some continuing experience (Law Society family mediator); minimal continuing experience (UK College family mediator).

- Continual assessment during training, no post-admittance monitoring (solicitor); benchmarked experience with detailed academic assessment of knowledge (Family Law Panel solicitor); recommendation by other professionals (Law Society family mediator); informed recommendation by family mediators (UK College family mediator).

- Transactional negotiation based practice within a business context (solicitor); in-depth family law knowledge, adherence to reflexive family focused practice with knowledge of mediation (accredited family solicitor); continued assessment against the initial training mediation value-based criteria (Law Society family mediator and UK College family mediator).

- Annual updating & refreshing (solicitor); annual updating & refreshing in specialism (Family Law Panel solicitor); additional family mediation updating & refreshing (Law Society family mediator); reflexive practice with refresher training (UK College family mediator).

As discussed in chapter six, the categories derived from the codes of conduct and best practice requirements indicate the relative importance placed on the role of legal norms within divorce matters by solicitors.[375] This in turn has an impact on the way in which a solicitor advises his or her client on appropriate settlement alternatives, as the solicitor should provide information then advice. To some extent, even family mediators recognise legal norms as a guide to a range of appropriate settlement arrangements. UK College family mediators consider law to be one of a set of normative frameworks that the clients may access to assist them in reaching a decision.[376] The UK College stresses the importance of facilitative approaches to mediation in which it is for the clients to

---

[374] See chapter 5 and in particular table 5.3 and following.

[375] See chapter 6 and in particular table 6.3 and following.

[376] Id.

seek value-laden views – advice from a solicitor or others, rather than for the family mediator to provide those views. The family mediator will provide the legal information that is appropriate to the clients in certain circumstances.

The Law Society code for family mediation adopts a half way approach; law is the final layer of protection. It requires Law Society family mediators to put clients on notice, if they are reaching an agreement that is not one that a court would normally reach in their situation, but leaves the clients free to go ahead with the arrangement after being reminded that they should seek legal advice before finalising the agreement.[377] This provides a degree of protection to the clients as it may mitigate the affects of reaching (or being persuaded to reach) an agreement on the basis of inadequate knowledge of one's legal entitlement, assuming that the Law Society family mediator has a full enough knowledge of the clients' situation to permit her to provide an assessment of divergence of any agreement from the legal standard.

The basis for decision-making is viewed differently by solicitors and family mediators – the former view decision-making in the context of the law (even for Law Society family mediators), the latter view decision-making in the context of consensus whether or not it conforms to legal entitlement. Solicitors have the final role of championing the client's case through the formal legal process if necessary, but the Family Law Protocol makes it clear that their role is not the role of an adversary, using whatever tactics they may legally employ in order to obtain the best deal for their client. Their role is to encourage, cajole and if necessary intervene to get clients to behave as responsibly as possible towards their families. This takes the solicitor away from the model of 'hired gun' for the client, towards a conciliator with knowledge of the law, of many previous divorces and of how to navigate the client through a difficult time. This is an interesting development in the role of the solicitor, influenced, some would say by the emergence of family mediation and the ethics of mediation.

The theoretical categories that have been developed from the codes of conduct and best practice statements area as follows. Once again, there is some overlap between the categories.

- **Partisan protector to the willing and free** (solicitor); **impartial guide to the willing & safeguard to the vulnerable** (Law Society family mediator & UK College family mediator).

- **Solid wall of protection** (solicitor); **protective buffer & legal crash barrier** (Law Society family mediator); **protective buffer** (UK College family mediator).

- **Legal adviser, guide & touchstone** (solicitor); **legal informer & backstop** (Law Society family mediator); **legal awareness raiser & sign poster** (UK College family mediator).

- **Third party issue awareness raiser & guide** (solicitor): **third party guide & facilitator** (Law Society family mediator); **third party guide & expert facilitator** (UK College family mediator).

---

[377] *Id.*

- ■ **Trusted adviser & secret keeper** (solicitor); **Trusted, private facilitator** (Law Society family mediator and UK College family mediator).

Thus far we have considered the categories by issue: training, accreditation and codes of conduct. Distinctions have been drawn between professional groupings, although the categories have not been clearly displayed by professional grouping. The following table places them together for all three types of literature – training, accreditation and codes of conduct and best practice statements by each professional grouping and is followed by an explanation of the core theory.

Table 7.1: Theoretical Categories by Professional Grouping

Solicitor

- Having potential ability followed by benchmarked level of competence in law and skills;
- An active partisan problem-solver;
- A partisan, protector & problem-solver;
- The framework is law;
- A legally knowledgeable, informed, problem-solving, communicator with business & financial acumen;
- Pre admission assessment after long term training and socialisation with no reaccreditation;
- Extensive pre-admittance experience;
- Continual assessment during training, no post-admittance monitoring;
- Transactional negotiation based practice within a business context;
- Annual updating and refreshing;
- Partisan protector to the willing and free;
- A solid wall of protection;
- Legal adviser, guide & touchstone;
- Third party issue awareness raiser and guide;
- Trusted adviser & secret keeper.

Family Panel Solicitor

Distinct from a non-Panel member as follows:
- A family law expert, competent, fair, legally acceptable consensual solution-facilitator;
- Expert professional assessment with periodic reaccreditation with minimum practice requirements;
- Extensive and continuing specialist experience;
- Benchmarked experience with detailed academic assessment of knowledge;
- In-depth family law knowledge, adherence to reflexive family focused practice with knowledge of mediation;
- Annual updating and refreshing in specialism.

Family Mediator Law Society

- Holding a solicitor qualification & inclination to mediate;
- An actively informed consensus solution-facilitator;
- An actively impartial non-directive facilitator;
- The legal back-stop;
- A family law expert, competent, fair, legally acceptable consensual solution-facilitator;
- Professional oversight and endorsement and minimum mediations undertaken with periodic reaccreditation or renewal;
- Some continuing experience;
- Recommendation by other professionals;
- Continued assessment against the initial training value-based criteria;
- Additional family mediation updating and refreshing;
- Impartial guide to the willing and safeguard to the vulnerable;

- Protective buffer and legal crash barrier;
- Legal informer and backstop;
- Third party issue raiser and (possibly) guide and facilitator;
- Trusted, private facilitator.

Family Mediator UK College

- Holding appropriate family mediator beliefs & values;
- An active consensus solution-facilitator;
- A passively impartial & fair facilitator;
- Law one possible framework;
- Knowledgeable and active in relation to child welfare;
- A competent, fair, impartial, consensual solution-facilitator;
- Professional oversight and endorsement, with at least a minimum mediations undertaken with periodic reaccreditation or renewal;
- Minimal continuing experience;
- Informed recommendation by senior family mediators;
- Continued assessment against the initial training's core mediation value-based criteria;
- Reflexive practice with refresher training;
- Impartial guide to the willing and safeguard to the vulnerable;
- Protective buffer;
- Legal awareness raiser and sign poster;
- Third party guide and expert facilitator;
- Trusted, private facilitator.

What do these theoretical categories indicate about what the professional bodies transmit about being a solicitor, an accredited family law solicitor, a Law Society family mediator and a UK College family mediator? The starting point for this study has been the rhetoric surrounding adversarial and consensus based approaches to dispute settlement as regards solicitors and family mediators. Thus far the thesis has focused on adversarialism and consensus as defined by the professions and the socio-legal literature; however, there is a psychological, sociological and criminological literature on adversarialism. This literature links adversarialism and mutualism (a more developed form of consensus based decision-making) to gender and gender traits. The literature links adversarialism to a traditional conceptualisation of the masculine identity[378] and mutualism to a traditional conception of a feminine identity.[379] Naturally, 'masculine' and 'feminine' are highly contested terms. Thornton provides an overview of the difficulties associated with these two. She argues that 'feminine' is a term used to denote a

> cluster of values conventionally ascribed to women, including care, corporeality, emotion, dependence and docility. Some of these terms have negative and disempowering connotations, and are the antithesis of notions of freedom, independence and autonomy. To stress the constructivist meaning of the feminine and to avoid its conflation with biological women, which all too often occurs within legal and other discourses, I used the term "fictive feminine."[380]

The term 'fictive feminine' has some difficulties associated with it, not least the charge of gender essentialism, however, Thornton uses the term as a label for a conception of feminine rather than to describe women, femininity or feminism. It is a short-hand expression of the depiction of the feminine in Western literature. She has labelled conceptions of the masculine with the same tradition as the 'imagined masculine', thus

> ...[C]ontrast the term with the "imagined masculine" which includes a cluster of characteristics likely to be ascribed to (benchmark) men and which carry more positive connotations – such as rationality, objectivity,

---

[378] See for example Karlberg, M. 'The Power of Discourse and the Discourse of Power: Pursuing Peace through Discourse Intervention' (2005) Vol. 10 No. 1 *International Journal of Peace Studies* 1, which discusses the link between adversarialism, conflict, competition and power, which obscure mutualism and its importance. This draws upon 'power as domination' discourse: Machiavelli, Weber, Bourdieu as well as feminist critiques of the 'power as domination model' and the development of a 'power with model' that characterises mutualism: 'Together, mutualistic power relations and adversarial power relations constitute two parallel and mutually exclusive relational categories...' at 9.

[379] Thornton draws upon Gilligan's discussion from *In a Different Voice: Psychological Theory and Women's Development* (Cambridge, Mass.: Harvard University Press, 1982) positing that the reason why feminist lawyers have found work within legal practice so difficult is associated with extreme adversarialism in legal practice. However, Gilligan's theory has been criticised due to concerns of gender essentialism. Thornton, M ' "Otherness" on the Bench: How Merit is Gendered' (2007) Vol. 29 *Sydney Law Review* 391 at 396.

[380] Thornton, M. 'Towards Embodied Justice: Wrestling with Legal Ethics in the Age of the "New Corporatism"' (1999) *Melbourne University Law Review* 28 in IV Femina, Feminine, Feminist.

independence, and strength. Within the Western intellectual traditional, these imagined values of masculinity and femininity have come to be associated with public and private and, in turn, with law and non-law binarisms that are themselves open to question.[381]

Thornton further argues that other values associated with the 'fictive feminine' are 'community, consultation, conciliation, compassion, consideration and care'[382] in contrast to those of the 'imagined masculine' that encompass 'competitiveness, adversarialism, and commitment to a cold and uncompromising vision of justice that extols means-ends rationality.'[383] Consequently, she argues that 'feminine' values are premised on mutualism – co-operation, equality and comparison and masculine are premised on adversarialism – competitiveness, assertion of right, individualism. Interestingly, different strands of feminism have interpreted the challenge of the 'fictive feminine' in different ways – some have sought to capitalise on the caring dimensions of this theory to promote a feminist ethic of care, such as that argued by Gilligan.[384] Others such as MacKinnon have been deeply critical of this approach, as it can be used to elide women with child-rearing and care for men as an inherent biological characteristic.[385] It is important to note that women and men will have aspects of the 'imagined masculine' and the 'fictive feminine' within them, and therefore the charge of essentialism need not derail the theory, as long as they are understood as labels for conceptions rather than labels for women and for men, which relate to dominant gender identity rather than biology.

Adversarialism and mutualism are also conceptions of interaction and decision-making that have different starting points.[386] The literature explains that adversarialism is reliant on autonomy, on objectivity and on the assertion of a right against another's position as well as being outcome focused, whereas mutualism relies on notions of mutual respect, co-operation and inter relationships and mutual trust and development, being process focused.[387] These features have been mirrored

---

[381] Id.

[382] Id.

[383] Id.

[384] See for example Gilligan, C. op. cit. note 378 and Noddings, N. Caring: A Feminine Approach to Ethics and Moral Education (Berkeley, University of California Press, 1984) and Cockburn T. 'Children and the Feminist Ethic of Care' (2005) Vol. 12 No. 1 Childhood 71.

[385] MacKinnon, C. Feminism Unmodified: Discourses on Life and Law (Cambridge, Mass.: Harvard University Press, 1987) at 39 and discussed by Thornton.

[386] For a discussion in a different context see Barak, G. 'A Reciprocal Approach to Peacemaking Criminology: Between Adversarialism and Mutualism' (2005) Vol. 9 No. 2 Theoretical Criminology 131.

[387] Mutualism, feminism and the ethic of care have been linked, as have adversarialism, objectivity and autonomy, which are have identified as masculine traits (see the discussion by Naffine in chapter 3). See further Cockburn T. op. cit. note 383 at 73 who cites the work of Curtin on this point, at 75 citing the work of Plumwood and Gilligan and at 78 citing Code who rejects adversarialism on the grounds that it starts from a point of autonomy and the assertion of right against another, rather than the point of relationship and mutual respect and co-operation.

in the professional and academic literature on the use of law and the use of mediation, although not in such explicit terms, as has been discussed in chapter three. The conclusions in this chapter reintegrate the theory of adversarialism and a weaker form of mutualism (consensus based decision-making) with their gendered conceptions, as the theory underpinning adversarialism and consensus explains the core theory that has emerged from the data. This section will take each of these professional groups in turn and provide an explanation of what the professional bodies' documentation has revealed about professional identity, with reference to the traditional 'masculine' and 'feminine' traits that have been associated with adversarialism and consensus.

7.2 Solicitor (Generalist)

The Law Society of England and Wales transmits the message that a generalist solicitor's identity is more closely associated with the 'imagined masculine' rather than 'fictive feminine' characteristics or traits.[388] A solicitor embodies mastery of a large body of knowledge. A solicitor is emotionally controlled – there is little emphasis on emotional intelligence or on active empathy, instead he is to be distanced and impersonal.[389] The distanced professional stance, in contrast to a more personally involved one, is reinforced by the way in which the solicitor is taught law and critiques and employs law.[390] There is a reliance on a non-empathic skills base

---

[388] For a discussion traditional conceptions of masculinist and feminist traits in a professional context see Collier, R. ' "Nutty Professors", "Men in Suits" and "New Entrepreneurs": Corporeality, Subjectivity and Change in the Law School and Legal Practice' (1998) Vol. 7 *Social and Legal Studies* 27; Webley, L. & Duff. L. 'Women Solicitors as a Barometer for Problems within the Legal Profession – Time to Put Values Before Profits?' (2007) Vol. 34 No. 3 *Journal of Law and Society* 374. For a discussion of the traditional definitions of gender and the difficulty of essentialism see Dowd, N. 'Resisting Essentialism and Hierarchy; A Critique of Work/Family Strategies for Women Lawyers' (2000) Vol. 16 *Harvard Blackletter Law Journal* 815. See further Sturm, S. 'From Gladiators to Problem-Solvers: Connecting Conversations about Women, the Academy and the Legal Profession' (1997) Vol. 4 *Duke Journal of Gender, Law and Policy* 119; Fuchs Epstein, C. *et al.* 'Glass Ceilings and Open Doors: Women's Advancement in the Legal Profession' (1995) Vol. 64 *Fordham Law Review* 291; Menkel-Meadow, C. 'The Comparative Sociology of Women Lawyers: The "Feminisation" of the Legal Profession' (1986) Vol. 24 *Osgoode Hall Law Journal* 987. For a critique in relation to masculinities see Collier, R. 'Reflections on the Relationship between Law and Masculinities; Rethinking the 'Man Question' in Legal Studies' (2003) Vol. 56 *Current Legal Problems* 354. See further for a critique Sommerlad, H. ' "Becoming" a Lawyer. Gender and the Processes of Professional Identity' in Sheehy, E. & McIntyre, S. (eds.) *Calling for Change: Women, Law and the Legal Profession* (Ottawa: University of Ottawa Press, 2006).

[389] Collier, R. 'The Changing University and the (Legal) Academic Career – Rethinking the Relationship between Women, Men and the 'Private Life' of the Law School' (2002) Vol. 22 *Legal Studies* 1 see 3-4 for a discussion of reconceptualising gender and the traditional understanding of the masculine.

[390] See Menkel-Meadow, C. *op. cit.* note 256. See further Menkel-Meadow, C. 'Portia in a Different Voice: Speculations on a Woman's Lawyering Process' (1985) Vol. 1 *Berkeley Women's Law Journal* 39. See further Economides, K. 'Cynical Legal Studies' in Cooper, J. & Trubek, L.G. (eds.) *Educating for Justice: Social Values and Legal Education* (Aldershot: Ashgate Publishing, 1997) 26.

(with the exception of relating skills required in order to secure information needed to formulate advice).[391] The solicitor is considered to be an outcome orientated problem solver. He is potentially adversarial but only when that is what is required in order to attain an appropriate outcome for the client. To achieve this, the solicitor is also firm, but fair, partisan and pragmatic as evidenced by the codes of conduct and best practice statements indicating when a solicitor must insist on certain conditions being met by the client or the client's former spouse or legal representative, if the retainer is not to be terminated by the solicitor. He is also deemed to be financially and business minded.[392] The solicitor is a reflective practitioner (during the training and accreditation stages) as this is required to enhance competence and to retain professional standing. In short, the solicitor is the traditional professional.[393]

7.3 Accredited Family Law Solicitor

The accredited family law solicitor is a step apart from the generalist solicitor although has similar traits. The differences stem from the way in which the family law solicitor relates to the client and the client's family law matter. The accreditation and best practice documentation suggest that an accredited family law solicitor begins her professional life by following the persona of the noble male solicitor but then puts on a thin 'emotionally understanding' cloak over this identity. The cloak obscures but does not obliterate the 'imagined masculine' traits, but instead displays a more 'feminine' identity to the client.[394] An accredited family law solicitor presents as a realistic negotiator. She aims to achieve a fair settlement for the family rather than solely for the client. Decision-making is as consensual as is possible between the solicitors for both clients, but the family law solicitor is also an expectation manager for her own client as there are some inherent value assumptions about what is right (although it is hoped that 'right' and 'legal' dovetail). Consequently, the 'masculine' has not been lost entirely. She is also partisan on the one hand while keeping an eye on the collective unit on the other (the individual should not profit to the real detriment of related others). She should also be able to foresee consequences for non-clients and focus the client on those. The family law solicitor is also

---

[391] Kanter, R. 'Reflections in Women and the Legal Profession: A Sociological Perspective' (1978) Vol. 1 Harvard Women's Law Journal 1. See further Gorman, E. 'Work Uncertainty and the Promotion of Professional Women: The Case of Law Firm Partnership' (2000) Vol. 8 Social Forces 865.

[392] Seron, C. 'Managing Entrepreneurial Legal Services: The Transformation of Small Firm Practice' in Nelson, R.L., Trubek, D. & Solomon, R. (eds.) *Lawyers' Ideals / Lawyers' Practices: Transformation in the American Legal Profession* (Ithaca & London: Cornell University Press, 1992) at 71; Patton, P. 'Women Lawyers, Their Status, Influence, and Retention in the Legal Profession' (2004-5) Vol. 11 *William and Mary Journal of Women and the Law* 173 at 182-3 for a discussion of the sociological literature on entrepreneurialism, the masculine and the feminine..

[393]See McGlynn, C. 'The Business of Equality in the Solicitors' Profession' (2000) Vol. 63 *Modern Law Review* 442 for a discussion of apparent gender neutrality and the masculine in relation to the profession, and further Rhode, D.L. 'The Profession and its Discontents' (2000) Vol. 61 *Ohio State Journal* at 8-9.

[394] For a discussion of gender differences, skills and leadership see Hegelsen, S. *The Female Advantage: Women's Ways of Leadership* (New York: Doubleday, 1990).

emotionally understanding yet sufficiently emotionally distanced in order to retain professionalism.[395] She will also employ a multi-agency approach when necessary, which is consistent with collegial working practices.[396] She should also be able to balance multiple interconnected issues and yet be able to separate these issues when required. She is still fundamentally outcome orientated (with the use of litigation if required), while taking into account the impact of the current process and the long term consequences of the process and the outcome once the solicitor has ceased to act. In sum, the accredited family solicitor is a newly feminised professional who retains the skeleton of her original 'imagined masculine' identity with emotional add-ons, who has a greater overview, but who is also consequently potentially less authoritative, as authority and empathy are often considered to be contradictory.[397]

7.4 Law Society Family Mediator

A Law Society trained family mediator has first been through training as a solicitor and has adopted the identity of the 'imagined masculine' professional. As a family mediator she is required to wear a thick humanising cloak that all but obscures her original identity and allows the family mediator to be an emotionally enlightened negotiation facilitator. The professional body assumes emotional aptitude and an ability to be impartial and facilitative, but it does not require the professional to believe in the values espoused by the family mediation movement. One could speculate that this is because belief in these values runs contrary to a traditionally masculinist view of professionalism that is borne out of Western liberalism.[398] Inclination to mediate is the key rather than a belief in family mediation as a process of transformation and empowerment for the clients. The Law Society recognises that family mediators may need training by way of resocialisation in emotional intelligence (some may say, rather uncharitably, emotional literacy).[399] Family

---

[395] Rhode, D.L. *The Unfinished Agenda: Women and the Legal Profession, The ABA Report on Women in the Profession* (2001) at 6 discusses her research finding that feminine characteristics and the characteristics expected of successful solicitors – assertiveness and competitiveness are often perceived to be in contradiction although these characteristics are more associated with commercial rather than family law practice. For a discussion of the changing face of masculinity and the profession see Collier, R. (2002) *op. cit.* note 388.

[396] See Webley, L. & Duff, L. *op. cit.* note 387 and Hegelsen, S. *op. cit.* note 393.

[397] For a discussion of cultural capital and how these traits are viewed within the profession see Sommerlad, H. & Sanderson, P. *Gender Choice and Commitment: Women Solicitors in England and Wales and the Struggle for Equal Status* (Aldershot: Ashgate Publishing, 1998). See further Kanter, R. *op. cit.* note 390. See Collier, R. (2002) *op. cit.* note 388 at 10 'assessment of women against a normative "ideal" employee, a figure understood simultaneously (and somewhat paradoxically) to be both distinctively gendered (as male/ masculine: assertive, rational, competent, unemotional and so on); and, equally, to be somehow gender-neutral in terms of the commitment and dependencies which are seen as "outwith" the field of paid employment.'.

[398] See Thornton's discussion *op. cit.* note 379.

[399] This may be what the profession considers to be necessary, whereas many studies in relation to women solicitors suggest that many women (and perhaps also men) have these skills and traits already although feel forced to repress them in a working environment, if they wish to advance within the profession at the rate associated with those solicitors who display

mediation is viewed as a process rather than a profession – process training is provided as well as the theoretical underpinning, but it is taught in a way that requires the solicitor to understand decision-making in an emotional context on the assumption that this is distinct from rational decision-making.[400] The Law Society family mediator never loses her solicitor identity and so is trained to be ever vigilant that the cloak may slip and reveal this to her mediation clients. This cloak assists with neutrality and the professional must constantly remind herself of the need to be non-partisan; the problem-solver must remember to be a facilitator. This raises an interesting paradox, as rationality and impartiality are generally associated with the 'imagined masculine' even though empathy and facilitation are more closely associated with the 'fictive feminine'.[401]

However, there are circumstances under which the Law Society family mediator is required to remove the cloak – when power imbalances between the clients are too great, or where the agreement that is being reached would offend against fundamental legal principles aimed at the protection of the clients. The Law Society family mediator thus always retains the solicitor identity underneath, including the solicitor's legal normative framework.

7.5 UK College Family Mediator

The UK College trained family mediator must have some of the markers of the family mediator identity before being permitted to undertake training. She must then adopt the full identity and maintain it with active adherence to a family mediator's beliefs and values. She is a true facilitator and in some circumstances may also be a transformer – the person who shows her clients how to change the way in which they interact and negotiate between themselves and with others. She is inherently impartial, unlike a Law Society trained family mediator who must remind herself of the need to be impartial when acting as a family mediator. She is provided with the knowledge that is necessary to be an effective family mediator, but all knowledge is of equal importance, for example, legal knowledge is given similar weight to the knowledge related to how to involve children in mediation sessions. Knowledge transmission is also very limited, although present. A UK College family mediator remains reflective as regards her professional development, although the UK College does not warn family mediators to beware of the influence of their previous professional identity – belief in family mediation may be so strong that it overwrites previous identities. This is reinforced through professional practice consultancy through which experienced family mediators oversee, assist and in part supervise other family mediators in their professional development. This is in-keeping with feminised professions, in which there is often greater supervision of members as, it has been argued, the greater the feminisation the more likelihood that members are viewed as less authoritative and thus in need of greater supervision.[402] The UK

---

more 'masculinist' traits. See for a discussion Webley, L. & Duff, L. *op. cit.* note 387. See further Hegelsen, S. *op. cit.* note 393.

[400] Collier, R. (2002) *op. cit.* note 388.

[401] For a discussion see Webley, L. & Duff, L. *op. cit.* note 387.

[402] Thornton, M. *Dissonance and Distrust – Women and the Legal Profession* (Oxford: Oxford

College family mediator is flexible, yet process controlling, empathic, and transformative and yet firm in the face of inappropriate behaviour. She encourages consensual decision-making, and she may suggest that her clients gain outside advice before they reach a final agreement – there is a deferral to outside authority on the one hand, while preserving the identity of the family mediation profession, which encompasses collegiality and loyalty. She should aim as far as possible to maintain a relative power balance between the separating couple, but there are virtually no circumstances under which she should challenge the clients' agreement unless the safety of one of the clients or a child is in danger, as there is no single normative framework against which an agreement is to be judged. The clients are the guardians of the norms, which are personal to them, and the family mediator is the guardian of the process and its integrity. Thus, the UK College family mediator embodies many of the characteristics associated with the 'fictive feminine' and is the most closely associated with this conception than the other professional groupings.

7.6 Final Conclusions

Returning to the original title of this thesis, "*Adversarialism and consensus? The messages professional bodies transmit about appropriate professional approach to solicitors and family mediators undertaking divorce matters*": to what extent is there evidence of adversarialism or consensus in the documentation that has been reviewed and what messages do the professional bodies send to their members? There is little evidence of adversarialism in the legal professional documentation, although partisanship is evident to a greater or lesser extent (in family law seemingly lesser than in non-family law areas). The move is towards consensual decision-making between solicitors rather than between clients, although that is unsurprising as decision-making between clients solely would normally be conducted without the need for retained solicitors. However, consensual decision-making is retained as the more desirable approach, with litigation being held in reserve if that fails – there is no evidence that litigation is championed, although negotiation is less evident in the context of generalist solicitors than for accredited family law solicitors.

Solicitors are expected to remain emotionally distanced and yet accredited family law solicitors are also required to be emotionally understanding. A solicitor never ceases to be a solicitor, but a family law solicitor does display her emotional credentials to empathise with her client and to assist her in reaching an agreement that works for the family. The Law Society family mediator makes regular use of her emotional skills as part of her identity as an impartial, consensus driven facilitator, however, she must discard her new identity and revert to her former identity of solicitor in the exceptional circumstance that one of the clients is on the verge of being severely prejudiced in legal terms or is in physical or emotional danger. The UK College documentation provides no evidence of adversarialism and no real evidence of obvious partisanship. The emphasis is very firmly placed on consensual decision-making. A UK College trained family mediator believes in the mediation project, eschews former training or professional identity and lives and practises as an emotionally intelligent, emotionally conversant impartial facilitator, who works in a

---

University Press, 1996). See further Thornton, M. *op. cit.* note 379 at 34 (in the web based version).

normative vacuum. She has the duty to protect decision-makers and the process (against violence, extreme power imbalance) but thereafter the process should yield a fair settlement, as any settlement is fair if not coerced.

Much of the public discussion of the role of solicitors (and in particular family law specialists) in the context of divorce matters is at odds with the messages transmitted by the Law Society about the professional identity and approach that their members should adopt.[403] In relation to professional body cues, family law practice is far more conciliatory than the non-academic literature would suggest. Family law solicitors are encouraged to adopt a conciliatory, multi-agency approach and to manage their client's expectations so as to develop a long term workable outcome for the family, rather than a short-term 'win' for the client. However, there are similarities between an extreme interpretation of a traditional generalist solicitor as partisan and adversary, even if the professional identity and approach of an accredited family law solicitor is virtually absent from the literature in all but the large scale empirical studies undertaken by academics such as Davis *et al.*, Eekelaar, Maclean and Beinhart and Ingelby.[404]

The generalist solicitor who undertakes family law work but has not received academic family law training, or family law exposure at the vocational stage of training, is heavily reliant on the messages sent to him by his colleagues when he was a trainee and young solicitor.[405] Generalist training remains emotionally distant; negotiation training is no longer a compulsory part of the LPC and PSC courses whereas litigation training is part of the core. There is little evidence in the empirical studies discussed in chapter three that divorce solicitors adopt an adversarial approach to family law practice. This may be in spite of, rather than because of, the messages that the Law Society transmits. It is, perhaps, understandable that the stereotype of the adversarial solicitor persists on this basis. Depictions of family mediators are more analogous to the messages transmitted by the professional bodies – the Law Society and the UK College; even if Dingwall suggests that family mediators may be more directive and interventionist than facilitative and impartial.[406] This is difficult to verify as few studies have observed family mediations and family mediators in England and Wales. There appears to be congruence between family mediator identity and the messages that professional bodies transmit about family mediator identity. One may speculate about why this may be the case – perhaps the relative youth and rapid expansion of the family mediation profession and the context in which it has developed.

What have we learned as a result of this study? It appears that the Law Society promotes the traditional professional, distanced identity that prizes problem-solving

---

[403] See chapter 1 and in particular sections 1.1 and 1.2.

[404] See chapter 3 and in particular section 3.5.

[405] See Boon, A. 'From Public Service to Service Industry: The Impact of Socialisation and Work on the Motivation and Values of Lawyers' (2005) Vol. 32 No. 3 *International Journal of the Legal Profession* 229.

[406] Dingwall, R. & Greatbatch, D. 'Behind Closed Doors. A Preliminary Report on Mediator/Client Interaction in England' (1991) Vol. 29 No. 3 *Family Court Review* 291.

and emotional distance through its generalist training, accreditation requirements and code of conduct. However, as family mediation has attracted more attention, so has the role of empathy and the skills of facilitation. The Law Society has attempted subtly to reengineer the professional identity of family law solicitors to become more feminised, more consensus orientated and less adversarial, even if adversarialism is less evident within the training, accreditation and codes of conduct for all solicitors than the literature would suggest. As the Law Society has embraced more traditionally feminised characteristics within the professional project, it has also felt the need to monitor accredited family solicitor expertise on a periodic basis. This may be purely a function of the expert status accorded to accredited family solicitors, rather than the concern to monitor feminised professionals more closely than the more usual distanced professional, although this is unclear.[407] The Law Society family mediator is a further extension of the feminised professional, rather than a believer in the family mediation project as is required by the UK College of its family mediators. The UK College's documentation appears to suggest an apparent obliteration of a family mediators' previous professional identity. It selects for and further inculcates the belief in family mediation values, even though family mediation is viewed by the Law Society as a process-orientated profession rather than a substantive one.

The messages transmitted by the Law Society to its solicitors have yet to filter down to the public, even if they have been evidenced within the profession by a number of empirical studies that have examined solicitors and family solicitors in some detail. The messages transmitted by the UK College to family mediators have also been transmitted to the public and have been picked up in the media, in political debates and in the academic literature. As little large scale observational empirical research has been undertaken on family mediation and on family mediation sessions in this country, it is difficult to know whether the messages sent by the professional body are shared and embraced by its professionals. That is an investigation for further study.

The Law Society appears to have adopted the 'feminine' traits and approaches that it considers to be constructive in the family law arena, and the UK College has embraced many of them whole-heartedly. Indeed, the Law Society had already begun to signal its support for these values even at the time when its members were being publicly chastised for their perceived adversarialism. It is clear that both professional bodies in a family context appear to be converging on a feminised conception of professional, which shuns latent adversarialism and prizes co-operation and settlement for the good of children and long term parenting arrangements. There may be fewer differences between family law solicitors and family mediators with respect to their professional approach than between generalist solicitors and family mediators, but the distinction between a legal normative framework for family law solicitors and no clear normative framework for family mediators persists.

This research has concentrated on the messages transmitted by the professional bodies in their conduct rules, admissions regime and training programmes in order to see how these messages compare with the existing literature on family law, family mediators and family lawyer mediators. It uses a grounded theory approach to bring

---

[407] See in particular tables 5.3 and 5.4 and the following text on this point.

the complexity of conduct, admissions and training into a set of clear themes which in themselves provide descriptors of professional intention at a conscious level. The research does not assess how closely the behaviour of the professionals themselves measures up to these norms or how the themes discovered relate to professional work and approach. Further research of an empirical nature will be needed to test these issues.

In a wider context this research adds a further methodology to the spectrum of methods employed to assess professional self determination and self regulation. It provides some new insights into comparisons between cognate occupations, and suggests the potential for such research in other professional areas of congruity. Within its own context it lays to rest some incorrect assumptions about family lawyer mediators which have continued since the early 1990s and thematically describes the approaches of such professionals in a new way.

Bibliography

Books & Published Research Reports

Abbot, A. *The System of Professions: An Essay on the Division of Expert Labour* (Chicago, Ill.: University of Chicago Press, 1988).

Abel, R.L. *American Lawyers* (Oxford: Oxford University Press, 1989).

Boulle, L. & Nesic, M. *Mediation Principles Process Practice* (London: Butterworths, 2001).

Burgess, R. *In the Field: An Introduction to Field Research* 4th Ed. (London: George Allen and Unwin, 1990).

Burton, F. Martin Clement, N., Standley, K. & Williams, C. *Teaching and Learning Manuals: Teaching Family Law* (Warwick: National Centre for Legal Education, 1999).

Coady, M. & Bloch, S. (eds.) *Codes of Ethics and the Professions* (Melbourne: Melbourne University Press, 1996).

Cockett, M. & Tripp, J. *The Exeter Family Study: Family Breakdown and Its Impact On Children* (Exeter: Exeter University Press, 1994).

Cooper, J. & Trubek, L.G. (eds.) *Educating for Justice: Social Values and Legal Education* (Aldershot: Ashgate Publishing, 1997).

Cownie, F. (ed.) *The Law School* (Aldershot: Ashgate Publishing, 1999).

Davis, G. *et al. Monitoring Publicly Funded Family Mediation: Final Report to the Legal Services Commission* (Legal Services Commission, 2000).

Davis, G. *Partisans and Mediators: The Resolution of Divorce Disputes* (Oxford: Clarendon Press, 1988).

Davis, G., Cretney, S.M. & Collins, J. *Simple Quarrels: Negotiations and Adjudication in Divorce* (New York: Oxford University Press, 1994).

Davis, G. & Roberts, M. *Access to Agreement* (Milton Keynes: Open University Press, 1988).

Davis, M., Davis, G. & Webb, J *Promoting Mediation: Report of a Study of Bristol Law Society's Mediation Scheme in its Preliminary Phase.* Research Study No. 21 (London: The Law Society, 1996).

Day Sclater, S. & Piper, C. (eds.) *Undercurrents of Divorce* (Aldershot: Dartmouth Press, 1999).

Denzin, N.K. & Lincoln, Y.S. (eds.) *Handbook of Qualitative Research* 2nd Ed. (Thousand Oaks, Ca: Sage Publishing, 2000).

Dingwall, R. & Eekelaar, J. (eds.) *Divorce Mediation and the Legal Process* (Oxford: Clarendon Press, 1988).

Durkheim, E. *Professional Ethics and Civic Morals* Brookfield, C. (*trans.*) (London: Routledge & Keagan Paul, 1957).

Economides, K. & Smallcombe, J. *Preparatory Skills Training for Trainee Solicitors* Law Society Research Study No. 7 (London: The Law Society, 1991).

Eekelaar, J., Maclean, M. & Beinart, S. *Family Lawyers: The Divorce Work of Solicitors* (Oxford: Hart Publishing, 2000).

Fisher, R. & Ury, W. *Getting to Yes: Negotiating Agreement without Giving in, Better Business Guides* 2nd Ed. (London: Hutchinson, 1982).

Folberg, J. & Milne, A. *Divorce Mediation, Theory and Practice* (New York: The Guildford Press, 1988).

Friedson, E. *Professionalism Reborn. Theory, Prophecy and Policy* (Cambridge: Polity Press, 1994).

Galanter, M. & Palay, T. *Tournament of Lawyers: The Growth and Transformation of the Big Law Firm* (Chicago, Ill.: University of Chicago Press, 1991).

Genn, H. *Paths to Justice: What Do People Think About Going To Law?* (Oxford: Hart Publishing, 1999).

Genn, H. *Hard Bargaining* (Oxford: Oxford University Press, 1987).

Gilligan, C. *In a Different Voice; Psychological Theory and Women's Development* (Cambridge, Mass.: Harvard University Press, 1982).

Glaser, B.G. *Basics of Grounded Theory Analysis: Emergence vs. Forcing* (Mill Valley, California: Sociology Press, 1992).

Glaser, B. & Strauss, A. *The Discovery of Grounded Theory: Strategies for Qualitative Research* (Chicago, Ill.: Aldine, 1967).

Hamnett, I. (ed.) Social Anthropology and Law (London: Academic Press 1977).

Hart, N. *When Marriage Ends: A Study in Status Passage* (London: Tavistock, 1976).

Haynes, J. *The Fundamentals of Family Mediation* (New York: Albany State University and New York Press, 1994).

Head, A., Head, M. & England, H. *Privately Funded Work in Family Mediation: Calculating the Volume of Privately Funded Family Mediation Cases:* A report prepared for the UK College of Family Mediators (London: UKCFM, December 2006).

Hegelsen, S. *The Female Advantage: Women's Ways of Leadership* (New York: Doubleday, 1990).

Hoggett H., Pearl D., Cooke E. & Bates P. *The Family, Law and Society Cases and Materials* 4th Ed. (London, Edinburgh, Dublin: Butterworths, 1996).

Holder, J. & O'Cinneide, C. (eds.) *Current Legal Problems 2005* (Oxford: Oxford University Press, 2006).

Laster, K. *Law as Culture* 2nd Ed. (Sydney: The Federation Press, 2001).

Laster, K. and Taylor, V.L. *Interpreters and the Legal System* (Sydney: The Federation Press, 1994).

Kennedy, D. (ed.) *Legal Education and the Reproduction of Hierarchy A Polemic Against the System: A Critical Edition* (New York: New York University Press, 2004).

Larson, M. *The Rise of Professionalism: A Sociological Analysis* (Berkeley: University of California Press, 1977)

Lewis, P. *Assumptions about Lawyers in Policy Statements: A Survey of Relevant Research* No. 1/2000 (London: The Lord Chancellor's Department, 2000).

Maclean, M. (ed.) *Making Law for Families* (Oxford: Hart Publishing, 2000).

Mackie, K. *A Handbook on Dispute Resolution: ADR in Action* (London: Routledge, 1991).

MacKinnon, C. *Feminism Unmodified: Discourses on Life and Law* (Cambridge, Mass.: Harvard University Press, 1987).

Maughan C. & Webb, J. *Lawyering Skills and the Legal Process* 2nd Ed. (Cambridge, Mass.: Cambridge University Press, 2005).

May, T *Social Research: Issues, Methods and Practices* 2nd Ed. (Buckingham: Open University Press, 2001).

Milne A., & Folberg, J. (eds.) *Divorce Mediation: Theory and Practice* (New York: Guildford Press, 1988).

Moorhead, R., Sherr, A. & Rogers, S. *Willing Blindness? OSS Complaints Handling Procedures, A Report to the Office for the Supervision of Solicitors* (London: Law Society, 1999).

Mulcahy, L. & Summerfield, L. *Keeping it in the Community: The Use of Mediation in Neighbour Disputes* (Norwich: Stationery Office, 2001).

Nelson, R.L., Trubek, D. & Solomon, R. (eds.) *Lawyers' Ideals / Lawyers' Practices: Transformation in the American Legal Profession* (Ithaca & London: Cornell University Press, 1992).

Noddings, N. *Caring: A Feminine Approach to Ethics and Moral Education* (Berkeley: University of California Press, 1984).

O'Donovan, K. *Family Law Matters* (London: Pluto Press, 1993).

Parker, S. & Sampford, C. (eds.) *Legal Ethics and Legal Practice: Contemporary Issues* (Oxford: Clarendon Press, 1995).

Parkinson, L. *Conciliation in Separation and Divorce* (London: Croom Helm, 1986).

Punch, K.F. *Introduction to Social Research* (London: Sage Publications Ltd, 1998).

Rhode, D.L. *The Unfinished Agenda: Women and the Legal Profession, The ABA Report on Women in the Profession* (American Bar Association: 2001).

Roberts, M. *Mediation in Family Disputes, Principles of Practice* 2nd Ed. (Aldershot: Arena, 1997).

Roberts, S.A. *Order and Dispute: An Introduction to Legal Anthropology* (Harmondsworth; Penguin, 1979).

Ross H.L. *Settled Out Of Court: The Social Process of Insurance Claims* (Chicago, Ill.: Aldine, 1970).

Sapsford R. & Jupp V. (eds.) *Data Collection and Analysis* (London: Sage Publications Ltd 1996).

Sarat, A. & Felstiner, W.L.F. *Divorce Lawyers and Their Clients: Power and Meaning in the Legal Process* (New York, Oxford: Oxford University Press, 1995).

Scott, J. *A Matter of Record: Documentary Sources in Social Research* (Cambridge: Polity Press, 1990).

Seneviratne, M. *The Legal Profession: Regulation and the Consumer* (London: Sweet and Maxwell, 1999).

Sheehy, E. & McIntyre S. (eds.) *Calling for Change: Women, Law and the Legal Profession* (Ottawa: Ottawa University Press, 2006).

Sherr, A., Lewis-Ruttley, H. and Webley, L. *A Training Skills Analysis for Family Lawyers* (London: Institute of Advanced Legal Studies, 1995).

Simpson, B. *Being There: Fathers after Divorce* (University of Newcastle Upon Tyne: Relate Centre For Family Studies, 1995).

Skeggs, B. *Formations of Class and Gender: Becoming Respectable* (London, Thousand Oaks, New Delhi: Sage Publications, 1997).

Sommerlad, H. & Sanderson, P. *Gender Choice and Commitment: Women Solicitors in England and Wales and the Struggle for Equal Status* (Aldershot: Ashgate Publishing, 1998).

Strauss, A. & Corbin, J. *Basics of Qualitative Research: Techniques and Procedures for Developing Grounded Theory* 2nd Ed. (Thousand Oaks, London, New Delhi: Sage Publications, 1998).

Test Design Project *Performance-Based Assessment: A Methodology, for Use in Selecting, Training and Evaluating Mediators* (US: National Institute for Dispute Resolution, 1995).

The Faculty of Law King's College *The Centenary of Family Law Collection of Essays* (London: Kings College of London, 1957).

Thornton, M. *Dissonance and Distrust – Women and the Legal Profession* (Oxford: Oxford University Press, 1996).

Tillet, G. *Resolving Conflict – A Practical Approach* 2nd Ed. (Sydney: Sydney University Press, 1999).

UK College of Family Mediators Directory & Handbook 1997-1998 (Glasgow, FT Law and Tax 1997).

Wallerstein, J.S. & Kelly, J.B. *Surviving the Break-Up: How Children and Parents Cope With Divorce* (London: Grant-McIntyre, 1980).

Weber, M. *The Theory of Social and Economic Organisation* (New York: The Free Press, 1964).

Webley, L.C. *A Review of the Literature on Family Mediation in England and Wales, France, Ireland, Scotland and the United States* (London: Lord Chancellor's Advisory Committee on Legal Education and Conduct, 1998).

Journal Articles & Papers

Abel, R.L., 'Why Does the ABA promulgate Ethical Rules?' (1981) Vol. 59 *Texas Law Review* 639.

Abel, R.L. 'Taking Professionalism Seriously' (1989) *Annual Survey of American Law* 41.

Abel, R.L. 'The Rise of Professionalism' (1979) Vol. 6 *British Journal of Law and Society* 82.

Astor, H. 'Mediator Neutrality: Making Sense of Theory and Practice' (2007) Vol. 16 *Social and Legal Studies* 221.

Barak, G. 'A Reciprocal Approach to Peacemaking Criminology: Between Adversarialism and Mutualism' (2005) Vol. 9 *Theoretical Criminology* 131.

Barrett, R. 'Mediator Certification: Should California Enact Legislation?' (1996) Vol. 30 *University of San Francisco Law Review* 617.

Barton, C. & Bissett-Johnson, A. 'The Declining Number of Ancillary Financial Relief Orders' (2000) *Family Law* 94.

Boon, A. 'From Public Service to Service Industry: The Impact of Socialisation and Work on the Motivation and Values of Lawyers' (2005) Vol. 12 No. 2 *International Journal of the Legal Profession* 229.

Boon, A., Webb, J. and Flood, J. 'Postmodern Professions? The Fragmentation of Legal Education and the Legal Profession' (2005) Vol. 32 No. 3 *Journal of Law and Society* 473.

Booth, M. 'The UK College of Family Mediators - An Update' (1997) Vol. 6 No. 2 *Family Mediation* 6.

Bowles, J. 'The Structure of the Legal Profession in England and Wales' (1994) Vol. 10 No. 1 *Oxford Review of Economic Policy* 18.

Brian, P.E. 'Reclaiming Professionalism: The Lawyers Role in Divorce Mediation' (1994) Vol. 28 *Family Law Quarterly* 193.

Caldwell, P.S. 'The Training of Arbitrators and Quality Assurance of Arbitration' (1992) Vol. 9 No. 3 *Journal of International Arbitration* 99.

Carey, T.V. 'Credentialing for Mediators-To Be or Not to Be?' (1996) Vol. 30 *University of San Francisco Law Review* 635.

Casper, J.D. 'Did You Have a Lawyer When You Went to Court? No, I Had a Public Defender' (1971) 7 *Yale Review of Law & Social Action* 4.

Cavenagh, P., Dewberry, C. & Jones, P. 'Becoming Professional; When and How Does it Start? A Comparative Study of First-Year Medical and Law Students in the UK.' (2000) Vol. 34 *Medical Education* 897.

Cockburn, T. 'Children and the Feminist Ethic of Care' (2005) Vol. 12 *Childhood* 71.

Collier, R. 'Reflections on the Relationship Between Law and Masculinities: Rethinking the "Man Question" in Legal Studies' (2003) Vol. 56 *Current Legal Problems* 345.

Collier, R. 'The Changing University and the (Legal) Academic Career – Rethinking the Relationship between Women, Men and the 'Private Life' of the Law School' (2002) Vol. 22 *Legal Studies* 1.

Collier, R. '"Nutty Professors", "Men in Suits" and "New Entrepreneurs": Corporeality, Subjectivity and Change in the Law School and Legal Practice' (1998) Vol. 7 *Social and Legal Studies* 27.

Cotterrel, R. 'Why Must Legal Ideas be Interpreted Sociologically?' (1998) Vol. 25 No. 2 *Journal of Law and Society* 171.

Cramton, R. 'The Ordinary Religion of the Law School Classroom' (1978) Vol. 29 *Journal of Legal Education* 247.

Davis, G., Macleod, A. & Murch, M. 'Undefended Divorce: Should Section 41 of the Matrimonial Causes Act 1983 be Repealed?' (1983) Vol. 6 No. 2 *Modern Law Review* 121.

Davis, G., and Roberts, M. 'Mediation and the Battle of the Sexes' (1989) *Family Law* 306.

Day Sclater, S. 'A Critical Approach to the White Paper on Divorce Reform' (1995) Vol. 4 *Web Journal of Current Legal Issues*.

Dingwall, R. 'Professions and Social Order in a Global Society.' (1999) Vol. 9 *International Review of Sociology* 131.

Dingwall, R. 'Family Mediation Researchers and Practitioners in the Shadow of the Green Paper: A Rejoinder to Marian Roberts' (1995) Vol. 17 No. 2 *Journal of Social Welfare Law* 199.

Dingwall, R. & Greatbatch, D. 'Behind Closed Doors. A Preliminary Report on Mediator/Client Interaction in England' (1991) Vol. 29 No. 3 *Family Court Review* 291.

Dingwall, R. & Fenn, P. "A Respectable Profession'? Sociological and Economic Perspectives on the Regulation of Professional Services' (1987) Vol. 7 *International Review of Law and Economics* 51.

Donohue, W.A., Drake, L. & Roberto, A.J. 'Mediator Issue Intervention Strategies: A Replication and Some Conclusions' (1994) Vol. 11 *Mediation Quarterly* 261.

Douglas, G. & Murch, M. 'Taking Account of Children's Needs in Divorce: A Study of Family Solicitors' Responses to New Policy and Practice Initiatives' (2002) Vol. 14 No. 1 *Child and Family Law Quarterly* 57.

Dowd, N. 'Resisting Essentialism and Hierarchy; A Critique of Work/Family Strategies for Women Lawyers' (2000) Vol. 16 *Harvard Blackletter Law Journal* 815.

Duncan, N. 'The Skills of Learning: Implications of the ACLEC First Report for Teaching Skills on Undergraduate Law Courses' (1997) Vol. 5 *Web Journal Current Legal Issues.*

Economides, K. Nicholson, D. & Webb, J. 'Ethics in Practice: Welcome!' (1998) Vol. 1 No. 1 *Legal Ethics.* 19.

Elston, E., Fuller, J. & Murch, M. 'Judicial Hearings of Undefended Divorce Petitions' (1975) Vol. 38 *Modern Law Review* 609.

Fisher, T. 'Training For Family Mediation' (1995) *Family Law* 571.

Fiss, O.M. 'Against Settlement' (1984) Vol. 93 *Yale Law Journal* 1073.

Finlay, H.A. 'Family Mediation and the Adversary Process' (1993) Vol. 7 *Australian Journal of Family Law* 63.

Folberg, J. 'A Mediation Overview: History and Dimensions of Practice' (1983) *Mediation Quarterly* 3.

Foster, N.J. & Kelly, J.B. 'Divorce Mediators; Who Should be Certified?' (1996) Vol. 30 *University of San Francisco Law Review* 667.

Friedman, L.M. 'The Law and Society Movement' (1986) Vol. 38 *Stanford Law Review* 763.

Friedman, G.H. & Silberman, A.D. 'A Useful Tool for Evaluating Potential Mediators' (1993) *Negotiation Journal* 321.

Fritze-Shanks, A. 'Some Models of Professional Behaviour for Family Lawyers and an Examination of the Strengths and Weaknesses of those Models' (1989) Vol. 3 *Australian Journal of Family Law* 202.

Fuchs Epstein, C. *et al.* 'Glass Ceilings and Open Doors: Women's Advancement in thee Legal Profession' (1995) Vol. 64 *Fordham Law Review* 291.

Galanter, M. 'World Of Deals: Using Negotiation To Talk About Legal Process' (1984) Vol. 34 *Journal of Legal Education* 368.

Glaser, B.G. 'Constructivist Grounded Theory?' (2002) Vol. 3 No. 3 *Qualitative Sozialforschung/Forum: Qualitative Social Research* www.qualitative-research.net/fqs/fqs-eng.htm.

Gorman, E. 'Work Uncertainty and the Promotion of Professional Women: The Case of Law Firm Partnership' (2000) Vol. 8 *Social Forces* 865.

Greatbatch, D. & Dingwall, R. 'Selective Facilitation Some Observations on a Strategy used by Divorce Mediators' (1989) Vol. 23 *Law and Society Review* 613.

Grillo, T. 'The Mediation Alternative: Process Dangers for Women' (1991) 100 *Yale Law Journal* 1545.

Habenstein, R.W. 'Critique of "Professions" as a Sociological Category' (1963) Vol. 4 No. 4 *The Sociological Quarterly* 291.

Haig, B.D. 'Grounded Theory as Scientific Method' (1995) *Philosophy of Education* at www.edu.uiuc.edu/EPS/PES-yearbook95_docs/haig .html.

Harper, B.N. 'Mediator Qualifications: The Trend Toward Professionalization' (1997) *Brigham Young University Law Review* 687.

Honeyman, C. 'A Consensus on Mediators' Qualifications' (1993) *Negotiation Journal* 289.

Hutchinson, A.C. 'Legal Ethics for a Fragmented Society: Between Professional and Personal' (1998) Vol. 5, Nos 2/3 *International Journal of the Legal Profession* 175.

James, R. & Seneviratne, M. 'The Legal Services Ombudsman: Form versus Function?' (1995) Vol. 58 No. 2 *Modern Law Review* 187

Johnstone, G. 'Liberal Ideals and Vocational Aims in University Legal Education.' (1999) Vol. 3 *Web Journal of Current Legal Issues.*

Karlberg, M. 'The Power of Discourse and the Discourse of Power: Pursuing Peace Through Discourse Intervention' (2005) Vol. 10 No. 1 *International Journal of Peace Studies* 1.

Kalter, N. *et al.* 'Predictors of Children's Post Divorce Adjustment' (1989) Vol. 59 American Journal of Orthopsychiatry 605.

Kanter, R. 'Reflections in Women and the Legal Profession: A Sociological Perspective' (1978) Vol. 1 *Harvard Women's Law Journal* 1.

Kelle, U. 'Theory Building in Qualitative Research and Computer Programs for Management of Textual Data.' (1997) Vol. 2 No. 2 *Sociological Research* at www.socresonline.org.uk/socresonline/2/2/1.html.

Kelly, J.B. 'Mediation and Psychotherapy: Distinguishing the Difference' (1983) *Mediation Quarterly* 33.

Kinach, B.M. 'Grounded Theory as Scientific Method: Haig-Inspired Reflections on Educational Research Methodology' (1995) *Philosophy of Education* at www.edu.uiuc.edu/EPS/PES-Yearbook/95_docs/kinach.html.

Maiman, R.J., McEwen, C.A. & Mather, L. 'The Future of Legal Professionalism in Practice' Vol. 2 No. 1 *Legal Ethics* 71.

Martin, P. 'The Hitch-Hiker's Guide to Mediation' (1995) *Family Law* 589.

Matz, D.E. 'Some Advice For Mediator Evaluators' (1993) *Negotiation Journal* 325.

McCarthy, P. & Walker, J. 'Mediation and Divorce Law Reform - The Lawyer's View' (1995) *Family Law* 361.

McCarthy, P. & Walker, J. 'Mediation and Divorce - The FMA View' (1996) *Family Law* 109.

McEwen, C. 'Competence and Quality' (1993) *Negotiation Journal* 313.

McGlynn, C. 'The Business of Equality in the Solicitor' Profession' (2000) Vol. 63 *Modern Law Review* 442.

Menkel-Meadow, C. 'Can a Law Teacher Avoid Teaching Legal Ethics?" (1991) Vol. 41 *Journal of Legal Education* 3.

Menkel-Meadow, C. 'Portia in a Different Voice; Speculations on a Woman's Lawyering Process' (1985) Vol. 1 *Berkeley Women's Law Journal* 39.

Menkel-Meadow, C. 'The Comparative Sociology of Women Lawyers: The "Feminisation of the Legal Profession"' (1986) Vol. 24 *Osgoode Hall Law Journal* 987.

Miles M.B. 'Qualitative Data as an Attractive Nuisance: The Problem of Analysis' (1979) Vol. 24 *Administrative Science Quarterly* 590.

Mnookin, R.H. & Kornhauser, L. 'Bargaining in the Shadow of the Law: The Case of Divorce' (1979) Vol. 88 No. 5 *Yale Law Journal* 950.

Moliterno, J.E. 'On the Future of Integration Between Skills and Ethics Teaching: Clinical Legal Education in the Year 2010' Vol. 46 No. 1 *Journal of Legal Education* 67.

Mulcahy, L. 'Can Leopards Change their Spots: An Evaluation of the Role of Lawyers in Medical Negligence Mediation' (2001) Vol. 8 No. 3 *International Journal of the Legal Profession* 203.

Mulcahy, L. 'The Possibility and Desirability of Mediator Neutrality: Towards an Ethic of Partiality' (2001) Vol. 10 *Social and Legal Studies* 505.

Nelson, R.L. 'Ideology, Practice and Professional Autonomy: Social Values and Client Relationships in the Large Law Firm' (1985) Vol. 37 *Stanford Law Review* 503.

Nicholson, D. 'Making Lawyers Moral? Ethical Codes and Moral Character' (2000) Vol. 25 No. 4 *Legal Studies* 601.

Pandit, N.R. 'The Creation of Theory: A Recent Application of the Grounded Theory Method' (1996) Vol. 2 No. 4. *The Qualitative Report* at www.nova.edu/sss/QR/QR2-4/pandit.html.

Parkinson, L. 'Divorce Reform and Family Mediation' (1993) Vol. 23 *Family Law* 643.

Patton, P. 'Women Lawyers, Their Status, Influence, and Retention in the Legal Profession' (2004-5) Vol. 11 *William and Mary Journal of Women and the Law* 173.

Pearson, J. 'Ten Myths about Family Law' (1993) Vol. 27 No. 2 *Family Law Quarterly* 279.

Platt, J. 'Evidence and Proof in Documentary Research: Some Specific Problems of Documentary Research' (1981) Vol. 29 No. 1 *Sociological Review* 31.

Powles, G. 'Taking the Plunge: Integrating Legal Ethics in Australia' (1999) Vol. 33 No. 3 *Law Teacher* 315.

Raitt, F. E. 'Informal Justice and the Ethics of Mediating in Abusive Relationships' (1997) Vol. 2 *Juridical Review* 76.

Rhode, D.L. 'The Profession and its Discontents' (2000) Vol. 61 *Ohio State Law Journal* 8.

Rhode, D.L. 'An Adversarial Exchange on Adversarial Ethics: Text, Subtext, and Context' (1991) Vol. 41 No. 1 *Journal of Legal Education* 21.

Rhode, D.L. 'Why the ABA Bothers: a Functional Perspective on Professional Codes' (1981) Vol. 59 *Texas Law Review* 689.

Richards, C. 'The Expertise of Mediating' (1997) *Family Law* 52.

Richards, C. 'A Knighthood or an Entry Pass? – What Does it Mean to Have Mediation Training?' (1997) *Family Law* 204.

Riskin, L.L. 'Understanding Mediator Orientations, Strategies and Techniques: A Grid for the Perplexed' (1996) Vol. 1 *Harvard Negotiation Law Review* 7.

Roberts, M. 'System of Selves? Some Ethical Issues in Family Mediation' (1992) Vol. 10 *Mediation Quarterly* 11.

Roberts S.A. 'The Path of Negotiations' (1996) Vol. *49 Current Legal Practice* 108.

Roberts, S.A. 'Decision-Making for Life Apart' (1995) Vol. 58 *Modern Law Review* 714.

Roberts, S.A. 'Alternative Dispute Resolution and Civil Justice: An Unresolved Relationship' (1993) Vol. 56 *Modern Law Review* 452.

Roberts, S.A. 'Mediation in the Lawyers Embrace' (1992) Vol. 55 *Modern Law Review* 258.

Roberts, S.A. 'Towards a Minimal Form of Alternative Intervention, International Developments in Divorce Mediation' (1986) Vol. 11 *Mediation Quarterly* 30.

Roberts, S.A. 'Mediation in Family Disputes' (1983) Vol. 46 No. 5 *Modern Law Review* 537.

Rose, C.M. 'Women and Property: Gaining and Losing Ground' (1992) Vol. 78 *Virginia Law Review* 421.

Russell, N.R. 'Mediation: The Need and a Plan for Voluntary Certification' (1996) Vol. 30 *University of San Francisco Law Review* 613.

Sherr, A. 'The Value of Experience in Legal Competence' (2002) Vol. 7 No. 2 *International Journal of the Legal Profession* 95.

Sherr, A. 'Legal Education, Legal Competence and Little Bo Peep' Inaugural Lecture by Professor Avrom Sherr as Woolf Chair in Legal Education (London: Institute of Advanced Legal Studies, 2001) accessible at sas-space.sas.ac.uk/dspace/bilstream/10065/246/1/AS_Woolf_Inaugural.pdf.

Snyder, F. 'Anthropology, Dispute Processes and Law: A Critical Introduction' (1981) Vol. 8 *British Journal of Law & Society* 141.

Sommerlad, H. 'Researching and Theorising the Processes of Professional Identity Formation' (2007) Vol. 34 No. 2 *Journal of Law and Society* 190.

Sommerlad, H. 'Managerialism and the Legal Professional: A New Professional Paradigm' (1995) Vol. 2 No. 3 *International Journal of the Legal Profession* 159.

Spiegelman, P.J. 'Certifying Mediators: Using Selection Criteria to Include the Qualified-Lessons from the San Diego Experience' (1996) Vol. 30 *University of San Francisco Law Review* 677.

Sturm, S. 'From Gladiators to Problem-Solvers: Connecting Conversations about Women, the Academy and the Legal Profession' (1997) Vol. 4 *Duke Journal of Gender, Law and Policy* 119.

Taylor, A. 'Concepts of Neutrality in Family Mediation: Contexts, Ethics, Influence and Transformative Process' (1997) Vol. 14 *Mediation Quarterly* 215.

The Chartered Institute of Arbitrators' Code of Professional and Ethical Conduct Final Draft (2001) Vol. 17 No. 3 *Arbitration* 273.

Thornton, M. '"Otherness" on the Bench: How Merit is Gendered' (2007) Vol. 29 *Sydney Law Review* 391.

Thornton, M. 'Towards Embodied Justice: Wrestling with Legal Ethics in the Age of the "New Corporatism"' (1999) *Melbourne University Law Review* 28.

Thornton, M. 'Technocentrism in the Law School: Why the Gender and Colour of Law Remain the Same' (1998) Vol. 36 *Osgoode Hall Law Journal* 369.

Thornton, M. 'Authority and Corporeality: The Conundrum for Women in Law' (1998) Vol. 6 No. 2 *Feminist Legal Studies* 147.

Twining, W. 'Alternative to What? Theories of Litigation, Procedure and Dispute Settlement in Anglo-American Jurisprudence: Some Neglected Classics' (1993) Vol. 56 No. 3 *Modern Law Review* 380.

Waldman, E.A. 'The Challenge of Certification: How to Ensure Mediator Competence While Preserving Diversity' (1996) Vol. 30 *University of San Francisco Law Review* 723.

Walsh, E. 'UK College of Family Mediators, Initial Training and Continuing Professional Development' (1997) *Family Law* 647.

Webb, J. 'Developing Ethical Lawyers: Can Legal Education Enhance Access to Justice?' (1999) Vol. 33 *Law Teacher* 284.

Webley, L. 'Divorce Solicitors and Ethical Approaches – The Best Interests of the Client and/or the Best Interests of the Family?' (2005) Vol. 7, No. 2 *Legal Ethics* 231.

Webley, L. & Duff, L. 'Women Solicitors as a Barometer for Problems within the Legal Profession – Time to Put Values Before Profits?' (2007) Vol. 34 No. 3 *Journal of Law and Society* 374.

Weckstein, D.T. 'Mediator Certification: Why and How' (1996) Vol. 30 *University of San Francisco Law Review* 757.

Wilensky, H.L. 'The Professionalization of Everyone?' (1964) Vol. LXX No. 2 *American Journal of Sociology* 137.

Winner, M. 'Capacity To Mediate' Vol. 7 No. 2 *Family Mediation* 17.

Wood, L. 'Mediation: A Backlash To Women's Progress On Family Law Issues' (1985) Vol. 19 *Clearing House Review* 431.

Conference & Seminar Papers

Bryant, A. 'Grounding Systems Research: Re-establishing Grounded Theory' *Proceedings of the 35th Hawaii International Conference on System Sciences* (Hawaii, 2000).

Divorce Mediation & Arbitration Centre Seminar Handout 10/5/1995, reproduced in *Skills for Legal Functions 1: Deciding Disputes* Legal Skills Working Papers (London: Institute of Advanced Legal Studies, 1996)

Douglas, G. 'Resolving Family Disputes' *The Nuffield Seminars in Civil Justice, Seminar 4*, (London: The Nuffield Seminar Series 4th March 2002).

Lord Mackay of Clashfern, The Lord Chancellor 'More Than Words - Divorce Reform And Marriage Support' *Speech To The Solicitors' Family Law Association* 7 November 1995.

Lowe, N. Grounds for Divorce and Maintenance Between Former Spouses, England and Wales www2.law.uu.nl/priv/cefl/Reports/pdf/England02.pdf' (Cardiff: University of Cardiff, October, 2002)

Wagenaar, H. 'The (Re-)discovery of Grounded Theory in Postpositivist Policy Research.' Paper prepared for the *ESF Workshop Qualitative Method for the Social Sciences* (Vienna: 28th-29th November 2003).

Rhoades, H. 'W(h)ither Advocacy? On Being a 'Good' Family Lawyer in a Shared Parenting Policy Environment' *Seminar at the Oxford Centre for Family Law and Policy* (Oxford: University of Oxford, August 16th 2007).

Official Policy Documents, Guidelines & Reports

Bartsch, H.-J. *Council of Europe-Leal Co-operation* (The Council of Europe, 1999).

Dearing Report: The National Committee of Inquiry into Higher Education: Higher Education in the Learning Society (Norwich: HMSO, 1997).

First Report on Legal Education and Training (London: ACLEC, 1996).

Hansard (HL), 11 January 1996.

HM Government *Judicial Statistics 2005* (London: Department for Constitutional Affairs, 2006).

Law Commission Report Number 192 *The Ground for Divorce* HC636 (London: HMSO, 1990).

Law Commission Report Number 170 *Facing the Future: The Ground for Divorce* HC479 (London: HMSO, 1988).

Law Commission Report Number 6 *Reform of the Grounds of Divorce: The Field of Choice* Cmnd 3123 (London: HMSO, 1966).

Law Discipline Network 'Why should law school focus on general transferable skills?' *Report on General Transferable Skills 1998* (The Law Discipline Network, General Transferable Skills in the Law Curriculum) at www.ukcle.ac.uk/resources/ldn/index.html.

Law Society *Trends in the Solicitors' Profession Annual Statistical Report 2006* (London: Law Society of England and Wales, 2007).

Law Society *Fairness for Families: The Law Society's Response to the Consultation Paper* (London: Law Society, 1994).

Law Society *Alternative Dispute Resolution Report Prepared for the Courts and Legal Services Committee* (London: Law Society of England and Wales, 1991).

Law-Subject Specific Benchmark Standards (Gloucester: Quality Assurance Agency for Higher Education, 2000).

Legal Aid Board *Franchising Family Mediation Services, The Legal Aid Board's Approach To The Piloting Of Franchise Contracts For The Provision Of Family Mediation Services* (London: Legal Aid Board, 1997).

Lord Chancellor's Department *Looking to the Future: Mediation and the Ground for Divorce: The Government's Proposals* Cm 2799 (London: HMSO, 1995).

Lord Chancellor's Department *Looking to the Future: Mediation and the Ground for Divorce: A Consultation Paper* Cm 2424 (London: HMSO, 1993).

Lord Woolf's *Access to Justice Interim Report* (London: Lord Chancellor's Department, 1995).

National Audit Office & Legal Services Commission *Legal Aid and Mediation for People Involved in Family Breakdown* HC 256 Session 2006-2007 (London: The Stationery Office, 2007).

National Family Mediation, *Looking to the Future: Mediation and the Ground for Divorce. A Response from National Family Mediation* (London; NFM, 2004).

Office for National Statistics *Social Trends No. 31* (London & Norwich: The Stationery Office, 2001).

Royal Commission on Legal Services Final Report Volume One Cmnd 7648 (London: HMSO, 1979).

Professional Literature: Law Society & UK College of Family Mediators

(In alphabetical order by document name.)

Solicitors

Law Society of England and Wales *Authorisation Guide* 2003 (as amended).

Law Society of England and Wales *CPE/Graduate Diploma in Law Courses CPE/GDL Course Providers* (Version 2).

Law Society of England and Wales *Guide to the Professional Conduct of Solicitors* 8th Ed. (as amended) (London: Law Society, 2003).

Law Society of England and Wales *Training Trainee Solicitors- The Law Society Requirements* (Version 7 July 2007).

Law Society of England and Wales *Legal Practice Course Providers* (2007) www.lawsociety.org.uk/becomingasolicitor/qualifying/legalpracticecourse/courseproviders.law.

Law Society of England and Wales *Legal Practice Course Provider Introduction* (Version 26 February 2007).

Law Society of England and Wales *The Legal Practice Course Written Standards* (Version 10 September 2004).

Law Society of England and Wales *Professional Skills Course Providers* (2007) www.lawsociety.org.uk/documents/downlaods/becomingpscexternalproviders.pdf.

Law Society of England and Wales *Professional Skills Course; Course Structure, Provider Information and Course Accreditation* (Version 3 August 2005).

The Law Society of England and Wales *The Training Regulations 1990* (Version August 2004).

Family Law Solicitors

Law Society of England and Wales *Family Law Panel: Application for Membership* (Version 1).

Law Society of England and Wales *Family Law Panel: Advanced Knowledge and Skills Criteria* (Version 1).

Law Society of England and Wales *Family Law Panel Advanced: Case Report Preparation and Submission Instruction* (Version 1).

Law Society of England and Wales *Family Law Panel Advanced: Case Study Preparation and Submission Instructions* (Version 1).

Law Society of England and Wales *Family Law Panel Advanced Chief Examiners Report* www.lawsoci.../fourth_tier.asp?section_id=6150&Caller_ID=N58 (as at 15th April 2004).

Law Society of England and Wales *Family Law Panel: Criteria and Guidance Notes* (Version 1).

Law Society of England and Wales *Family Law Panel Procedures* (Version 1).

Law Society of England and Wales *Family Law Panel: The Law Society's Family Law Panel Assessment* (Version 1).

Law Society of England and *Wales Family Law Protocol* (Version 1, 2001).

Law Society of England and *Wales Family Law Protocol* (Version 2, 2006).

Law Society Family Mediators

Law Society of England and Wales *Family Mediation Accreditation Scheme: Criteria and Guidance Notes* (Version 1).

Law Society of England and Wales *Family Mediation Panel: Application for General Membership* (Version 1).

Law Society of England and Wales *Family Mediation Panel: Application for Practitioner Membership- Development / Direct Route Questionnaire* (Version 1).

Law Society of England and Wales *Family Mediation Panel: Application for Practitioner Membership – Passport Route Questionnaire* (Version 1).

Law Society of England and Wales *Family Mediation Panel: Criteria and Guidance Notes* (Version 1).

Law Society of England and Wales *The Standards of Competence for the Accreditation of Family Mediators* (Version 1).

Law Society of England and Wales *Family Law Protocol* (Version 1, 2001).

Law Society of England and Wales *Family Law Protocol* (Version 2, 2006).

Law Society of England and Wales *Family Mediation Panel: Procedures & Conditions for Panel Membership* (Version 1).

Law Society of England and Wales *Family Mediation Panel: Standards of Competence for Accreditation of Family Mediators* (Version 1).

Law Society of England and Wales *Family Mediation Training Standards* (Version 1).

UK College of Family Mediators

UK College of Family Mediators *Approved Training for CPD Points*.

UK College of Family Mediators *Children, Young People and Family Mediation – Policy and Practice Guidelines* (September 2002).

UK College of Family Mediators *Code for Family Mediators* (April 2000).

UK College of Family Mediators *Competence Assessment for Family Mediators: Portfolio Guidelines, Specification and Template* (November 2005).

UK College of Family Mediators *Complaints' Procedure and Disciplinary Code* (January 2006).

UK College of Family Mediators *Continuing Professional Development – Scheme Requirements.*

UK College of Family Mediators *Domestic Abuse Screening Policy.*

UK College of Family Mediators *Notes for Guidance in Respect of Court Proceedings & Form E (financial settlement terms* (February 2004).

UK College of Family Mediators *Policy on Conflicts of Interest and Similar Conflicts and Good Practice Guidelines* (2000).

UK College of Family Mediation *Professional Practice Consultancy for Family Mediators: A Guide to Roles and Responsibilities* (June 2003).

UK College of Family Mediators *Recommended and Required Curriculum and Teaching Methods for Foundation Training Courses* (April 2003).

UK College of Family Mediators *Requirements for the Providers of Foundation Training – and the Guidelines to the Requirements for Providers of Foundation Training* (June 2005).

UK College of Family Mediators *Requirements for Providers of Professional Practice Consultancy – and Guidelines as to the Requirements of Professional Practice Consultancy* (April 2003).

UK College of Family Mediators *Requirements for the Registration of Mediators* (October 2005).

UK College of Family Mediators *The Policies and Standards of the UK College of Family Mediators - Objects and Functions of the College.*

Overseas Professional Literature & Literature from other Professional Bodies

Academy of Family Mediators, Standards of Practice for Family and Divorce Mediation, 1998.

Academy of Family Mediators 1983, Standards of Practice, Part XI. Training and Education and VII. Professional Advice A. B. and C.

CEDR *Model Mediation Procedure Guidance.*

Solicitors Family Law Association Divorce Procedure Fact Sheet at http://www.sfla.org.uk/factsheetdisplay.php?id=18. The SFLA has subsequently been renamed Resolution.

Solicitors Family Law Association Code of Practice (now Resolution) See http://www.sfla.org.uk/code_practice.php.

Family Mediation & Legal Profession Press

Acland, A.F. 'Simply Negotiation with Knobs On' (1995) *Legal Action* 8.

Adam, S. 'Quality Assurance within NFM – A Summary' (1995) Vol. 5 No. 3 *Family Mediation* 5.

Ap Cynan, R. 'Why Train Lawyers As Mediators?' (1993) Vol. 90 No. 36 *Law Society Gazette* 2.

Blacklock, R. & Roberts, M. 'Professional Standards in the Selection of Family Mediation' (1995) Vol. 5 No. 1 *Family Mediation* 10.

Booth, M. 'The UK College of Family Mediators - An Update Family Mediation' (1996) Vol. 6 No. 2 *Family Mediation* 6.

Cretney, S. 'Joseph Jackson Memorial Lecture 1996 Family Law – "A Bit Of A Racket"?' January 26th 1996 *New Law Journal* 91.

Elliot, D. 'Supervision in Changing Times' (1997) Vol. 7 No. 2 *Family Mediation* 19.

'Fault Lines Rock Act' February 2001 *Law Society Gazette* 26.

Gibb, F. 'Challenge Looms In Divorce Reform Test' March 30th 1998 *The Times*.

Gibbons, J. 'Legal Aid - Controlling The Budget Or Controlling The Lawyers' February 16th 1996 *New Law Journal* 220.

Gupta, Y. 'The Mediation Screening and Orientation Program' (1996) Vol. 6 No. 1 *Family Mediation* 13.

Hester, M. & Pearson, C. 'Domestic Violence and Mediation Practices. A Summary of Recent Research Findings' (1997) Vol. 7 No. 1 *Family Mediation* 10.

Logan, A. 'Market in Mediation' 25th October 1995 *Law Society Gazette* 14.

Norrie, R. 'Family Mediation (Role Of Lawyers In Family Mediation Services, 1996 Act Eligibility And Training)' (1997) *Legal Executive* 42.

Richards, C. 'Domestic Violence: What Is There For Mediation? A Conference Report' (1996) Vol. 6 No. 3 *Family Mediation* 8.

Richards, C. 'Why Go Through with it? - Accreditation with NFM' (1995) Vol. 5, No. 1 *Family Mediation* 11.

Roberts, M. 'Quality Control of Professional Standards by NFM' (1994) Vol. 4 No. 2 *Family Mediation* 18.

Roberts, S.A. 'The Trajectory of Family Mediation (Concerns about NFM Services Being Drawn into Closer Association with Civil Justice under the Legal Framework in 1996 Act' (1997) Vol. 7 No. 2 *Family Mediation* 4.

Tsang, L. 'Separating the issues - mediation is no longer seen as sounding the death knell for family lawyers as it appeared to do when the Family Law Bill was published in 1995' 21st July 1999 *Law Society Gazette General News Section*.

Ward, S. 'Some of the issues topping the conference agenda, as solicitors congregate to discuss 'Fitting the Profession for the Future'' 8th October 1997 *Law Society Gazette General News Section*.

Westcott, J. 'The Importance of Being Regulated (but not in the Family Law Act)' (1997) Vol. 7 No. 1 *Family Mediation* 18.

Legislation

Administration of Justice Act 1985

Children Act 1989

Civil Procedure Rules (including updates)

Courts and Legal Services Act 1990

Family Law Act 1996

Solicitors Act 1974

The Training Regulations 1990 (as amended)

Quid Pro Books

Dissertation Series

www.quidprobooks.com